Cover photograph

The River Tees in winter spate. The houses of Middleton One Row stand high on the river bank, as they and their forerunners have done for over 800 years.

"All objects are as windows, through which the philosophic eye looks into infinitude itself"
From <u>Sartor Resartus</u> by Thomas Carlyle

MIDDLETON ST. GEORGE

WINDOWS ON THE EVOLUTION OF A TEES VALLEY PARISH

ALAN PALLISTER

Copyright is lodged with the author, A. F. Pallister.

Published 2007 by The History of Education Project
(Durham Initiative for Employment and Training)

The Miners' Hall
Red Hill
Durham
DH1 4BB
Tel/Fax: 0191 370 9941
Email: gordon.batho@btopenworld.com
www.dur.ac.uk/g.r.batho

Copies are available from the above address

ISBN 978 1 870268 28 8

Produced by A. F. Pallister

Printed by Prontaprint

P1.1 The site of the deserted medieval village of Middleton St. George or Low Middleton, looking towards Church House Farm and the old parish church of St. George. This picture was taken in 1967 when the earthwork remains of the houses and tofts could still be seen.

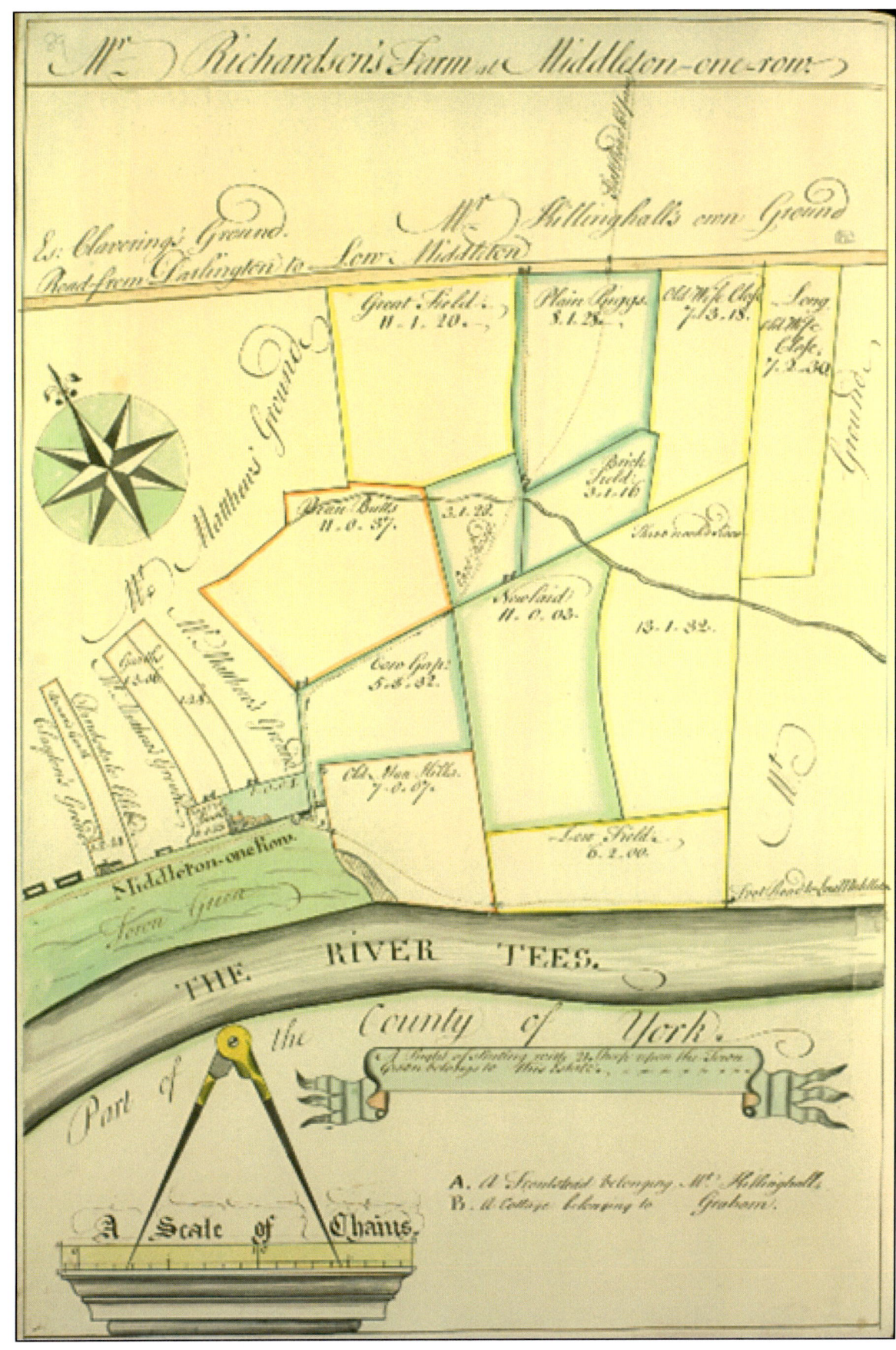

Pl.2 Mr. Richardson's farm at Middleton One Row in 1757 – part of the Killinghall Estate. Later known as Middleton One Row East Farm.

In memory of my parents George and Doris Pallister,
sharers in this history, and without whom this book could not have been produced.

We are the music-makers,
And we are the dreamers of dreams,
Wandering by lone sea-breakers,
And sitting by desolate streams;
World-losers and world-forsakers,
On whom the pale moon gleams:
Yet we are the movers and shakers
Of the world for ever, it seems.

(From "Ode" by A.W.E. O'Shaughnessy)

FOREWORD

Writing this account has been a chastening experience. My original concept of compiling the definitive history of Middleton St. George soon fell apart, as the scale of the task became all too apparent. The modified, but more realistic, objective has been to put together an ever-changing picture of the parish, integrating information from widely dispersed available sources with some fruits of my own research.

Besides being of interest to local people, it is hoped that this book also has something to offer to local and social historians in general. I have attempted to avoid a purely parochial view, and to put the local situation and events into the broader regional and national scene.

A general history of Middleton St. George is long overdue, as none has ever been published. The paucity and fragmentary nature of the early sources have probably been a disincentive to aspiring local historians. Various county compilers have included Middleton St. George in their volumes, and the monumental work of Robert Surtees in particular has contributed greatly to local research. The accent in all these works is on the descent of the manors and on the landed gentry, with other aspects largely neglected. The Victoria County History is biased in the same direction. Some more recent local researchers have made very useful contributions in their privately produced works, as included in the bibliography.

Of great significance, although often not appreciated, is the fact that the present shape of the community within the parish bears no resemblance to that which existed up to the middle of the nineteenth century. The coming of the ironworks was responsible for the industrial village, which has developed into the community we know today. This abrupt transition may sometimes have been seen as a barrier between the recallable past and the hazy distant history of the rural community which existed previously.

Throughout all the changes, whether slow development or more dramatic events, there runs a continuous thread, and, as we look back at the surrounding history, we are in our own lives continuing to make the history and extend the thread.

There is ample scope for deeper investigation of subjects I have dealt with in this account, and for study of many related aspects which have been mentioned only briefly or not at all. My study has been taken up to the present day, but the treatment of the last century is more a selective outline view than a fully detailed account. This period, well within the memories or hearsay of many people, affords numerous fascinating lines of enquiry which could profitably be pursued, allowing the story of the parish to be more comprehensively covered. If this account provides a framework within which this can be done, I shall feel that at least one objective has been achieved.

Alan Pallister

ACKNOWLEDGEMENTS

A great number of people have contributed wittingly or unwittingly to this book, and I am grateful to them all.

Firstly I must express my appreciation to Professor Gordon Batho, who has undertaken the publication under the auspices of the History of Education Project, and has given encouragement and guidance on the content and presentation. His administrator, Rebecca Ashby has finalised the production for the printer, following the formatting by Kevin Finch, a volunteer at the Project.

My wife Philippa has critically read the script, and has also put up with my frequent absence from gardening duties! I am particularly grateful to my son Calum, whose help in overcoming the perils of IT and putting everything into digital form has been crucial to this work ever seeing the light of day. My brother Richard, with his local knowledge, has scrutinised the text, and made constructive comments. With my home now being away from the area, the contribution from my cousin Adrian Anderson has been valuable in keeping me informed of items in the local press which would otherwise have escaped me.

Research has been facilitated by the helpful staff of Durham County Record Office, Durham University Library Archives and Special Collections, North Yorkshire County Record Office and the public libraries at Darlington and Middlesbrough.

The archaeological content, adding much to our knowledge, would not have been possible without the co-operation of the farmers concerned. The excavations at West Hartburn were by permission of the late Mrs. Mary Pattison and subsequently by Mr. George Pattison. Mr. Harry Brown allowed survey and examination of the unexcavated half of the village. Survey of the deserted village of Low Middleton was carried out by permission of Major Chetwynd-Stapylton, and access for more recent field examination has been readily given by Mr. Thomas Harker and Mr. Anthony Harker.

On a personal note, I acknowledge my debt to the late Dr. David Reid of the University of Durham, whose inspiration over many years channelled my wandering interest in local history into more structured and systematic research.

I also owe much to the late Leslie Still, who brought the resources of the Teesside Archaeological Society into action at West Hartburn and who, in the course of the excavations, taught me a great deal about archaeology.

Many others, too numerous to mention individually, have contributed with memories and other material and in giving me access to their houses and property. I have noted elsewhere known providers of photographs. To all these I am greatly appreciative.

Any errors and omissions are entirely my own. Bringing any such to my notice will help correct the record for the future.

CONTENTS

LIST OF FIGURES IN THE TEXT		12
LIST OF ILLUSTRATIONS		13
INTRODUCTION		17
CHAPTER 1:	EARLY HISTORY	21
	Roman Footmarks and Anglo-Saxon Obscurity	
CHAPTER 2:	THE MIDDLE AGES	25
	Manorial Lords and Peasant Farmers	
CHAPTER 3:	THE SIXTEENTH CENTURY	51
	New Patterns of Religion, Estates and Farming	
CHAPTER 4:	THE SEVENTEENTH CENTURY	61
	No Escape from Civil Strife	
CHAPTER 5:	THE EIGHTEENTH CENTURY	79
	Slow Rural Progression	
ILLUSTRATIONS		91
CHAPTER 6:	THE FIRST HALF OF THE NINETEENTH CENTURY	109
	Spa and Railway Hasten Changes	
CHAPTER 7:	METAMORPHOSIS 1860 – 1880	133
	The Coming of the Ironworks and the Creation of a New Village	
CHAPTER 8:	FROM THE NINETEENTH CENTURY INTO THE TWENTIETH 1880 – 1914	147
	Continued Development through Troubled Times	
CHAPTER 9:	THE TWENTIETH CENTURY AFTER 1914	163
	A Sketch of the Unfolding Scene to the Present Day	
POSTSCRIPT:	INTO A NEW MILLENNIUM	173
REFERENCES		175
BIBLIOGRAPHY		187
INDEX		195

NOTE ON DATES

Unless direct quotations, years given in dates up to 1752, when the Julian calendar was in use, have been adjusted where necessary to conform with the Gregorian calendar in use today.

LIST OF FIGURES IN THE TEXT

		Page
Fig.1	Area and location maps	16
Fig.2	The parish of Middleton St. George and adjoining parishes	18
Fig.3	Middleton St. George at mid-twentieth century	19
Fig.4	The Roman Road	20
Fig.5	Supposed Anglo-Saxon sundial from St. George's Church	23
Fig.6	Manorial Middleton	26
Fig.7	Suggested opposing lines of settlement determining the eastern boundary of the Parish of Middleton St. George	28
Fig.8	The site of the medieval village of Low Middleton or Middleton St. George	31
Fig.9	Descent of the manor of Low Middleton or Middleton St. George up to c.1400	33
Fig.10	The deserted medieval village of West Hartburn	35
Fig.11	West Hartburn houses	37
Fig.12	The ten village holdings recorded at Middleton One Row in 1598 and still distinguishable in the twentieth century	41
Fig.13	The old way between Low Middleton and West Hartburn by St. George's Church	43
Fig.14	Suggested plan of the thirteenth century church of St. George	46
Fig.15	Descent of the manor of Low Middleton or Middleton St. George after c.1400	53
Fig.16	Conjectural reconstruction of the Killinghall manor house in the seventeenth century	78
Fig.17	Red Hall Farm in 1726 - now Oak Tree Farm (North Yorkshire County Record Office, with permission of Sir Mark Havelock-Allan)	80
Fig.18	Palm Tree House Farm in 1727 (North Yorkshire County Record Office, with permission of Sir Mark Havelock-Allan)	81
Fig.19	Baptisms, burials and marriages in the parish of Middleton St. George 1650-1800	85
Fig.20	Plan of St. George's Church - the old parish church of Middleton St. George	114
Fig.21	The farms of Middleton St. George in 1837 (from the tithe map)	116
Fig.22	Forster Field Farm in 1837 - now Foster House Farm - showing field names	119
Fig.23	Tariff for the Dinsdale Spa Hotel 1835	122
Fig.24	The bath house of the Dinsdale Spa about 1835	122
Fig.25	Coal to the coast - proposed routes by water and rail between Darlington and Stockton	124
Fig.26	Origin of ironworkers, brick workers and related trades at Middleton St. George from 1871 census	136
Fig.27	The ironworks and other industrial enterprises at Fighting Cocks at the end of the nineteenth century	150

Ordnance Survey maps are conventionally orientated with north at the top of the map.

LIST OF ILLUSTRATIONS

		Page
Pl.1	The site of the deserted medieval village of Middleton St. George or Low Middleton.	5
Pl.2	Plan of Richardson's farm at Middleton One Row in 1757. (North Yorkshire County Record Office, with permission of Sir Mark Havelock-Allan).	7
Pl.3	The residential agglomeration of Middleton St. George as seen from the air.	91
Pl.4	The twelfth century motte near Middleton One Row, which overlooked the medieval river crossing.	92
Pl.5	Low Middleton from the air, showing the extent of the medieval village.	92
Pl.6	The site of the medieval village of West Hartburn from the air. (By permission of Cleveland Archaeology)	93
Pl.7	The excavated House D at West Hartburn.	93
Pl.8	Font at St. George's Church.	94
Pl.9	Carved head beneath corbel of thirteenth century chancel arch.	94
Pl.10	Cocks armorial window in chancel.	94
Pl.11	St. George's Church, before demolition of the tower.	95
Pl.12	St. George's Church today.	95
Pl.13	St. George's Church, interior.	95
Pl.14	Castle Hill, the oldest house at Middleton One Row.	96
Pl.15	White House Farm, at the northern end of the parish.	96
Pl.16	Low Middleton Hall, the manor house of the Killinghalls in its c1721 rebuilt form.	97
Pl.17	Middleton Hall, built by the Rev. William Addison Fountaine around 1820.	97
Pl.18	St. Laurence's Church at Middleton One Row, built in 1871.	98
Pl.19	The Weslyan chapel built in 1869 between Killinghall and Fighting Cocks.	.98
Pl.20	The former bath house of the spa, in use as the club house of the Dinsdale Spa Golf Club.	99
Pl.21	The Dinsdale Spa Hotel, built in 1829.	99
Pl.22	Hodgkin's 1926 painting of the Middleton (Dinsdale) Ironworks. (By permission of Darlington Borough Council)	100
Pl.23	The engine house just before its demolition in 2004.	100

LIST OF ILLUSTRATIONS continued

		Page
Pl.24	The ironworks site redeveloped for new housing.	100
Pl.25	Ironworkers and managers, possibly soon after the re-opening of the works in 1900	101
Pl.26	The blast furnaces during demolition in 1947. (Northern Echo)	101
Pl.27	The view today across the playing field.	101
Pl.28	Two saddle tank shunting engines making their final appearance in front of the rapidly disappearing works they had served.	102
Pl.29	Salmon fishing at Low Middleton ferry c1880.	102
Pl.30	Fighting Cocks Station on 30 June 1887, its last day of operation. (Photograph provided by the late Mrs Burdy.)	103
Pl.31	The new Dinsdale Station on 1 July 1887, its opening day. (Photograph provided by the late Mrs Burdy.)	103
Pl.32	Robert Pallister, the wheelwright, with his wife and Thomas Knott, the smith, outside their premises at Fighting Cocks. (Photograph provided by the late Mrs Anne Gould, the wheelwright's great-granddaughter)	104
Pl.33	The smithy at Fighting Cocks prior to its demolition.	104
Pl.34	An early ironworks cricket team on the field opposite to Almora Hall	105
Pl.35	Almora Hall, the house of Jonathan Westgarth Wooler, around 1880. (Darlington Centre for Local Studies)	105
Pl.36	The Square around 1914. (Darlington Centre for Local Studies)	106
Pl.37	The Lyric Cinema in Station Road after closure.	106
Pl.38	A Lancaster bomber with its crew and ground staff at Goosepool c 1944.	107
Pl.39	Steam locomotives awaiting scrapping on sidings by the ironworks site.	107

Most of the illustrations are from the author's own photographs. Where illustrations are from photographs or documents kindly provided by others, this is acknowledged in the list. In the case of a few of the older photographs, the origins are unknown, but whoever preserved them has contributed to this record.

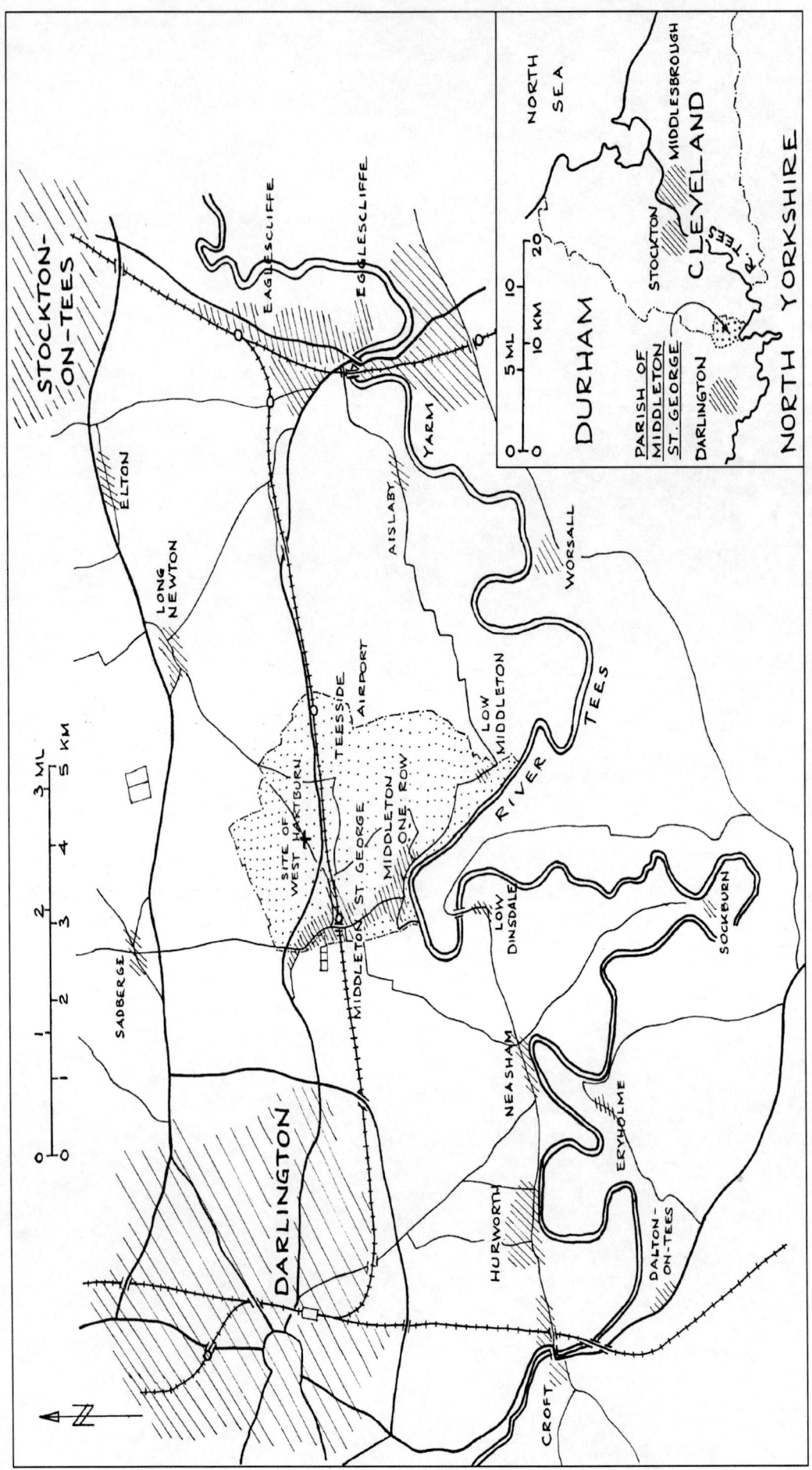

Fig.1 Area and location maps

INTRODUCTION

The geographical scope of this history is generally the parish of Middleton St. George. However, parish boundaries do not always define functional limits, and it is sometimes appropriate to step across them, as is the case here. Middleton St. George is situated in County Durham, on the north side of the river Tees, winding its sinuous way to the sea. The nearest town is Darlington, with its centre about four miles to the west. The general location and surrounding area are shown in Fig.1. The soil is a heavy clay, except for some lighter, low-lying land by the river. Until the nineteenth century, the parish was devoted almost entirely to agriculture.

The relationship between Middleton St. George and the adjoining parishes is shown in Fig.2. The present village of Middleton St. George, as distinct from the parish, is a creation of the nineteenth century, and extends on the west into the parish of Dinsdale. Middleton One Row stands on its ancient site on the high bank of the river. It is still nominally a separate village, but for all intents and purposes is effectively integrated with the village of Middleton St. George (see Pl.3). The Goosepool farms, although always part of the Middleton manorial estates, were previously in Long Newton parish, before adjustment of parish boundaries brought them into Middleton St. George at the end of the 19th.century. With the more recent re-organisation of counties, the eastern boundary of the parish is now also the county boundary between County Durham and Cleveland. The map in Fig.3 shows the parish as it was in the mid-twentieth century.

The early development of the parish is undocumented. This is neither unusual nor surprising, in view of the lack of written records at the time when villages were being created and parishes established. Moreover, as a result of its location in County Durham, Middleton is at a further disadvantage, in that the starting point for many village histories, Domesday Book, is of no assistance. William the Conqueror's survey of 1086 set out to cover the whole country. Unfortunately, events shortly before had led to the "Harrowing of the North", which left the northern countryside devastated and the lands virtually worthless. In these circumstances, William's officials did not even bother to cross the Tees, and the northernmost counties were omitted from the survey.

Nearly a hundred years later, in 1183, the Bishop of Durham, Hugh Puiset, carried out his own survey of all the lands belonging to the bishopric, which became known as the Boldon Book. Again the local historian is deprived of any help as far as Middleton is concerned, as Middleton did not come under the bishop's control until 1189, and is therefore excluded from his survey.

Without any early survey information, we must turn to such other documentary records which begin to appear around this time. The first reference to Middleton dates from 1166. The continuing record is sparse and spasmodic, but is supplemented by archaeological evidence, to give a general view of the parish and its people in the Middle Ages. It is not until the Tudor administration of the sixteenth century that a more intimate insight becomes possible. Thereafter, the increasing extent of written information affords scope for a deeper study of the population up to the present day, when records can be complemented by the memories of those who in their own time helped to shape this history.

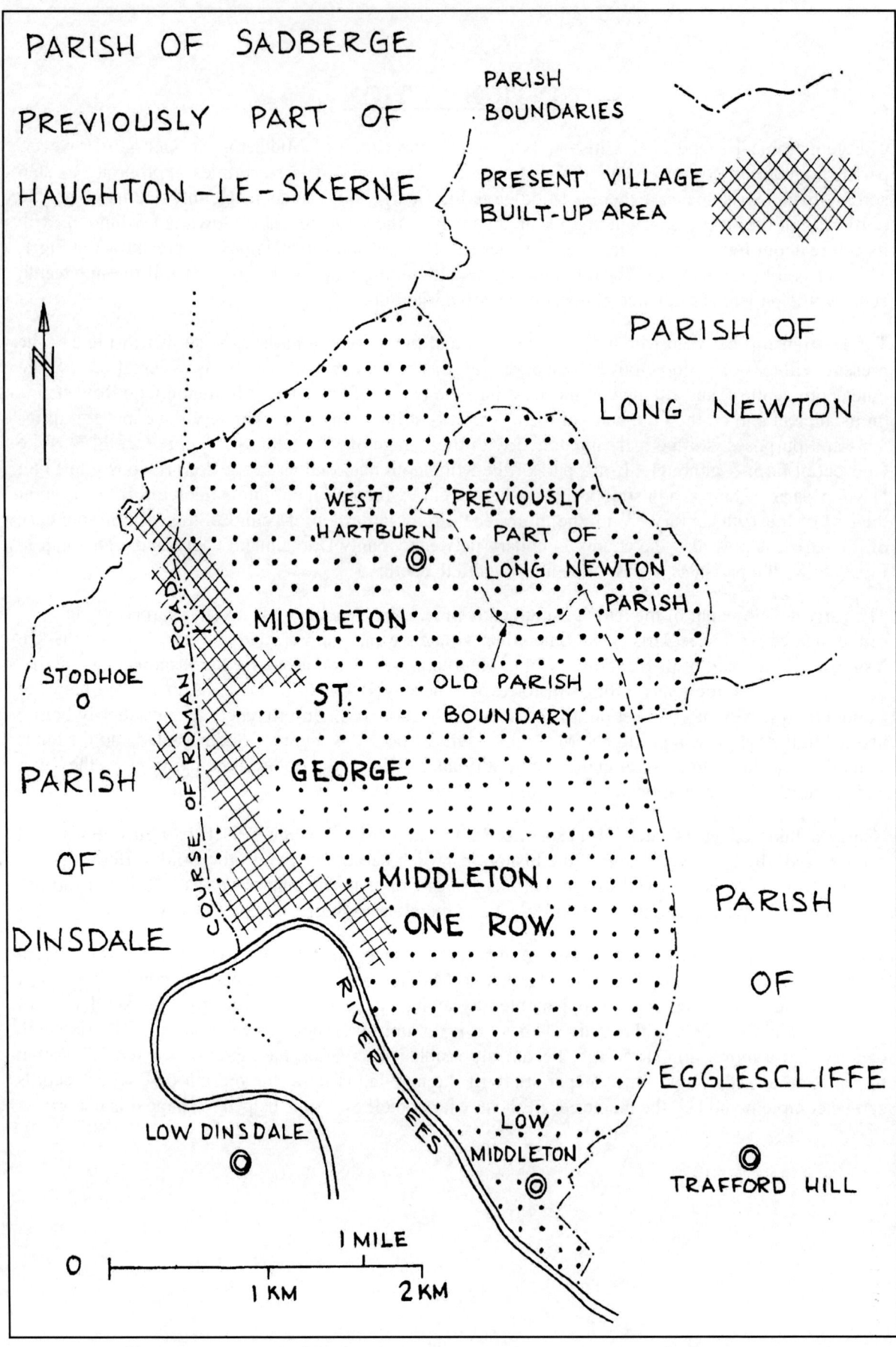

Fig.2 The parish of Middleton St.George and adjoining parishes

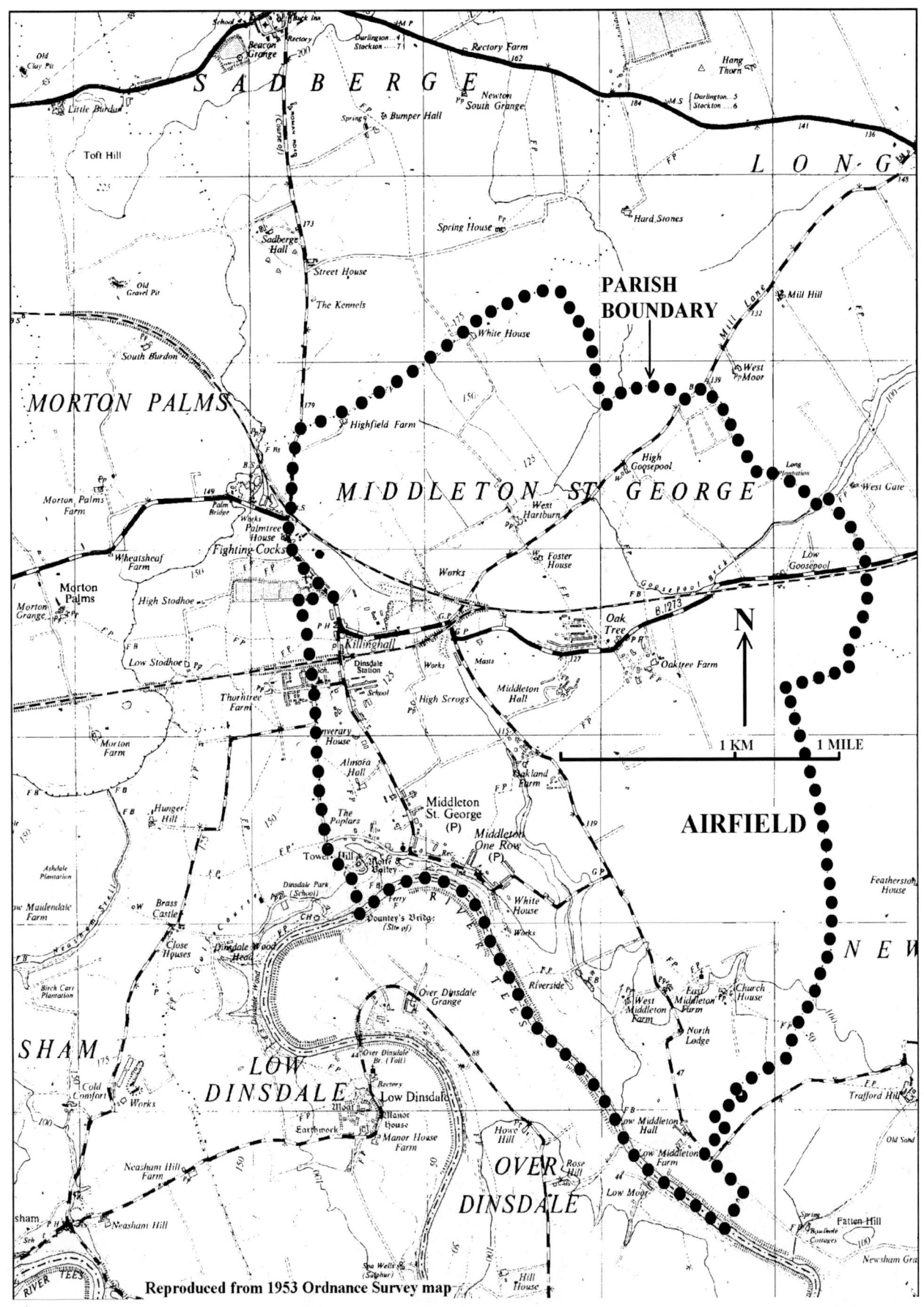

Fig. 3　　Middleton St. George at mid-twentieth century

The Roman Road by Middleton St. George
(Reproduced from the 1953 Ordnance Survey Map)

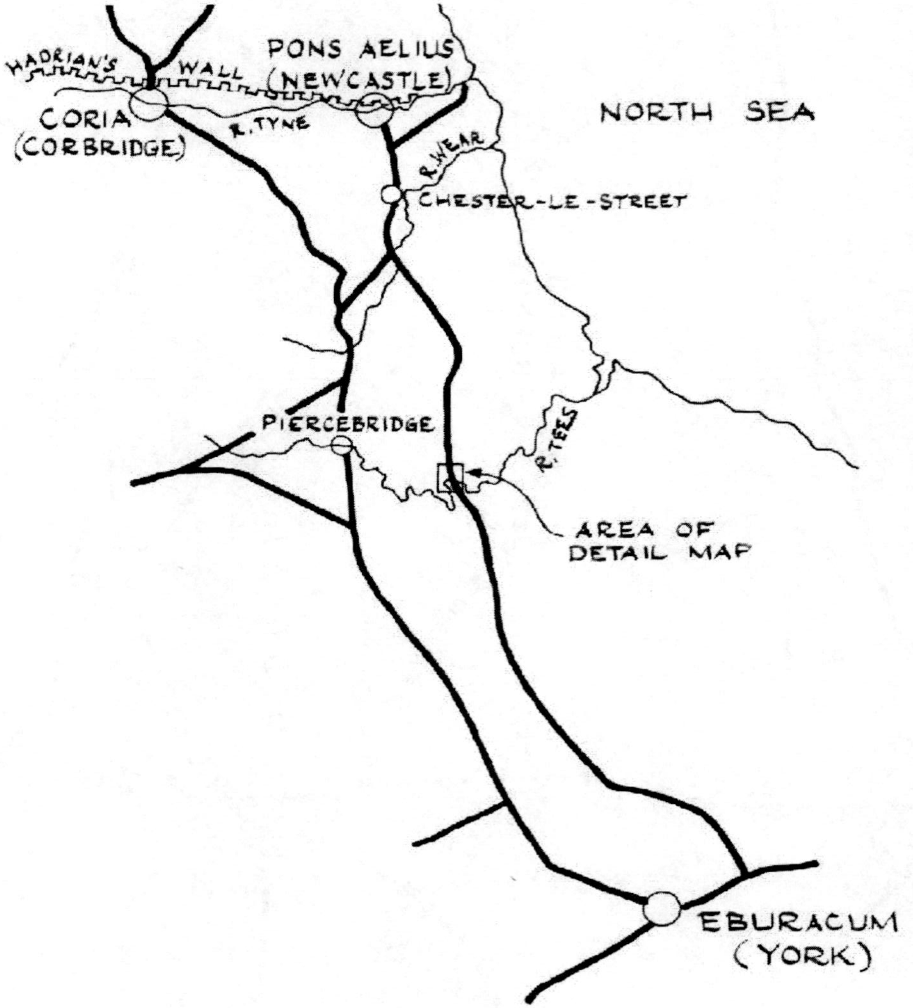

Roman Roads between York and the Wall

Fig. 4 The Roman Road

CHAPTER ONE - EARLY HISTORY

ROMAN FOOTMARKS AND ANGLO-SAXON OBSCURITY

The tangible history of Middleton St. George begins with the Romans, who, in the years after their first century AD invasion, pushed northwards and established lines of communication to support their advanced garrisons. Middleton is on one such route. The western boundary of the parish is the Roman road from east of York to the eastern end of Hadrian's Wall, running parallel to the better known road through Piercebridge (See map in Fig.4). The course of the road is generally well attested, and some sections are still in use today. The road crossed the river Tees about half a mile west of where Middleton One Row was later to be established. Tradition claims there to have been a bridge, Pons Teys, at the river crossing, and this may well have been the case.

The course of the road by Middleton is well defined by later features which have perpetuated the original line. Fig.4 shows the line of the road in relation to the present village. After crossing the river from the south, the road led up the steep river bank on the course of the present road. This section is shown on earlier Ordnance Survey maps as Pountey's Lane, preserving in corrupted form the name of the supposed bridge. At the point where the modern road turns towards Middleton One Row, the Roman road continues straight on, along a field track known locally as the Black Path. After following another short stretch of present road by Thorntree Gardens, the old road again continues in a straight line marked by the boundaries of twentieth century properties - the school and more recent housing developments. Obliterated for a short distance by the construction of the reservoirs, the Roman road can be seen to recommence in the field opposite Station Road, where it is marked by old hedge line and cultivation ridges. The old road then runs beneath some modern houses, before rejoining the present public road at the point where Palm Tree House Farm stood until relatively recently, just short of the Fighting Cocks Inn. It then continues northwards on the generally straight course of the present road to Sadberge and beyond.

Middleton lies in the area leading up to the military zone of the Wall, without the splendours and sophistication of Roman civil life found further south. Nevertheless, recent research has shown that the Tees valley had substantial farmsteads in the Roman period, which in some cases may have been a continuation of earlier iron age settlements. One such farmstead, not so far away at Dalton-on-Tees, is in a very similar environment to Middleton, and another has very recently been discovered at Ingleby Barwick.

Evidence for a settled Roman presence at Middleton was provided when two small pottery lamps of the period were found during the excavation of foundations for the house called The Friary in the late nineteenth century [1]. The lamps bear the stamp of the potter "Anniser", who operated in the third century, and whose products are to be found in Italy and southern France. It is very unlikely that these had been left by someone just passing by, and almost certainly they belonged to an established settlement. The find site is very close to the later medieval motte, in a commanding position overlooking the river crossing and with an extensive view of the approach from the south. To the north the Roman road ran to the next obvious control point on the hill top at Sadberge. In this strategic position, and with the evidence of the lamps, it is entirely reasonable to postulate a Roman camp at Middleton with living quarters, and this is supported by a report that "various fragments of Roman tiles, bricks, &c were found by workmen when digging in Mr. Barnard's grounds" [2].

After the departure of the Romans early in the fifth century, settlement of Angles, Saxons and Jutes impinged on the native population to re-shape society. It is generally recognised that a pattern of nucleated communities, the forerunners of the villages we know today, began to be established in the Anglo-Saxon period. With the spread of Christianity, more tangible signs have come down to us. Pagan and Christian Anglo-Saxon cemeteries at Norton-on-Tees are evidence of early settlement, and the small cross fragment to be seen in Croft church was part of a free-standing stone cross erected around 800 for the community living there at that time [3].

The coming of the Vikings from the beginning of the ninth century had a very significant impact on the area, as witness the number of villages and hamlets having the Danish "by" ending, e.g. Thornaby, Maltby, Aislaby, Girsby. Opinions differ as to whether the implication of this is that these places were established by the Danish incomers, or whether it was more a matter of giving Danish names to existing settlements.

The river Tees provided a ready means of ingress for the sea-borne invaders and settlers. Insufficient is known about the river conditions at the time to assess how far upstream boat travel was possible. It has been propounded that the Romans used water transport as far upstream as Piercebridge, but this would have depended upon river management works of an extent not likely to have been available at any other time in the distant past [4].

Many stone crosses or fragments of crosses bear testimony to the dominant Danish influence in the tenth and eleventh centuries. "Hog back" tombstones similarly stem from the same Danish period. Good examples of these evidences can be seen at nearby Low Dinsdale and Sockburn. Even before the Danish period, Sockburn was a religious centre of some status, being the place noted in the Anglo-Saxon Chronicle where Hygebald was consecrated Bishop of Lindisfarne in 780 [5].

Domesday book entries for Yorkshire show an established pattern of manors and landholdings on the south bank of the Tees at the time of the Norman Conquest - at Worsall, Girsby, Over Dinsdale, Eryholme and Croft [6]. While similar evidence is not available for the north bank, it is hardly likely that the situation there would have been significantly different.

The old church of St. George at Low Middleton used to be fondly referred to as the "Saxon church". However, nothing is identifiable in the existing building to support this appellation, and its origin remains obscure. The only artefact cited as evidence for settlement in the parish in the pre-Conquest period is a sundial, from St. George's, which is said to be Anglo-Saxon. The dial was built into the outer chancel wall, near the priest's door [7]. It was mounted upside down, having been presumably incorrectly re-fixed after some of the wall reconstruction which is much in evidence. Sometime in the last century it was moved to the new church at Middleton One Row.

The dial is a very simple one, plainly incised on a single block of stone, which has subsequently been fractured and lost its middle section. This means that any sign of fixing for the gnomon has also gone. The sketch in Fig.5 shows the details. In view of the significance of its suggested early dating, some discussion of the reasoning for this is appropriate.

A. R. Green, in an authoritative article on Saxon dials [8], described most of the known examples in this country, but was only able to note that he had not succeeded in locating that which was recorded elsewhere as existing at Middleton St. George. The Victoria County History includes the dial in its section on Anglo-Saxon remains, but without description or comment [9]. It would seem, therefore, that the dial has generally been regarded as Anglo-Saxon, although the authority for the dating is uncertain.

A common mistake in attempting to attribute a sundial to the Anglo-Saxon period arises from confusion with the later medieval "mass clocks". In Mr. Green's article, the basic differences are explained, but a few examples remain difficult to classify. So it is with the Middleton dial. The divisions marked on the dial are of prime importance. The Anglo-Saxon day was divided into eight tides, and the dials could have four, eight or twelve subdivisions to the half day. The mass dials were based on our present clock, and the half day was therefore usually divided into twelfths. It can be seen from the sketch that the Middleton dial is divided in the significant bottom half, which can be taken as representing the half day, into tenths. It does not, therefore, fit into either of the foregoing classifications. (The upper half of the dial need not be seriously considered, as this was never in a position to be effective, and served a purely decorative purpose.)

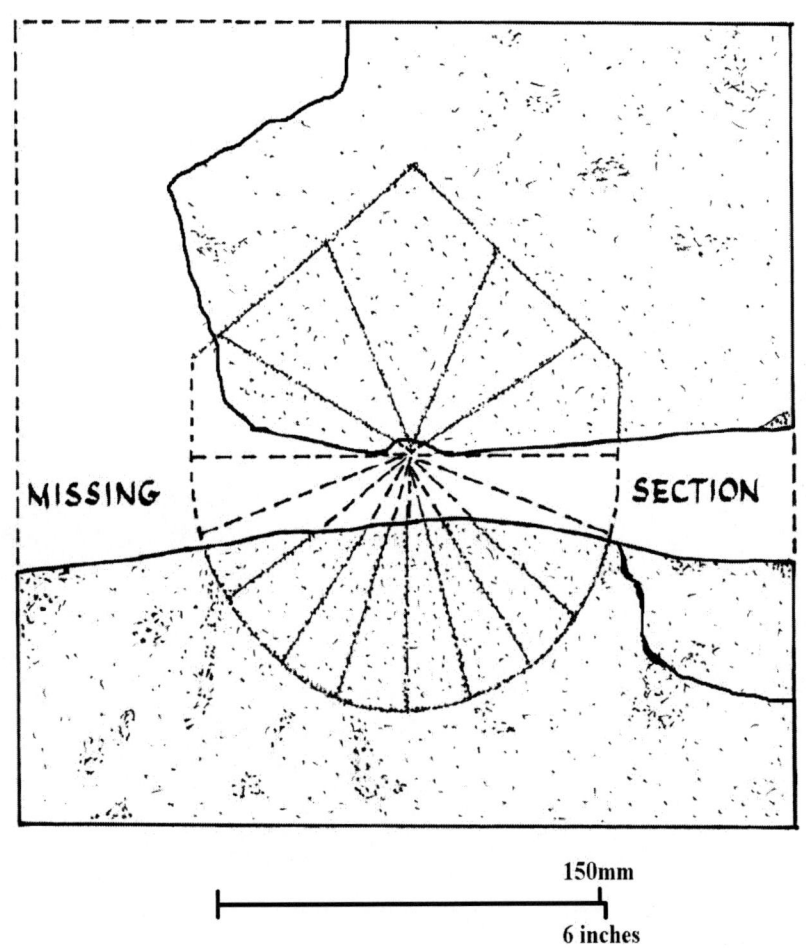

Fig.5 Middleton St.George Sundial

However, in Mr. Green's list, there appears one dial found near Old Byland in North Yorkshire, which is effectively subdivided into tenths. This dial is without any doubt of the Anglo-Saxon period, as it bears an inscription of that era. In contrast, no mass clock is known with decimal subdivisions.

It may be significant that Middleton and Old Byland are only about 25 miles apart, and both were in the Danish sphere of influence in the pre-Conquest period. Hence, if a decimal system of time measurement existed in the area at the time, the link between the dials at the two places is quite reasonable. One cannot draw a definite conclusion from the similarity in this one respect of the Middleton and Old Byland dials, but it does add some weight in favour of an Anglo-Saxon origin for the Middleton example, which in turn would support the case for a pre-Conquest origin for Middleton. Even more similar to the Middleton dial is another Yorkshire example with ten divisions, at Kirkburn near Driffield, but this does not have conclusive dating evidence. [10]

CHAPTER TWO - THE MIDDLE AGES

MANORIAL LORDS AND PEASANT FARMERS

Middleton lay within the anciently established Wapentake of Sadberge. Wapentakes were administrative districts in Yorkshire, and Sadberge is the sole example inexplicably occurring north of the Tees. Its origins are unknown, but it clearly was established before the Norman Conquest. The inclusion of Middleton in the Wapentake of Sadberge is the reason why it was excluded from the Boldon Book. Not being part of the bishopric at the time, its returns were made to the royal exchequer, and were for convenience registered with Northumberland.

Middleton emerges into written history in 1166 with an entry in the so-called Red Book of the Exchequer.

"…..Willelmus filius Siwardi…….me de vobes tenere quandam villam, Goseford nominatum, et aliam quandam dimidian quae Milletone dicitur, pro feodo et sevitio j militis….."[1].

In translation from the Latin, William, son of Siward, declares that he held of the king (Henry II) one knight's fee in Gosforth and half of Middleton. It is known that Gosforth was reckoned as two-thirds of a knight's fee, and hence William's half of Middleton was one third of a knight's fee [2]. This holding was what became known as Over Middleton or Middleton One Row.

Another entry of the same date accounts for the other half of Middleton, also recorded as a third of a knight's fee, and held by Godfrey Baard [3]. This became distinguished as Low Middleton.

A significant event occurred in 1189, when Richard I (The Lionheart), looking for ways to finance his crusading activities, sold the Wapentake of Sadberge to the Bishop of Durham, Hugh Puiset. Thereafter, the wapentake maintained its courts and officers, but the administration became more and more integrated with that of the bishopric. Middleton, together with the other constituent parts of the wapentake, joined the rest of the county under the bishop's jurisdiction.

In the legal document recording the transaction between king and bishop, the service of the son of Godfrey Baard was included for two parts of a knight's fee in Middleton and Hartburn [4]. There are two points of interest in this statement. Firstly, the two parts of a knight's fee appear to be the summation of the two holdings recorded in 1166, but only the Baard name is given, with no mention of a separate holder for Middleton One Row. The Victoria County History suggests that one name had been omitted, or that, at the time of the transaction, Baard was responsible for the whole of the service [5] Secondly, the name Hartburn appears for the first time. More precisely defined as West Hartburn, it was always in medieval times linked with Low Middleton.

The fact that the services of Godfrey Baard were specifically included in the document for the bishop's acquisition of the Wapentake of Sadberge is interesting. The reason for this is that other places in the Wapentake, including Dinsdale and Long Newton, had the powerful Bruce and Balliol families as overlords. Middleton did not, and the bishop presumably wanted to make it clear that the service for Middleton was due directly to him.

From these earliest documentary references, it is clear that the component parts of the parish were already established by the twelfth century. Although there are no means of knowing the precise boundaries, supporting information from later records and the archaeological evidence combine to allow the general layout of the parish around the year 1200 to be broadly reconstructed with a good degree of confidence, as shown in Fig.6. This overall manorial framework endured for some four centuries longer, although the details of the arrangements within it were doubtless subject to progressive change.

Throughout the Middle Ages, the local unit of organisation and administration was the manor. The map shows the parish to have been made up of three manors. However, the definition of West Hartburn as such requires some clarification. Low Middleton and Over Middleton or Middleton One Row, were manors in their own right, each with its own manorial administration. West Hartburn is

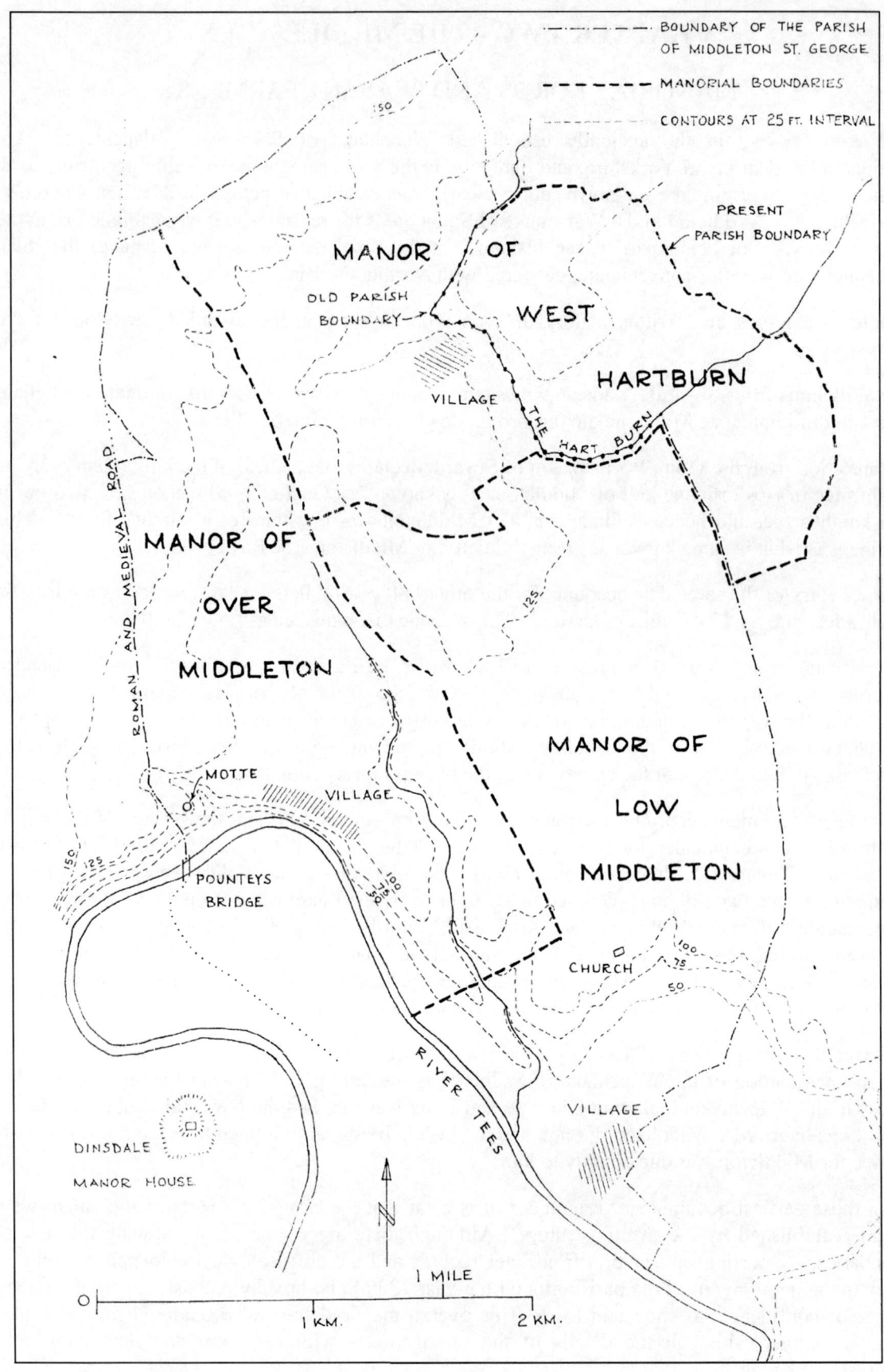

Fig.6 Manorial Middleton

also frequently referred to as "the manor", and had its own identity and village nucleus. However, it was always held principally by the lords of Low Middleton, and was effectively controlled by them.

At this stage, a note on nomenclature may be appropriate. In the earliest records the name Middleton appears alone without any distinguishing prefix. Later the manor on the eastern side is called either Middleton St. George or Nether Middleton. The present hall, farm and cottages carry on the latter name as Low Middleton, which name is generally adopted in this account when referring to the manor, to avoid confusion with the parish. The other Middleton, on the western side, became more specifically Over Middleton or various forms of Middleton One Row.

The map shows the settlements in relation to the physical features of the parish - the river, other watercourses, and elevation contours. Low Middleton and Middleton One Row have frontages on the river, and it is suggested that both were established at a relatively early stage. A recent study states that," The framework of the county's settlement system is likely to be pre-Conquest" [6], and Low Middleton and Over Middleton may have been part of that early framework. Low Middleton extended northwards from its river frontage to the higher ground where St. George's Church stands. By the twelfth century, when pressure on land was becoming a significant factor, the likely scenario is that the manor had expanded much further into the land to the north. The manor house and village of Low Middleton were at the extreme south-east of the manorial lands, and functional convenience was undoubtedly the main factor behind the setting up of the subordinate "manor" of West Hartburn, as a separate unit in the northern extension. Attempts have been made to quantify the convenience factor, and it has been suggested that when the most distant arable land was more than one mile from the village it became more economic to establish a satellite or daughter settlement on the far lands [7]. On this basis, the setting up of West Hartburn would be well justified, as its arable land extended to over two miles from the parent village at Low Middleton.

Even a cursory view of the map highlights a considerable problem of interpretation. The village of Low Middleton nestled comfortably in a large low-lying basin, bounded by the river on the south and by abruptly rising ground elsewhere. This favourable location suggests a place for primary settlement, but if this were the case, the settlers would have tilled the lighter soil, eminently suitable for cultivation, all around the village, and established their boundaries accordingly. This is completely at odds with what has come down to us. The parish boundary is hard up against the eastern edge of the village, and cuts the low-lying basin into two, the western part being in Middleton St. George parish, and the somewhat larger eastern part in Egglescliffe parish. The likely explanation is that there was, at some indefinable moment in the past, pressure on the desirable land from both sides, east and west, with the parish boundary marking an agreed division between the two interests.

The land to the east of the parish boundary belonged to the manor of Trafford, within the parish of Egglescliffe, and it must be assumed that there was early competition for the Middleton basin, resolved by compromise agreement with the contesting party in the east. The village of Low Middleton may have been an independent settlement, or perhaps a planted settlement to establish and maintain the foothold of the landowning interests to the west - possibly the predecessors of the medieval lords of Dinsdale and Over Middleton. The suggested line of settlement expansion is shown diagrammatically in Fig.7. The inference from the disproportionate division of the Middleton basin is that the settlers from the east were either stronger than those from the west, or, more likely, were established first.

This proposition also provides some reason for the name "Middleton", which is not otherwise explicable. The very common name means the middle farm, settlement or village, and could well be applied to a new settlement set up at the interface between already existing settlements to east and west.

It is very likely that the definition of the eastern parish boundary had been established no later than the mid-twelfth century, when the pattern of Middleton manors was firmly in place. It could have

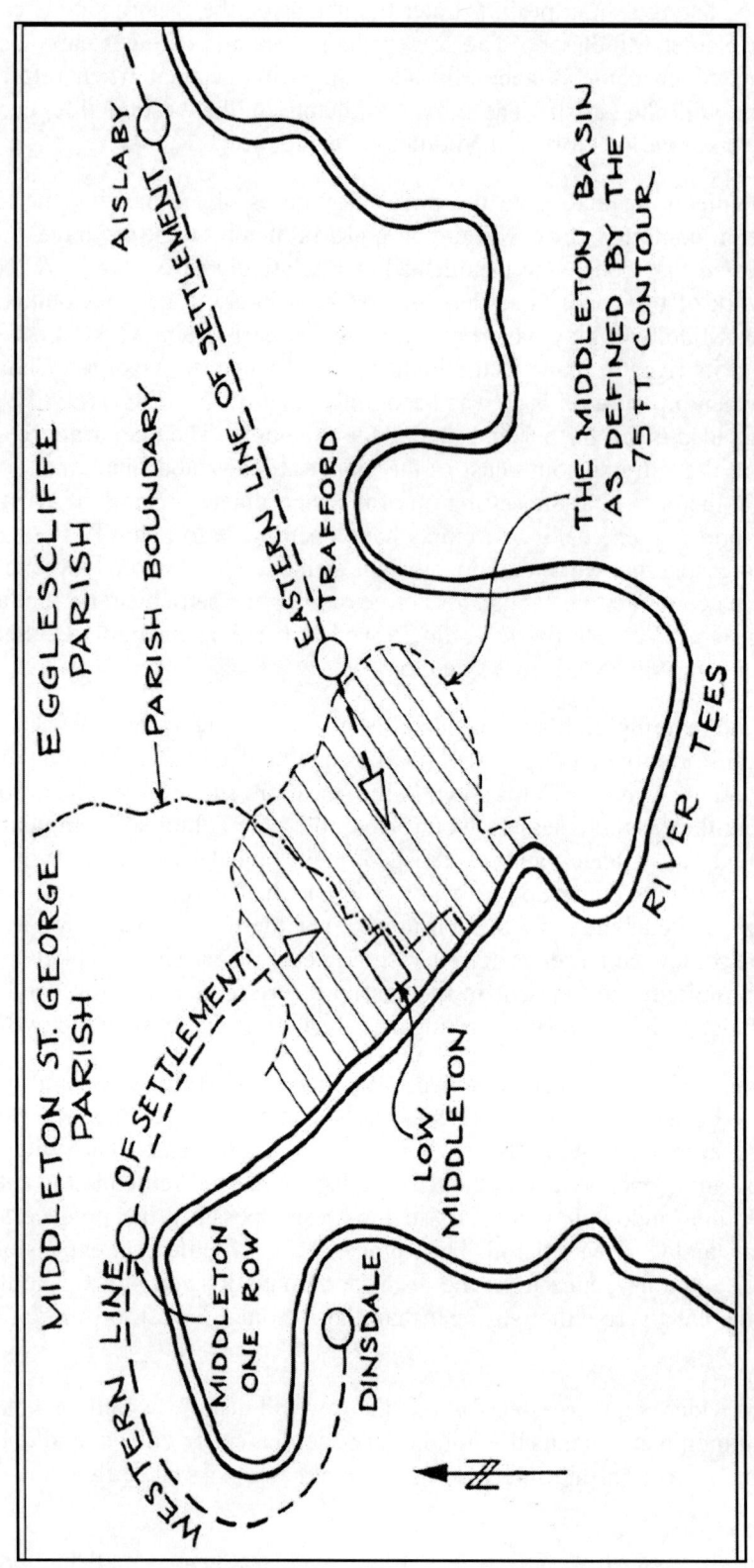

Fig. 7 Suggested opposing lines of settlement determining the eastern boundary of the parish of Middleton St. George

been established very much earlier, but the absence of information on the formation of parishes precludes any closer view. The boundary may have been defined as a demarcation between estates, before the existence of a church for Middleton, in which case it would have pre-dated the formation of the parish. When the Middleton settlements did acquire a church, the setting up of a separate parish would rationally follow, making use of the existing estate boundary.

The establishment of the western parish boundary would have been less contentious than on the east, as it lay entirely within the province of the lords of Dinsdale. Being the dominant influence on the western side, they would have played a major part in determining the parish boundary, which also formed a domestic division between their home manor of Dinsdale and their holding of Over Middleton. It is significant that the customary rights of tenants of Over Middleton included the use of land at Stodhoe, in the parish of Dinsdale. This was probably a very early established practice, which was maintained after the parish boundary was drawn up.

Before looking at the constituent manors in the parish of Middleton St. George, it is worth reviewing briefly the typical characteristics of the rural landscape in the Middle Ages, in the form which pertained to Middleton's location in lowland Durham.

The arable lands of the manor were arranged in large open fields, normally three in number, but sometimes subject to variation in that respect. The fields were tilled in rotation, and, in the normal three field system, one remained fallow each year. Each farmer had his land in the form of long narrow strips, intermixed with those of the other tenants, and spread throughout the fields. Cultivation was in common, with each farmer providing his share of resources, in way of labour, plough beasts and equipment, proportionate to the size of his holding. For example, a farmer with a very modest holding might provide one ox towards an eight ox plough team. All had to work to the same time scale and routine for ploughing, sowing and harvesting.

The arable fields usually surrounded the village. Beyond them lay the common pasture land of the manor. Each farmer had a right to graze a defined number of cattle, horses and sheep. Herdsmen and shepherds were appointed to look after the herds and flocks, and to prevent them straying onto the unfenced arable land.

In the normal pattern, the houses of the farmers were grouped together in the village, and not dispersed as are the farmhouses of today. Each house had its own toft or yard, where hens and pigs might be kept, and often also its own croft, which was an attached cultivated plot where vegetables and other crops could be grown.

If the manor had a resident lord, his house was normally close by the village. The land which the lord of the manor kept in his own hands was called the demesne. This was sometimes scattered throughout the fields with the lands of his tenants, but often it was gathered together for greater convenience in a separate demesne parcel. The tenants had customary obligations to work the demesne lands of the lord.

Normally, the manor court regulated the whole of the working of the manor, and also dealt with disputes and petty crimes. The lord of the manor appointed a bailiff or steward as his representative, to look after the detail management on his behalf. Other minor officials, such as the hayward, could be appointed to deal with specific functions. It has to be noted, however, that in the particular circumstances of Durham the system of local courts is far from clear [8]. The bishop's halmote court, meeting at Sadberge, would for some matters have included Middleton within its jurisdiction, but the more domestic issues were probably dealt with by manor courts at Low Middleton and Over Middleton (or Dinsdale).

It must be emphasised that the foregoing is only an outline of typical manorial arrangements. The traditional view that such a system persisted virtually unchanged throughout the Middle Ages is now discredited. The general pattern did indeed continue, but modern research shows progressive changes occurring all the time. Sometimes separate farmsteads existed outside the basic common field pattern, and, even within the traditional open fields, amalgamation of strips often led to an individual's land coming together in one or more fenced closes.

There is no reason to believe that the Middleton manors did not follow, at least in essence, the typical functional layout, although each doubtless had its own particular features. It is now appropriate to look at each of the three manors in turn.

LOW MIDDLETON

The isolated position of St. George's Church has sometimes brought forward the suggestion that there must once have been a village there. There is, however, no evidence that this was ever the case. As indicated on the manorial map in Fig.6, the medieval village was sited in and around the area where Low Middleton Hall stands today. The remaining earthworks in the form of low banks in a small paddock on the opposite side of the road to the Hall were surveyed by the writer in 1963. (See Pl. 1) These banks were the last signs of the village to be seen on the ground. They are now ploughed out, and whatever remains of the medieval village lies hidden beneath the earth. At the time of the survey, the small paddock was the only area on that side of the road which had remained uncultivated and in grass since the desertion of the village. Subsequent ploughing all around had long before destroyed all other signs of the old village. However, the recorded earthworks do give an accurate position of one line of village street, and from this the likely layout of the village as a whole can be determined.

The most common form of village in the locality comprised two roughly parallel rows of houses with a green area between. Middleton One Row was so named because of its unusual single row layout, and to distinguish it from Low Middleton, which was presumably of the normal double row arrangement. Where then was the second row at Low Middleton? The clue probably lies in the alignment of a field boundary to the north of the road with the edge of an artificially raised rectangular area south of the road. This area has an 18th.century dovecote at its south-east corner, and was probably part of the landscaping scheme around the Hall, carried out in that period. The likelihood is that the landscaping made use of whatever earthworks remained from the medieval village, and simply flattened them out, regularising the shape to create the raised area visible today. The flattened earthworks on that side would represent the second row of houses. From this consideration of the evidence, the layout of the medieval village of Low Middleton can be reconstructed generally as shown on the plan in Fig.8. (See also Pl.5)

It can be seen that the parish boundary takes a conscious turn around the north-east corner of the village area. At the south-west corner, the western building line probably continued, but has been subsequently masked by the present Low Middleton Hall and Farm. Where the manor house was situated in those early times is uncertain. It almost certainly lay within or adjacent to the grouping of village houses, and quite possibly, on the same site that the Hall or Farm occupies today.

The earthworks previously visible conformed to a typical pattern of medieval settlement for the area, and generally over much of lowland England. The houses fronted onto a village green, and were elevated slightly on raised platforms, probably the accumulation of a succession of buildings on the same site. Low banks, originally with fences, divided the plots, and shallow ditches carried away water and waste. Houses would have been single storey, generally of one or two rooms, with animals often under the same roof.

Only one actual house site was identifiable at Low Middleton. This can be seen on the plan, adjacent to a pair of present-day houses immediately north of the road. From the size of the mound, this had been a relatively substantial building. It stood in its own enclosure, and was separated by a small ditch from two similar enclosures in the same alignment to the north. The surface indications were not, however, revealing enough for any other houses to be recognised.

Based on the assumed arrangement of the village, it would have comprised about 10-12 households, with perhaps a population of some 40-60 people. We have no specific knowledge of any individual inhabitants, but the lives of all would have been devoted to the seasonal cycle of agricultural work, and the often precarious maintenance of their livelihoods and their families.

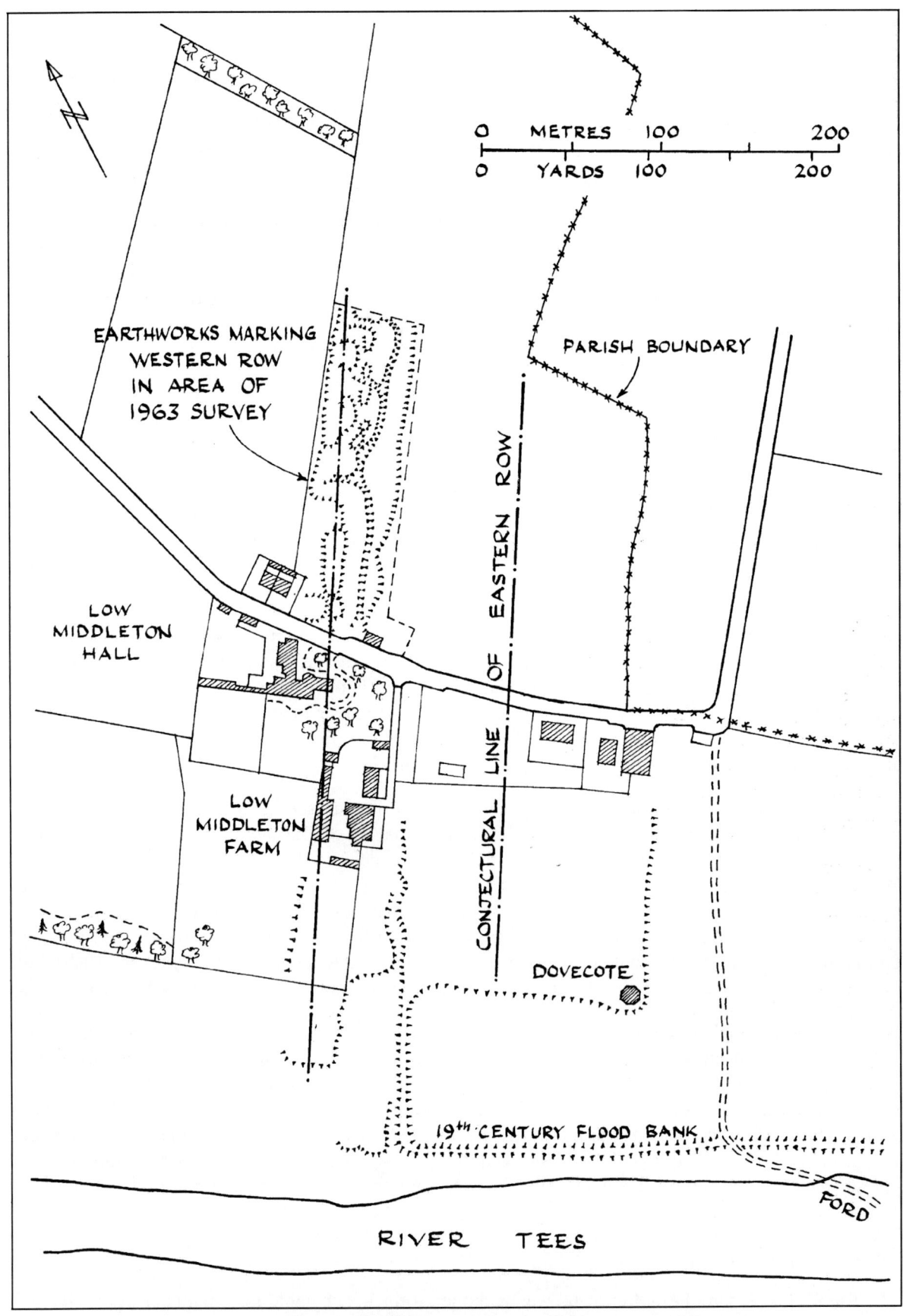

Fig.8 The site of the medieval village of Low Middleton or Middleton St.George

Beyond the little plots attached to their houses, lay the open fields which they tilled communally. These must have been laid out, initially at least, on the low-lying land in the river basin to the north, south and west of the village, as the land there is light, and on that account attractive to early settlers for their crops. The ancient pattern of the open fields is long lost, but it is likely that, as the population increased, it became necessary to extend the tilled area to the higher surrounding ground, where the heavy clay soil was a greater challenge. Moving still further away from the village, lay the common pastures, where the animals of lord and people were grazed.

The Victoria County History cites the various documentary references pertaining to the descent of ownership of the manor. The picture these present is far from simple. What is clearly established is that the manor was held in two parts or "moieties". When Godfrey Baard answered for his lands in 1166, it was said that these were half of an estate, the other half being held by Roland Baard, probably Godfrey's brother [9]. As mentioned earlier, Ralph Baard, the son of Godfrey, was noted as being accountable for the whole of Middleton in 1189. However, the division of Low Middleton into two parts appears consistently thereafter in the line of succession until they were united at the beginning of the seventeenth century. The two lines can be separately considered.

The Baard Portion

Around 1210 another Ralph Baard, probably the son of Roland, held one sixth of a knight's fee, half of the one third of a knight's fee for the whole of Low Middleton. About a century later, in 1320 or thereabouts, another Roland Baard died, holding a moiety of the manor of Low Middleton. The last of the Baard name to be in possession of the half share of the manor was yet another Ralph in 1367 [10].

However, some family connection continued, when William Walworth was recorded as being in possession in 1378 [11]. He seems to have been a relative of the Baards [12], and was a notable character on the national stage. His family had earlier held lands in Darlington, but he himself had been a fishmonger, rising up the ladder of trade to become mayor of London. He was knighted by the young Richard II, after his unsaddling of Wat Tyler at Smithfield culminated in the latter's death, and led eventually to the ending of the Peasant's Revolt in 1381.

By the 15th.century, the Killinghall family had appeared on the scene, but again some continuity seems to have been maintained, as Longstaffe in his "History of Darlington" links the Killinghalls with the Walworths. He remarks that the Killinghalls had acquired the Darlington possessions of the Walworths, and assumes that this was by marriage to a Walworth heiress [13]. Presumably the acquisition of Low Middleton came by the same or a similar route. The other connection pointed out by Longstaffe is in the coats of arms, both families sharing the corn sheaves motif for their shields. Even more significantly, the ancient coat of arms of the Killinghalls bore three kelyngs (codfish), not only a play on their name, but also a sign of the fish trade connection, shared with the Walworths [14].

In 1417 John Killinghall was recorded at his death as holding the manor of Nether Middleton [15]. In 1385 he had been clerk to Bishop Fordham's justices itinerant [16], and by 1413 had become a travelling justice himself, hearing cases at local courts on behalf of the bishop, Cardinal Langley [17]. His son and grandson were both also called John. One or other of them was one of the squires who took an oath before the bishop, Cardinal Langley, in 1434 "not to maintain evil-doers, as prescribed by parliament" [18]. The third John was succeeded by his son Thomas, who was in turn followed by his son Hugh. On Hugh's death in 1509, he was said to have held two thirds of the manor of Nether Middleton [19].

The Cambe Portion

The Ralph Baard, son of Godfrey, who was reckoned to be accountable for the manor at the time of the bishop's purchase of the Wapentake of Sadberge in 1189, would appear to have been more specifically the holder of the second moiety of Low Middleton. Soon afterwards this part of the manor had come into the possession of Walter and Robert de Cambe, nephews of Bishop Hugh Puiset's chamberlain.

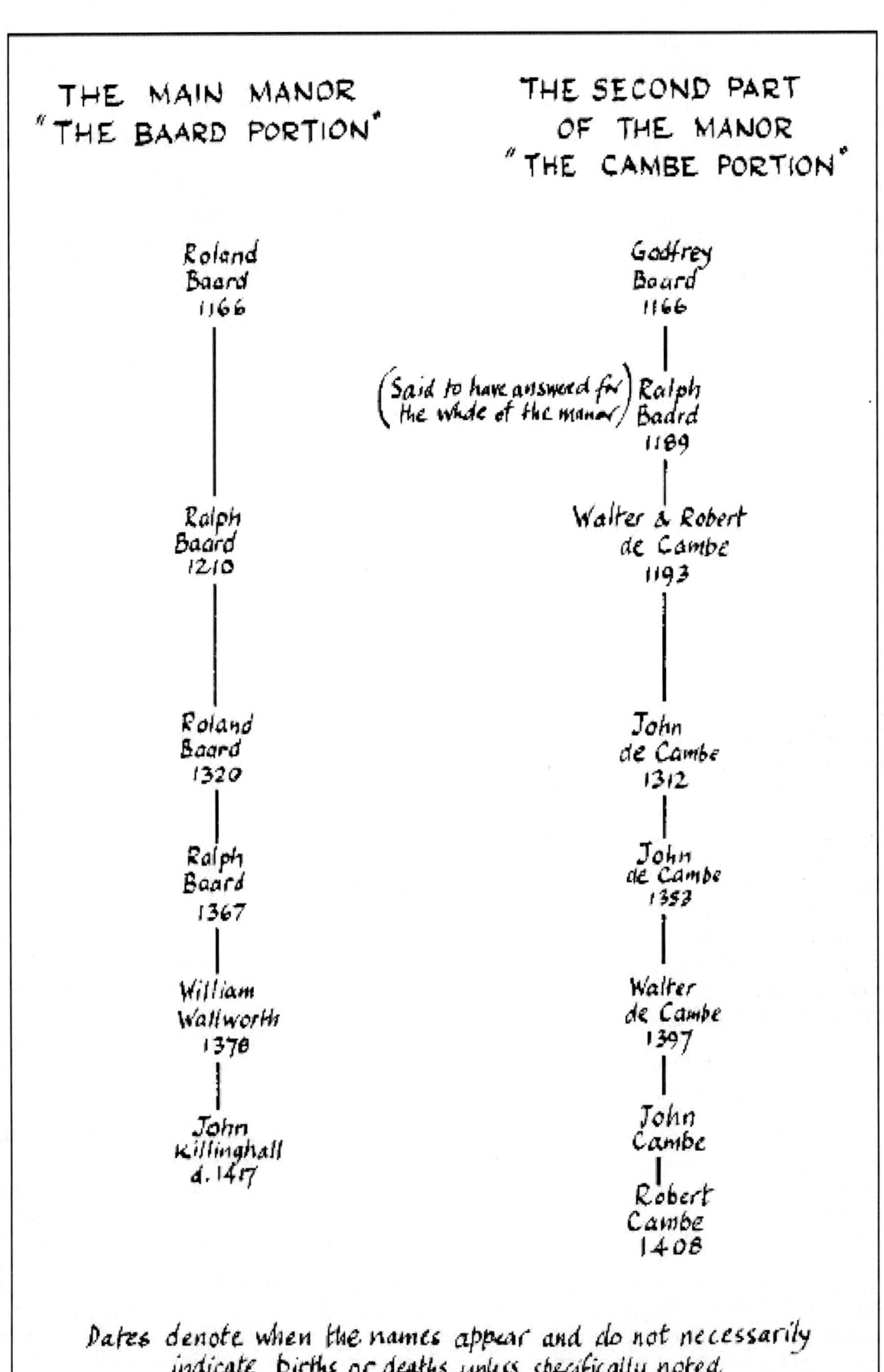

Fig. 9 Descent of the manor of Low Middleton or Middleton St. George up to c.1400

The Victoria County History suggests that this acquisition was by marriages to two Baard heiresses [20]. Through Walter de Cambe, the lands descended in the Cambe family for over three centuries.

An insight into medieval tenurial arrangements is obtained by looking at a typical example from the Durham archives, recording the situation when Walter de Cambe died in 1397, and was succeeded by his son John. Walter was said to have held a capital messuage and ten oxgangs of land in Nether Middleton in fee tail and two oxgangs in fee simple [21]. His total of twelve oxgangs corresponds with what was recorded at other times. Very roughly, this represented arable land of about 180 acres. Inherently associated with this were commensurate rights on the grazing land. A capital messuage meant a chief house, possibly the manor house. Holdings in fee tail had inheritance restrictions, while those in fee simple were unencumbered in that respect. Looking at the terms of tenure, Walter de Cambe was said to have held his lands from the bishop by knight's service, suit of court at Sadberge, and 13d. rent. Knight's service was the feudal form of tenure, whereby lands were granted by the overlord in return for the service of a stipulated number of knights. For various reasons, and particularly when the knight's fee was a fractional quantity, as at Low Middleton, the service was often commuted to "scutage", which was a money payment. The "suit" element was a requirement that Walter had to confirm his tenure at the bishop's court at Sadberge. The 13d. rent, was a nominal amount, rather than reflecting the value of the lands.

The chart in Fig.9 shows the general progression of the two lines of descent of the medieval manor, without attempting to detail the full succession of holders. From the detailed evidences, it would appear that the unfolding development of the estates was not as simple as the chart might indicate, but the "backbone" lines are clear, as shown. The eventual coming together of the two lines is shown in the continuation of this chart in Fig.15 in Chapter 3.

WEST HARTBURN

The "manor" of West Hartburn extended over most of the northern part of the parish. It takes its name from the stream running through its lands, the Hart Burn, known today in this section of its course as Goosepool Beck. The stream continues eastwards as Coatham Beck and then Hartburn Beck, before running into the Tees between Stockton and Billingham. It flows through the existing Hartburn Village, more properly East Hartburn, which is now enveloped by Stockton. Goosepool, the eastern portion of West Hartburn was in the parish of Long Newton until comparatively recent times, when it became part of Middleton St. George.

Although only a small stream at its western end, the Hart Burn was undoubtedly important as the water supply for the village of West Hartburn, which lay on a gently rising slope to the west of the stream. The village site straddles the present-day road, which, until recent reshaping of the road system, ran between the modern village of Middleton St. George and Long Newton. Today, all that can be seen are the mounds and depressions in the grass field to the south of the road. (Pl.6) Similar evidence to the north of the road has been ploughed out. Prior to this, the whole site was surveyed and the village layout recorded, as shown in Fig.10.

The layout is conventional, with a central village green, flanked by a row of houses on each side. The houses stood in their own little enclosures, with perimeter banks and ditches. Between the green and the houses on the south side was a sunken road, worn down by the passage of people, animals and carts over the centuries. There may have been a similar track on the north side of the green, but any signs of it have been obliterated by the present roadway.

Making up for the absence of any written description of the village, there is archaeological evidence for the houses of the villagers to supplement the field survey information. Excavations were carried out on three house sites between 1962 and 1968 [22, 23, 24]. All that remains are the buried lowest courses of the houses, but that is sufficient to allow us to form a picture of how they looked and how they were used.

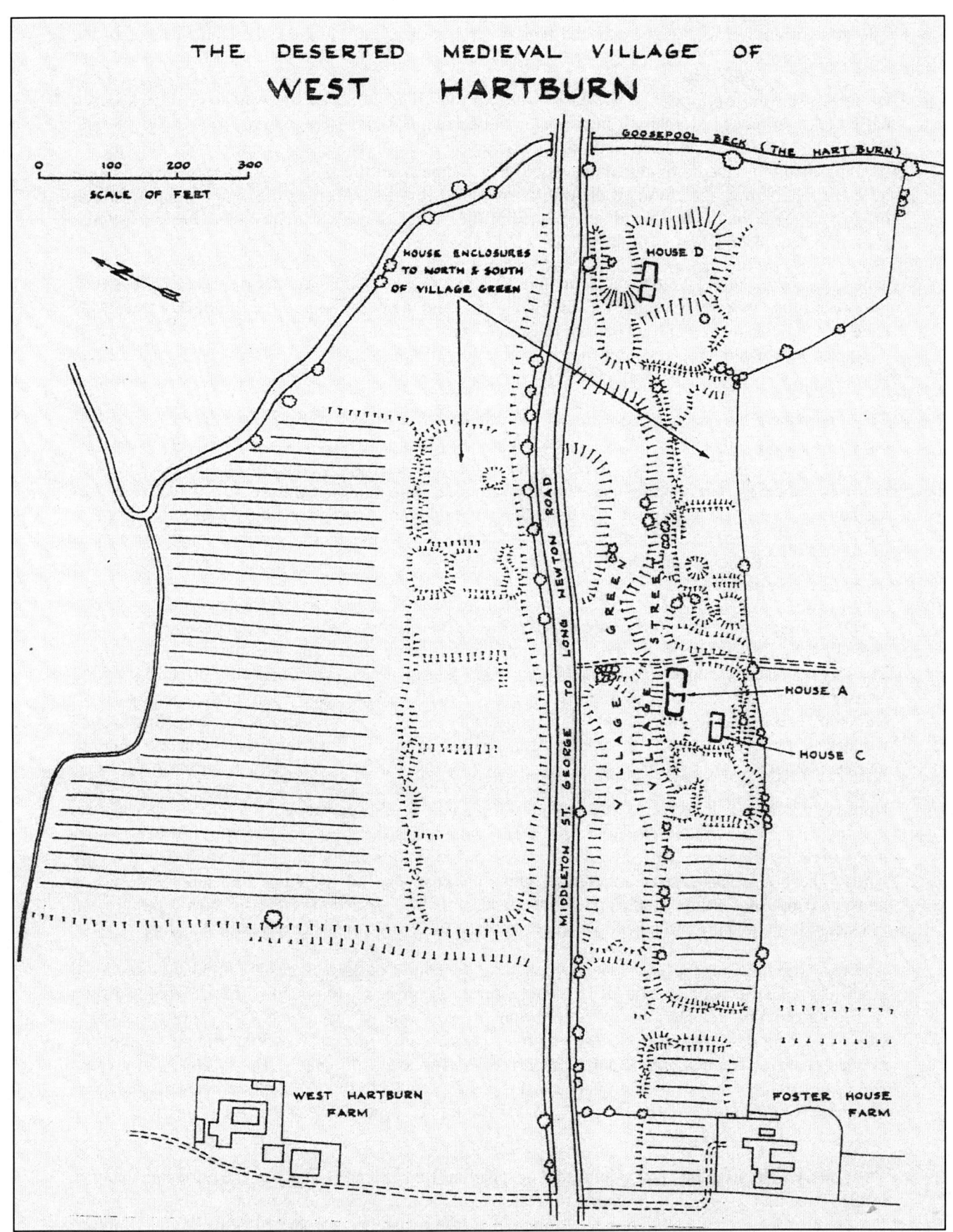

Fig. 10 The deserted medieval village of West Hartburn

The ground plans of the three excavated houses are shown in Fig.11, using the nomenclature of the original reports.

House D, shown in Pl.7, was at the eastern end of the village, and its site was marked by a raised earthwork platform. Externally it measured about 58 feet (17.7 metres) long by 20 feet (6.1 metres) wide. Its low walls had been carefully constructed of undressed river stones, with clay as the bonding medium. The building stones would have come from the river Tees, at its nearest about a mile and a half away. The stone walls would have been very low, forming the base for upper walling of clay or wattle and daub. Nothing remained of the timber framing which would have supported a roof of thatch. All the houses in the village would have been of only one storey.

This is a good example of a typical "long house", a two room dwelling, with a cross passage between the two rooms. One of the rooms was the living area, and the other housed the livestock when it was necessary to keep them inside. There were two doorways into the house, one at each end of the cross passage. No trace remained of the flimsy partitioning dividing the house. Both rooms had earthen floors.

The room where the family lived and slept was about was about 17 feet (5.2 metres) by 14 feet (4.3 metres) in size, and had a central hearth set into the floor. In its later stage, as uncovered by excavation, a disused mill stone had been used to form the hearth. A drainage channel for the slops ran from the hearth, through the intermediate partitioning, and into the cattle space at the other end of the house. The house was on a very slight slope, with the animal section, for reason of drainage, at the lower end. From a central sump a stone lined and capped channel ran through the outer wall to discharge outside the house. The animal end, 31 feet (9.5 metres) long, was appreciably larger than the family living end.

An interesting feature from this house was a saltire form of cross, carved on a small sandstone block embedded in a former door sill. This must have been of some significance, as decorative carving of any sort is not to be expected in a medieval village house. The suggestion is that it is a "witching cross", in the same tradition as the "witch posts" found in some early farmhouses in the North Yorkshire Moors, not too far distant [25]. Traditionally the cross was regarded as a protection against witches, stopping the witch in the course of her passage from the doorway, past the hearth, and out up the chimney.

House A was also a "long house" of two rooms with a cross passage between. Slightly larger in size, it was similar in construction to House D. What remained of the lower walling was, however, rather more irregular, due to collapse in places of one or both stone faces which had sandwiched a clay core. The house had clearly undergone numerous changes, but the same division of the house between people and animals had applied over most of its life. The living end had had a central hearth in its clay floor, and the animal end had had a cobbled walkway alongside the cattle standing.

At a relatively late stage, probably not long before the demise of the village, structural and functional modifications reflected domestic changes and aspirations for better living conditions. What had been fragile partitioning between the living and animal ends, was replaced by a more substantial cross wall. The central hearth was done away with, and replaced by a fireplace with a chimney against the new cross wall. The quagmire floor in the animal end was consolidated in rough stone and given a new clay surface. The assumption is that this room was added to the domestic accommodation, with the animals moved to an outbuilding. A coal store in one corner showed the use of this fuel, which was also evidenced in House D.

The pottery finds from this house indicated occupation from at least as early as the thirteenth. century to the sixteenth century, with probably several rebuilds in that period. The dating findings for House D were broadly similar. A silver penny found in House A had been produced at the Durham mint of Bishop Ruthall (1509-1523). Amongst the other finds were many items of iron, evocative of the lives of the inhabitants. Unusually, these included spurs and stirrups, indicative of an owner of some status. Sherds of pottery occurred widely over the site, many with the typical medieval green glaze.

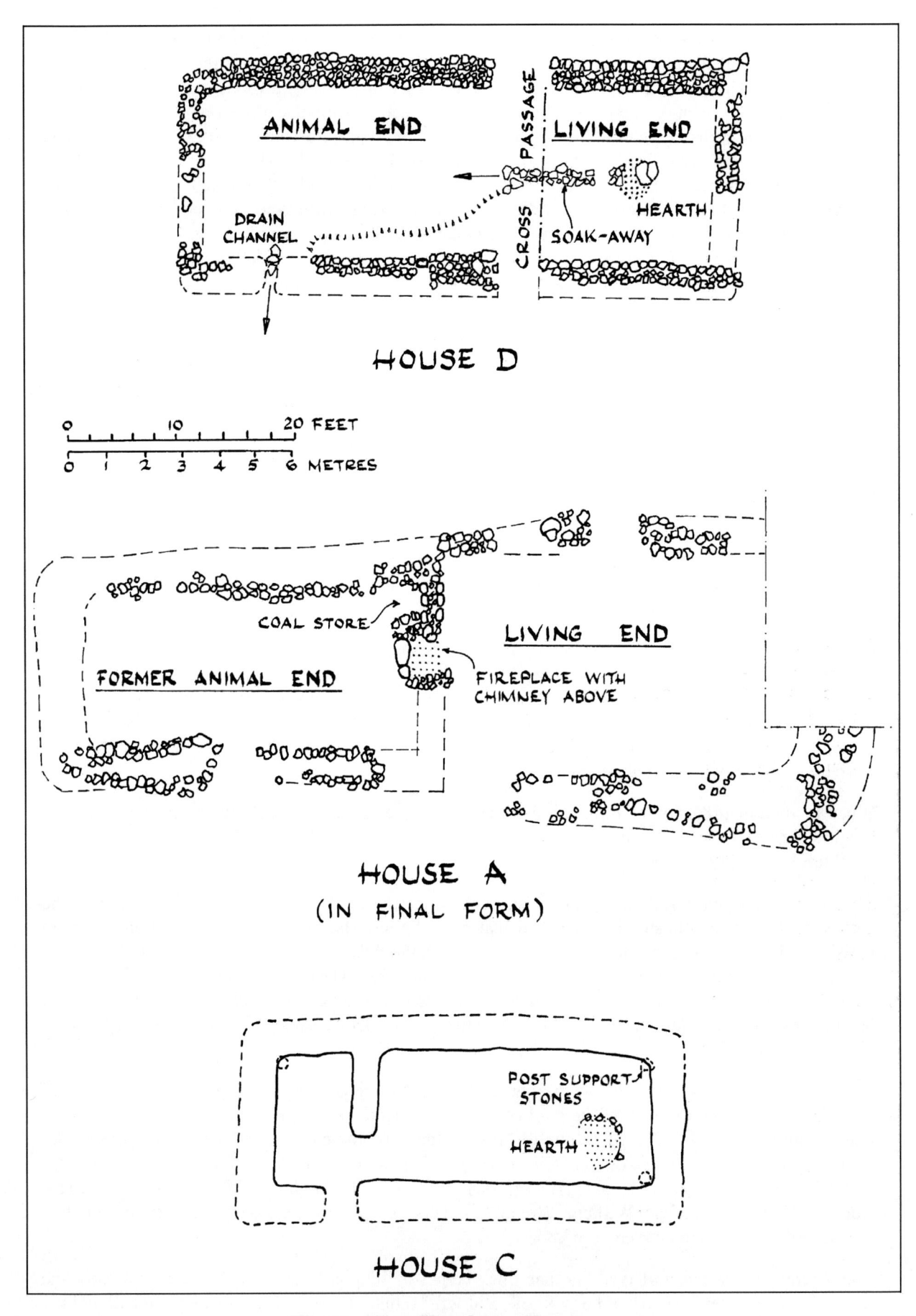

Fig.11 West Hartburn Houses

Both House A and House D were substantial dwellings, albeit primitive by modern standards. This presumably reflected the status of their respective inhabitants. In contrast, the building labelled House C was of a much more humble type. It was essentially of one room only, although there appeared to have been a small sub-division at one end. Virtually no stone was used in its construction, the walls being entirely of clay or wattle and daub. Post holes with base stones in the corners had been sockets for the timber framing supporting the roof. The house had clearly been burned down, the lines of the walls being demarcated by the burnt and fallen thatch. Again there was an open hearth, set into the floor near to the end wall. Standing within the same enclosure as House A, this smaller building may have housed other members of an extended family. Alternatively, the relatively large size of the hearth suggests that it may have served as a bakehouse or brewhouse. A re-making of the earthen floor, with the obliteration of the hearth, was probably associated with a change of use.

A very interesting find from this building was a silver brooch, with a crudely inscribed Latin inscription, reading in translation, "Jesus the Nazarene / King of the Jews". This may have been acquired as a pilgrim token, or may simply have been a valued possession of someone of modest affluence. It was found beneath the floor level, where it had probably been hidden. Similar brooches have been found in hoards near the border in Scotland, thought to have been hidden at the time of extensive border warfare in the early fourteenth century [26]. It may be that, in similar circumstances south of the border, the West Hartburn brooch takes Middleton back into direct involvement with the era of Robert the Bruce and the Wars of Scottish Independence.

West Hartburn has afforded an opportunity to appreciate something of the otherwise elusive medieval village house. Similar forms of buildings no doubt prevailed also at Low Middleton and at Over Middleton or Middleton One Row.

In 1189 Ralph Baard's two-thirds of a knight's fee was said to be in "Middleton and Hartburn". The latter is West Hartburn, which was in the Middle Ages always in the possession of the holders of Low Middleton. It was similarly divided in terms of ownership, into two parts. It follows that one part of West Hartburn descended in the Baard line and the other part in the Cambe line, as for Low Middleton. In the same pattern of succession, as explained later, the two parts of West Hartburn were by about 1520 in Killinghall hands.

When he died in 1486, John Killinghall had held "140 acres called West Hartburn" of the bishop by knight's service and suit [27]. In 1526 his great grandson William died, holding the manor of West Hartburn by knight's service [28].

This is nothing like the full territorial extent of West Hartburn. Apart from the split ownership, the picture is further complicated in respect of that part of West Hartburn which was in Long Newton parish. In 1210 Robert de Cambe held one twelfth of a knight's fee [29], and this is probably the same as the one twelfth of a knight's fee said in 1306 to be due from Hartburn "formerly John de Balliol's land" [30]. The Balliols had been lords of Long Newton, and hence the land in question must have been the part of West Hartburn within Long Newton parish. This corresponds to the present farms of High and Low Goosepool.

Around 1348-60 licence was given to John de Meynill to acquire a fourth part of the "manor of Goosepool" [31]. The location of the land concerned is identified by the legal confirmation in 1421 that Thomas Ashby of Sadberge had held Hartburn lands "on the east side of the brook" of Sir John Conyers, and on the west side of John Killinghall [32]. The Killinghall ownership seems subsequently to have extended to Goosepool, as in 1547 the wife of Francis Killinghall sold 290 acres "on the east side of West Hartburn" to William Wrenn [33]. This equates to the combined area of the two Goosepool farms which later emerged.

The Wrenn interest had started earlier than this. Francis Killinghall's wife was Katherine Wrenn, and her widowed mother Margery in her will of 1540 left "....unto my sonn Frauncys Kylynghall and my doughter Kateryn his wyffe all my corne sowen and unsowen and xij drawe oxen with waynes, ploughes and other appurtenances which I have at Middleton George, and xij stootes, vij scoure shepe and foure going at Wynghous besides his awne goodes which he hathe going at Hartbone......"[34]. There is no mention of any land, but the Wrenns would appear to have been in beneficial possession. The actual ownership of land passed to them in the later transactions of 1547 and 1548. The Killinghall selling of their Goosepool lands in 1547 to William Wrenn, was followed in 1548 by the relinquishing to him of the remainder of the Baard portion on the west side of West Hartburn [35]. The Killinghall family, however, retained the Cambe portion, also on the west side, not disposing of this until 1595 [36] as noted in the next chapter.

OVER MIDDLETON

Over Middleton or Middleton One Row differs in two respects from Low Middleton and West Hartburn - firstly in its medieval overlordship, and secondly in the fact that the village still exists today. It is the only one of the three medieval settlements to have survived.

The manor of Over Middleton occupied the western side of the parish of Middleton St. George, where it abutted on the parish of Dinsdale, with which it was closely associated. It has already been seen that in 1166 William, son of Siward and lord of Dinsdale, held one third of a knight's fee in Over Middleton.

Dividing the parishes of Middleton St. George and Dinsdale is the Roman road which crossed the Tees near the northern extremity of one of the sinuous loops of the river. Tradition has it that there was a Roman bridge, Pons Teys, at the crossing point, and this has been perpetuated in the name Pontesse or Pounteys applied to the later forded crossing and the land nearby. Although there is no evidence to support the existence of a Roman bridge, there is no doubt that there was a medieval bridge. What is clear is that the old road continued to be used as one of the important routes northwards. The river crossing, bridged or forded, was a strategic control point. High on the northern river bank, on the eastern side of the road, stands the motte [37] which gave the adjacent Victorian house the name Tower Hill. The motte, shown in Pl.4, is an earthwork mound, which would have been surmounted by a timber tower, and provided a position of strength overlooking the river crossing. An associated enclosed area, the bailey, would have provided space for horses and for all the related activities of defence and everyday living. Any traces of enclosing banks and ditches have been obliterated by housing developments, and the mound itself is masked by trees which would not originally have been there. From its type, the motte is likely to have been constructed around the middle of the twelfth century or slightly later, possibly by the William, son of Siward, known from the records, or at least by someone quite close to him in time, and also probably in family connection.

The village of Middleton One Row stands a short distance east of the motte, and was no doubt under its protection. There has been a good deal of modern expansion, but the ancient layout which gave it its name is still the core of the village, a single row of houses on the high northern bank of the river Tees. These houses in the Middle Ages would have been very much of the same form as those excavated at West Hartburn.

A very significant document relating to the physical make-up of the village records the sale in 1598 of the Surtees Over Middleton estate to Anthony Felton of Jarrow. The property is described as "The manor, ten messuages, ten cottages, ten gardens, ten orchards, 100 acres of arable, 100 of meadow, 200 of pasture, 100 of moor, 40 of furze and bryer, in Over Middleton and Stodhow" [38]. This is a classic description of how manorial land was divided between the tenants in the early pattern of organisation. The precise details may be questioned, but the documentary description is invaluable, as it provides a revealing link between the Middle Ages and the present day. The ten messuages, with their cottages and appurtenances, had probably made up the village of Over Middleton or Middleton One Row since the first mention of it in the twelfth century. Throughout the intervening centuries changes would undoubtedly have taken place, but the basic pattern is likely to have remained the same.

Just as we can look back at Middleton One Row over at least four centuries from 1598, we can also look forwards over a similar span of time to the present day. The 1897 Ordnance Survey map still shows the same ten messuages as the basis of the village, as shown in Fig.12. This is convincing proof of the veracity of the 1598 description of the village layout four centuries earlier. Only in the last few decades has modern building disturbed the picture. Even so, the remnants of the ancient pattern are still visible, as a remarkable example of continuity over some 800 years.

Reverting to consideration of the medieval village, the 1598 document presents a conventional picture of peasant landholding in the Middle Ages. Each messuage, together with its garden and orchard, comprised a consolidated holding, in the form of a long narrow enclosed area, extending from the row of houses to a small stream running parallel to the river. Between the houses and the steep river bank ran the rough access road. The arable land would have been in common fields, divided in intermingled strips between the villagers and perhaps also the lord of the manor in the usual way. The ridge and furrow grassland to be seen today beyond the stream may be the residual sign of the former open fields. The meadow could have been within the open fields or in separate well-watered plots elsewhere. The pasture land normally lay outside the open fields on the perimeter of the manor, but at Middleton One Row some grazing was available on the river bank, as witness the grazing rights which have come down to the present day, although no longer utilised.

The basic village structure as conveyed by the 1598 document is not in question. However, caution must be exercised in reading the details, as the description is too regular and the figures too rounded to be taken entirely at face value. There was a tendency in legal transactions to use formalised long-standing descriptions, not necessarily reflecting changes that had taken place, and this was doubtless the case here. Properties and lands were defined on the ground, and accurate measurements were not at that time regarded as essential. Based on what has come down to us, the messuage boundaries were far from regular, and the plots they enclosed were by no means equal in size

Another factor indicating departure from a regular arrangement is the reference in the 1598 document which says that the manorial lands were "in Over Middleton and Stodhow". Stodhoe is in fact in the parish of Dinsdale, and was part of the Surtees manor of Dinsdale in the Middle Ages. However, the inhabitants of Over Middleton had established rights there. A document of 1552 relating to the Surtees lands refers to "the several closes of Stodoo, wherein the tenants and inhabitants of Over-Myddleton hath used to have entercommon" [39]. This term is applied to rough grazing or moor, which the Over Middleton people were entitled to share, and perhaps also to gather some of the whins and briars mentioned in the later document. It has been suggested earlier that the customary use of land at Stodhoe may well have originated before the parish boundary was established.

William, son of Siward, is the earliest identifiable lord of both the manor of Dinsdale and also the manor of Over Middleton. The latter estate was reckoned as one third of a knight's fee. He is also the first member of the family who took their name "Super Teisam" or Surtees, from the river whose winding course formed a substantial section of the boundaries of their lands. The present old manor house of Dinsdale stands within the earthworks of the still more ancient fortified manor [40].

The long line of William's Surtees successors at Dinsdale also maintained their ownership of Over Middleton. The documented stages of the succession can be followed in the Victoria County History [41]. Dinsdale itself was in the early Middle Ages part of the Balliol overlordship, but Over Middleton was held directly of the king until 1189, when it passed into the hands of the bishop. When he died in 1435, Sir Thomas Surtees was recorded as having held the whole vill of Over Middleton from the bishop by fealty and 4s.6d. rent [42].

Although the manors of Over Middleton and Low Middleton were quite separate, their contiguous location in the same parish led to a good deal of cross leasing of lands. For example, in 1367 Gocelin Surtees held 6 oxgangs of land in Low Middleton of the heirs of John de Cambe, paying a rent of one pound of cumin and 2d [43]. This appears to have been a substantial part of Low Middleton, at a very nominal rent, and arrangements between the two parties were probably deeper than the bald figures suggest.

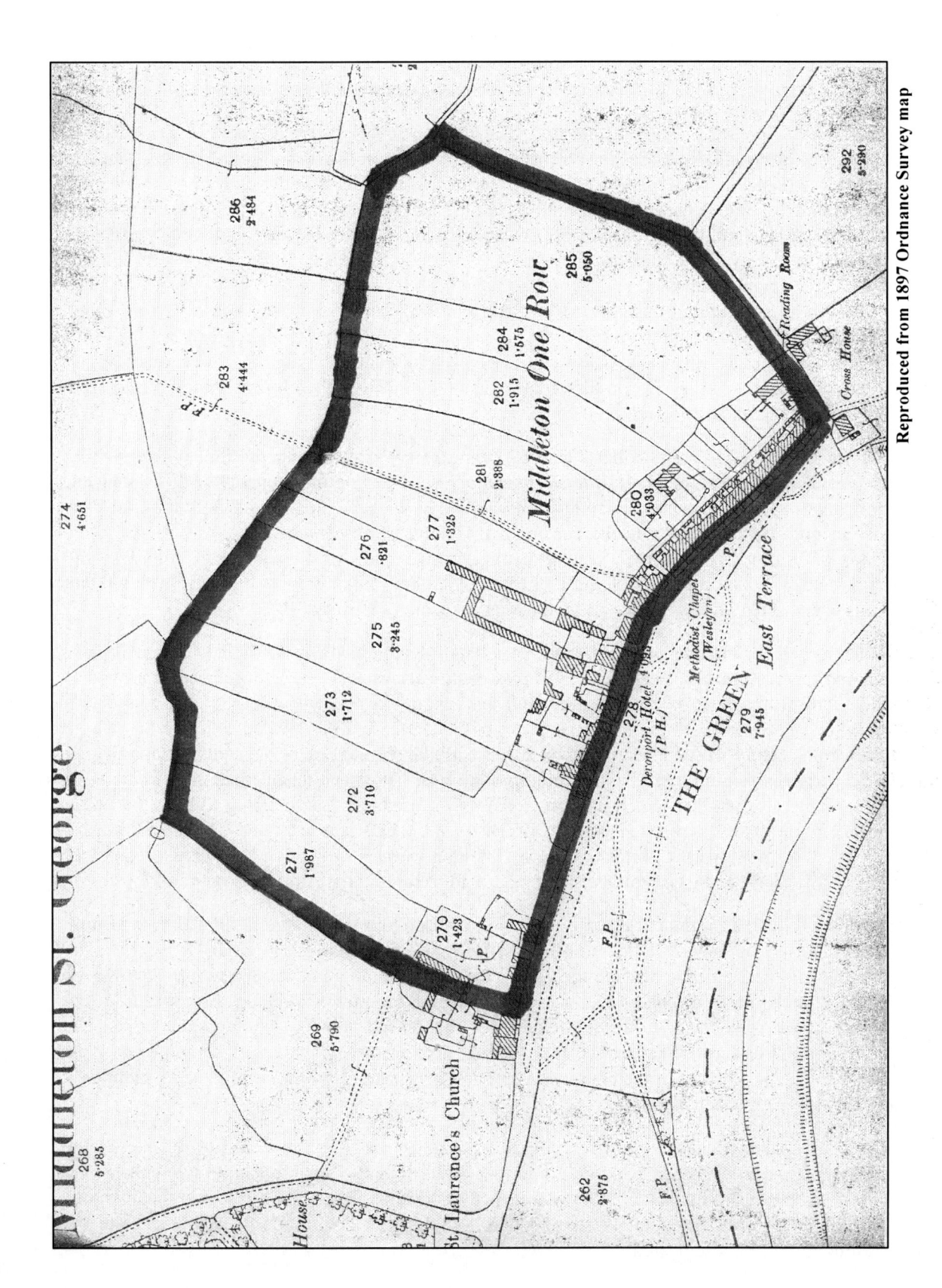

Fig. 12 The ten village holdings recorded at Middleton One Row in 1598 and still distinguishable in the twentieth century.

Reproduced from 1897 Ordnance Survey map

Gocelin was also in possession of land in both ownership portions of West Hartburn, one oxgang from the heirs of John de Cambe, as for Low Middleton, and another oxgang from Ralph Baard [44]. Conversely, in the next century, John Killinghall, who died in 1417, is recorded as having held four messuages and eight oxgangs in Over Middleton from Sir Thomas Surtees [45]. This could hardly have been a straightforward exchange, as the two instances were not contemporaneous, and it is difficult to imagine the reason for such an arrangement. Other factors, such as perhaps under-age heirs, could have been responsible.

Sometime in the thirteenth century a church was built or re-built on the rising ground overlooking the village of Low Middleton, presumably under the patronage of the Low Middleton lords of the manor. This approximate dating is based on the architectural style of the chancel arch, the only ancient dateable feature of the building. It does not necessarily follow that there was not a church on the site before that time. Many early churches were of very crude construction, and consequently did not survive in their original form. There must always have been the incentive to re-build, either because it was structurally necessary, or simply to keep up with improved standards and evolving styles. What remains of the ruined church at nearby Sockburn is also of the thirteenth century, but the many pre-Conquest sculptured stones within the church make it virtually certain that there was a much earlier building there. The early sun-dial found at Middleton has already been cited as possible evidence for an Anglo-Saxon church on the site.

The Victoria County History says that "the site is an ancient one, but no portion of the existing structure is older than the second half of the 13th.century". Accepting the accuracy of this statement, an earlier church must have existed, as two rectors, John and William, attested a charter around 1200, and other incumbents are known in the first half of the thirteenth century. As early as 1240, the Archbishop of York was called upon to give a ruling on the status of the advowson, following the death of a rector [46]. Another possible pointer to an older church is the font (Pl.8), for which a late 12th.century date is tentatively suggested by the Victoria County History [47].

The dedication to St. George is significant. An Anglo-Saxon dedication to St. George is very unlikely, and there are no firmly attested examples of this elsewhere. St. George became a popular symbolic figure at the time of the crusades, and his veneration reached a peak with Edward III's creation of the College of St. George and the Order of the Garter in 1348. A dedication to St. George in the thirteenth century would be entirely consistent with the chronology of the saint's popularity. If the church had been re-built then, the opportunity may well have been taken to adopt a fashionable dedication in place of another which had previously been used. It is interesting to note that in an early document the church is referred to as St. Gregory's [48]. The Victoria County History passes this off as a not uncommon mistake, but it is just possible that it was a projection backwards to an older dedication, particularly as St. Gregory was a popular patron saint in the Anglo-Saxon period.

The church is sited in a prominent elevated situation overlooking the village. Its position is also on the direct route linking Low Middleton and West Hartburn, as shown on the plan in Fig.13. The sunken path of the road leading through the village of West Hartburn can be seen to turn southwards towards the church, one and a half miles away, and then on to Low Middleton. Coming from the other direction, the road out of Low Middleton can be identified on aerial photographs leaving the village in a north-eastern direction, before turning northwards towards the church and West Hartburn [49]. The positioning of the church was probably influenced by the need to serve both these villages, as well as Over Middleton.

The church as it stands today is shown in Fig.20 in Chapter Six. (Pls.11, 12 &13) In the Middle Ages it was even smaller than it is now, but almost certainly had the same simple two-cell layout, with an aisleless nave and a chancel. As noted earlier, the origin of the church is lost in the unknown past, and its progressive evolution is also obscure. However, Fig.14 suggests how the medieval church building may have appeared.

The original church probably had a nave and chancel set symmetrically about the axis of the chancel arch, in whatever form that took at the time. The chancel is likely to have been much smaller than at present, serving essentially as a sanctuary to house the altar.

Reproduced from the 1954 Ordnance Survey map

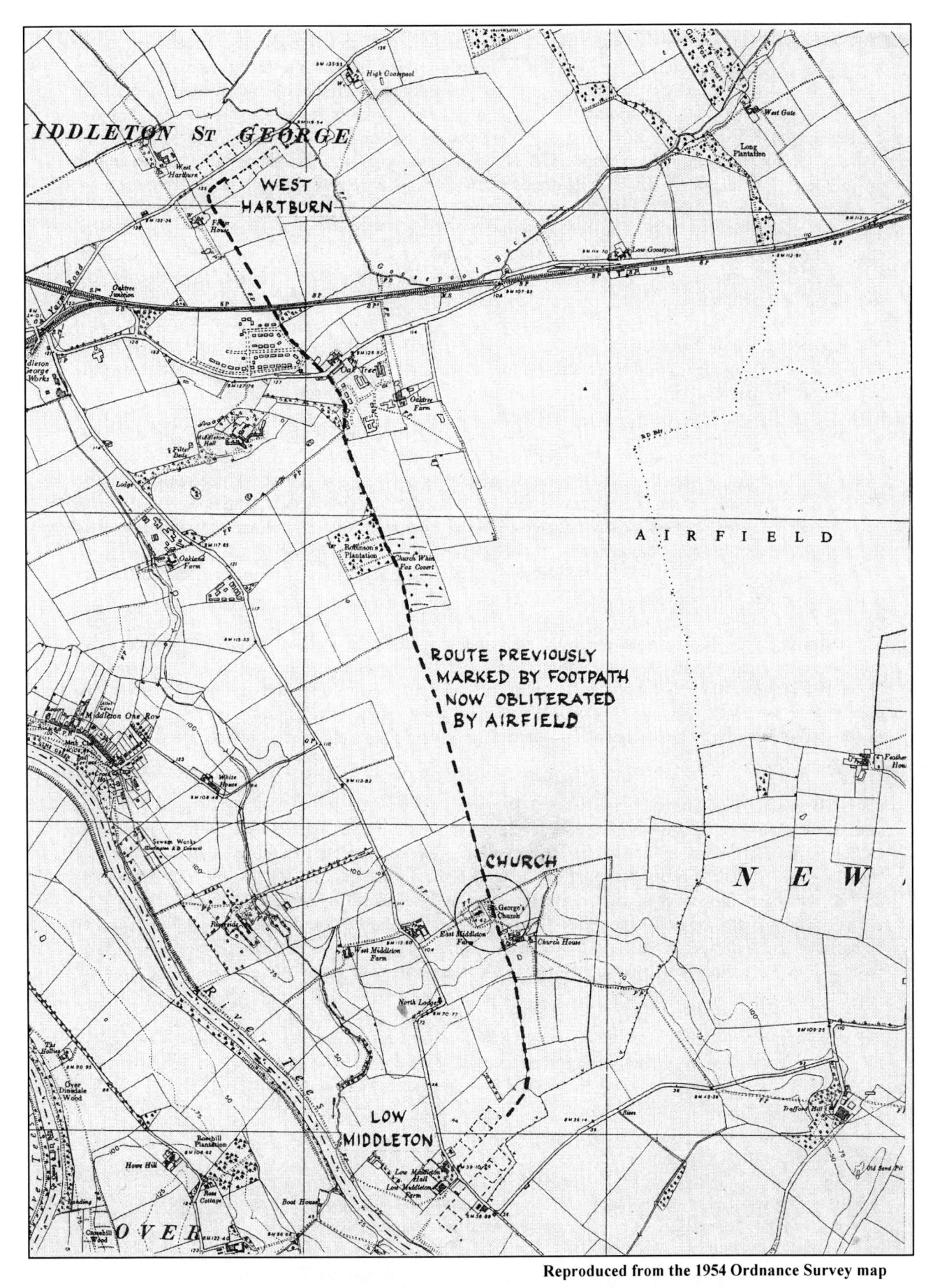

Fig. 13 The old way between Low Middleton and West Hartburn by St. George's Church.

43

The thirteenth century was a great period of rebuilding of parish churches, to accommodate increasing populations, and also to keep up with fashion and the new Gothic style of architecture. There are no means of knowing whether any such rebuilding at Middleton involved increasing the size of the nave, but it would certainly have provided the opportunity to enlarge the chancel, both for greater spiritual display, and also to afford more scope for the manorial lords to be buried in the church. John Killinghall, in his will of 1572, stipulated that he was "to be buried in the parish church of Middleton" [50], and there can be little doubt that this practice was prevalent in earlier centuries.

The new chancel arch was built in the contemporary style. It has plain voussoirs with chamfered edges. Two carved heads embellish the springing corbels, a woman with her tongue out at one side, and a man at the other (Pl.9) These are the only examples of stonemason's decorative creativity now to be seen in the church.

The internal length of the medieval nave was 29 feet (8.8m), as at present, and its internal width was 17 feet 9 ins. (5.4m), against 24 feet 4 ins. (7.4m) now. It is impossible to even hazard the size of the chancel, as the medieval lines have been lost in the nineteenth century rebuilding.

The walls are a great mixture of stone materials, reflecting the original construction and also subsequent repairs and rebuilding. The south and west walls of the nave and the section of cross wall pierced by the chancel arch pre-date the major rebuilding at the beginning of the nineteenth century. They are built mostly of the red sandstone available locally from outcrops in the banks of the river Tees, roughly dressed and erratically coursed. The buttress with base mouldings at the SE corner of the nave, built to help react the thrust from the chancel arch, would appear to have been an original thirteenth century feature, at least in its lower portion. The corresponding buttress at the SW corner is less substantial as it does not have thrust to react.

The main entrance doorway, at the west end of the south nave wall, is probably in its original position, and the porch may well be contemporary with the thirteenth century church. Early windows have been largely obliterated in the re-building, and only one retains a hood moulding dateable to the sixteenth or seventeenth centuries, a sign of an intermediate stage of rebuilding. A priest's doorway in the south wall of the chancel pre-dates the rebuilding, and was clearly re-used in the reconstruction, possibly in its original position.

The only medieval monuments are two broken grave cover slabs, now displayed outside the west wall of the church. One is the upper section of a gravestone, and the other a lower part. They appear to belong to each other, although one authoritative opinion suggests that they do not. The upper section bears a floriated cross design at the head of a shaft, with the hilt of a sword to its right and a bird to the left. The lower section bears the fleur-de-lys base of a cross shaft and the blade of a sword. The designs are consistent with a dating to the first half of the fourteenth century [51]. The slabs have had a chequered history, being at one time built into a wall at Middleton Hall [52], then removed to St. Laurence's Church, before finally returning to their original home at St. George's Church.

The appointment of clergy was the prerogative of the lords of the manor of Low Middleton. It has already been seen that the manor was divided into two "moieties". The advowson, or right to present to the rectory was similarly divided. It follows that there were two incumbents, one being a nominal rector and the other a working rector. Thus in 1312 the sinecure rectory was held by William de London, who had been presented by Ralph Baard, and the working rector was John de Cambe, who had been presented by his father [53].

The list of known clergy up to the time of the Reformation is as follows [54]. Dating gaps suggest that it is incomplete. The dates given are not necessarily terminal dates, but simply years in which the names appear in records.

Incumbent rectors		Sinecure rectors	
William de Auclet	1223/28	William	1215/19
William	1240	John	1215/20
John de Middleton	1248/60	William Baard	1228
Geoffrey de Shilveden	1288	Hugh	1214/60
John de Cambe	1312	Nicholas Brito	1260
Alan de Shuttlington	1339	Peter de Cirisy	1288
Richard (or Ralph) de Settrington	1363	John de Welton	
		William de London	1312
William de Merrington	1365	Thomas de Herdwyk	1338
William Saddler	1466	John de Hothwaite	1338
John Todd	1501	Robert Killinghall	1419/34
William Rippon		Robert Bolton	1434
James (or John) Orpyn	1531/77	Christopher Conyers	
		Robert Redmayne	1570

The Cambe line of owners of Low Middleton presented to the incumbent or working rectory, providing the clergy responsible for the services and other parochial duties. The Baard/Killinghall line presented to the sinecure rectory, which was a titular position, without duties, but drawing the associated endowment.

In both lines of office, there are instances of preferment within the family. John de Cambe in 1312 had been presented by his father to the incumbent rectory, as already noted, and Robert Killinghall, a younger son of John Killinghall, was presented to the sinecure rectory by his father in 1434 [55].

It was clearly common for clergy to have as part of their title an associated place name. John de Middleton presumably came from the immediate locality of the parish. Others bore various Durham and Yorkshire place names.

After Elizabeth Killinghall's acquisition of the Cambe portion of Low Middleton (See later - Chap.3), she presented James Orpyn, the last pre-Reformation working rector, prior to his institution in 1532 [56]. Thereafter, the Killinghalls and their successors were responsible for all appointments to the working rectory. This arrangement lasted until the advowson was transferred to the Bishop of Durham in 1900 [57].

It would be fascinating to have some insight into the lives of these priests and the discharge of their duties in the small church overlooking the village. In the period, there was general complaint about the qualifications and competence of parish clergy. Some, it was said, could do little more than recite the services, in Latin they hardly understood, and were incapable of giving meaningful instruction to their congregations and parishioners.

As early as 1215 the Fourth Lateran Council made a serious effort to address these deficiencies, and to see that men ordained to the priesthood had an acceptable level of education. To correct another alleged shortcoming, the manner of administering the sacraments was defined. The Council also came out against absent vicars and pluralism, and insisted on a decent standard of living for parish clergy. The Oxford Council of 1222 considered five marks (£3.33) a year a sufficient income for a vicar, but many had less. Much later, in the time of Henry VIII, the Valor Ecclesiasticus named James Orpyn, noted above, as rector of Middleton George, with a nett income of 73s.(£3.65) a year. This included the value of his house and two acres of glebe land [58].

We have no means of knowing to what extent the Middleton St. George clergy conformed with the intended standards, but the fact that on numerous occasions they attested charters is a sign at least of literacy and some status. What may sometimes be more in doubt is any commitment to live in the parish. The sinecure rectors had no obligation in that respect (William de London would hardly seem to have been a resident in 1312), but even some of the incumbent rectors would have had difficulty in meeting any residency qualification.

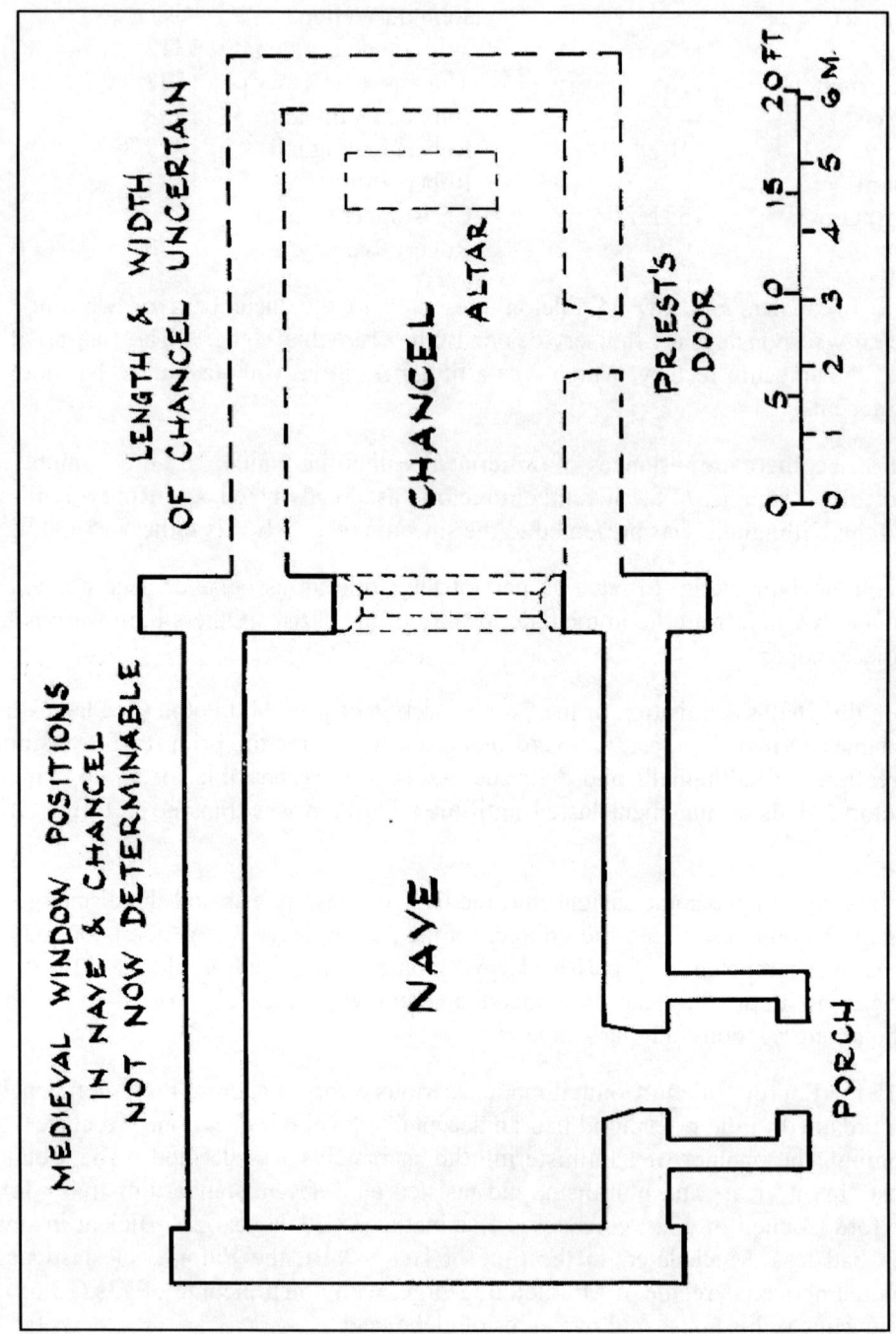

Fig.14 Suggested plan of the thirteenth century church of St.George

For instance, this must have been the case with Alan de Shuttlington, rector in 1339, who also had benefices elsewhere, was Master of Sherburn Hospital, and Keeper of the Halmote Court at Durham. In his absence, a poorly paid curate was doubtless deputed to carry out the duties - the very situation that the legislation aimed to prevent.

An example of the incumbent taking an active part in the affairs of the diocese is provided in 1507, when a synod during an episcopal vacancy was recorded as being attended by the "rector of Middelham George" [59]

Turning to the topic of communications, the Roman road forming the western boundary of the parish has been noted in Chapter 1. Whether or not there was a bridge at the crossing of the Tees in Roman times, it is clear that the road continued to be used as a main route northwards for many centuries afterwards, and reference has already been made to the twelfth century motte which guarded the river crossing. At some stage, probably as early as the period of occupation of the motte, a bridge was built to facilitate passage. This bridge continued in use throughout most of the Middle Ages.

The building of a bridge over a wide river was a considerable task, and testifies to the importance of the road and the river crossing. The bridge at Middleton and one at Yarm provided the only bridged crossings of the lower Tees in the early Middle Ages.

Robert Surtees, the great historian of County Durham, cites the evidence for the bridge, hazarding the opinion that it was "probably the first arch that was thrown across the Tees" [60]. Be that as it may, he does show that it was maintained by the Convent of Durham, as an important entry into the bishopric. The Sacrist's Book includes entries for the costs of repair and maintenance of the bridge, and in a charter Walter Cambe gave an oxgang of land in West Hartburn for the same purpose. In 1380 Alexander Surtees imposed a rent charge of one mark on the chaplain of St. Mary's Chantry in Dinsdale church for repair of Pountey's Bridge.

There was a chapel by the bridge, dedicated to St. John. This "Capella de Puntasia" is mentioned around 1200, and there are records of later presentations to the chapel.

1312	William Turner
1402	John Teysedell
1440	John Consclyffe
1444	William Sadbyere

John Teysedell is described as "capellan capellae S Johanni super Pontem Teyse", or "chaplain of the chapel of St. John on Tees Bridge". If taken literally this would indicate that the chapel was actually on the bridge. For this to have been the case, the bridge must have been a substantial structure.

Surtees also quotes a document of 1426, addressed to William Brydelawes, hermit, and referring to his hermitage of Pountesse. The inference is that this was different from the chapel, but it seems a little surprising if there were two religious houses in such close proximity. The activity at the crossing point is further emphasised by another reference from Surtees, when he recalls that one of his long-distant ancestors gave to the Convent of Durham land there, for the establishment of a house of hospitality and charity.

In its period of great importance, the bridge and road must have witnessed an impressive procession of travellers - kings, prelates, pilgrims, adventurers, soldiers, traders, magnates and common people. When in 945 the coffin of St. Cuthbert was taken from Chester-le-Street, as a safeguard against Danish raids, the monks carried the body of the saint to Ripon, and then returned four months later to his final resting place at Durham. These travels involved crossings of the Tees, and the direct line may well have taken the monks over the river at Middleton ford, assuming there was no bridge there at that time.

Longstaffe, in his History of Darlington, instances the passing of Edward I and his army in 1299. On 28 November he celebrated mass at Appleton Wiske, before continuing on to Darlington, by the inferred "old pass of Pounteys Bridge" [61]. Edward was on his way to put the Scots in their place, but the traffic in that long-running conflict was not all one way. For instance, in the great Scots incursion of 1318, one branch of their army is thought to have crossed the Tees at Yarm or Low Dinsdale [62]. If the latter were the case, the crossing point was probably at Pountey's Bridge, where fording the huge army and baggage train would not be necessary. The road northwards from the bridging point divides the parishes of Middleton St. George and Dinsdale (Low Dinsdale civil parish).

The demise of the bridge is not documented, but it would appear not to have survived into the sixteenth century. Several factors contributed to its decay. The chief of these was the development of a route a little further west, with a bridge built in the fifteenth century at Croft. It is said that this route was safer for travellers than the wooded passage up from Pountey's Bridge. Another major adverse factor was the diminished status of Sadberge on the route north from the bridge. In the early Middle Ages, the wapentake court sitting there had dispensed justice and made it a place of considerable importance. The subsequent decline of its administrative functions, and eventually their complete transfer to Durham, removed much of the need to travel by the route through Sadberge. Surtees stated that the foundations of the squared stone abutments of the bridge could still be seen in his day, but recent investigations have found nothing visible today. Stonework from the remains of the bridge was said to have been used in the construction of the nearby spa bath and in house building.

The aim in the previous sections of this chapter has been to give a picture of the villages and manors from around the second half of the twelfth century, when documentary evidence begins to be available to us, to a very general terminal date around the middle of the sixteenth century, when the process of change from the old feudal arrangements was well advanced. Legal documentation, mainly concerned with inheritance of estates, has also allowed some insight into the manorial families concerned. What is lacking is information about the lives of the common people, apart from the indications of life style which can be gleaned from the archaeology. However, the outline sketched earlier of the typical routine of the medieval villager can be given more depth by reference to some of the events and influences contributing to the changes which took place over the four centuries between about 1150 and about 1550.

The early part of the period falls into a time of expansion of settlements over the whole country, with a growing population and consequently increasing pressure on land. The disruption following the Norman Conquest was over, and a strong framework of feudal estates had been established. This organisational structure facilitated controlled utilisation and development of the land.

Aided by good conditions in the cyclical weather pattern, existing settlements were expanded by pushing into the hitherto waste land, and new settlements were founded. However, by the thirteenth century the availability of land was becoming a limiting restraint on expansion. The situation changed dramatically in the fourteenth century, when the deterioration of the weather cycle combined with other factors to halt and even to reverse some of the progress which had already been made.

In a subsistence economy, life for the peasant population must always have been precarious. In the early fourteenth century, natural disasters emphasised this fragility. Disease among sheep was prevalent between 1313 and 1317, and this was followed by cattle murrain for several years. In addition to the direct loss of animal products, a secondary effect was a shortage of draught oxen, making it impossible to plough all the arable land, with a drastic effect on corn production. When starving mouths were fed, there was nothing left for next year's seed. The difficulties were compounded by several years of excessive rainfall in the same period. No specific record of these afflictions is extant for Middleton, but the manors were hardly likely to have escaped their effects.

In addition there were man-made depredations resulting from the ever-present conflict between the Scots and the English, reaching a climax in the years leading up to Bannockburn and Scottish independence. An example has already been quoted of the marching of the English army under Edward I into Scotland.

In the opposite direction, there were numerous damaging incursions of Scots into northern England, and reference has already been made to the invasion of 1318. One branch of the Scots army, having ravaged Hartlepool, made their way to the Tees, which they crossed at Low Dinsdale or Yarm, before penetrating into Yorkshire. Whichever the actual crossing point, the effect must have been the same; pillaging, stealing of cattle, and burning of houses and crops over a wide swathe in the path of the invaders. In recognition of the losses and resulting hardships, tax concessions were made. In 1291 the valuation for the sinecure rectory of Middleton St. George was £9.6s.8d. and for the vicarage (the incumbent rectory) £4. In 1318 these had been reduced to £4.13s.4d. and £2.6s.8d. respectively [63].

Even when Scotland's independence was established after Bannockburn, the border counties remained vulnerable to intermittent warfare, disputes and disruption. In the autumn of 1399 there was a Scots border raid, and Henry IV, who had recently seized the English crown, aimed to make a retaliatory show of force, and at the same time to pursue his claim to homage from Robert III of Scotland. In these circumstances, the support of the northern lords and their tenants was crucial. As part of the preparations for attack and defence, a martial array was held on Gilesgate Moor, outside the city of Durham, on 24 March 1400. From the record of attendance, it seems that the clergy of the district were instructed to appear with a token of the fighting force available from their respective parishes. Accordingly the rector of Middleton St. George was there, accompanied by one archer [64]. It was a long trek from Middleton to Durham, and the nominal showing was no doubt regarded as representative of the support expected from the parish. When circumstances required, the routine of the agricultural year had to give way to the overriding demands of national security. When Henry's rather abortive invasion took place in August, the crossing of the Tees by his army, and its support in passage, would no doubt have imposed further disruption and burdens on the local communities.

Human afflictions, in the form of periodically recurring outbreaks of plague, were another factor in the rural economy and social conditions. The worst and best known occurrence was the nation-wide Black Death of 1348, when one third of the population may have died. The outbreak is documented for several nearby areas to east and west [65], but for Middleton the record remains silent. However, as the outbreak was so widespread it is unlikely that Middleton escaped its ravages. The Black Death and resulting loss of population have been blamed for the desertion of villages elsewhere, but it did not have this effect at Middleton, where the three villages all recovered from any effects and survived for another two hundred years or so.

One of the long-term effects was a weakening of the feudal system. The system had provided an effective framework for the collective cultivation of the land and the administration of the countryside. It was however a straightjacket to progress outside its rules, preventing individual enterprise towards improvement. This had been recognised from an early stage, and gradual encroachments into the system had inevitably taken place. This movement was accelerated by the problems of the fourteenth century. In the aftermath of the plague, there was no shortage of land, but instead a shortage of tenants, who frequently used the situation to attempt to escape the bonds of villeinage. Legislation was passed seeking to maintain customary service obligations and to control wages, but economic pressure often led to wages higher than the statutory level, and landlords sometimes resorted to leasing out their demesne land to others looking for a bargain in time of depression. Another avenue was to convert arable land to pasture for sheep and cattle, as grazing was less labour intensive. This aspect, as it affected Middleton, is dealt with in the next chapter.

CHAPTER THREE - THE SIXTEENTH CENTURY

NEW PATTERNS OF RELIGION, ESTATES AND FARMING

The coming of the Tudors in 1485 is conventionally regarded as marking the end of the Middle Ages, and the century which followed is distinguished by far-reaching changes in land ownership, agrarian practices and religious belief, with associated effects on the appearance of the countryside and the life of the rural population.

Entering the sixteenth century, the dominant power in the parish was held by the Killinghalls of Low Middleton, with the Cambe family owning the lesser portion of the manor. Over Middleton or Middleton One Row continued under Surtees lordship as a separate manorial estate within the parish.

Hugh Killinghall died in 1509 in possession of the main part of the manor of Low Middleton or Middleton St. George, usually referred to as two thirds of the manor, and was succeeded by his son William. On William's death in 1536, the estate passed to his son Francis. His position as captain in the garrison at Berwick may indicate that his outlook was other than that of a landed proprietor. In any event, in 1548 he sold his West Hartburn lands to William Wrenn, and in 1569 he sold his Low Middleton estate, termed two-thirds of the manor of Middleton, and the manorial title to Ralph Tailbois [1]. Thus the Killinghalls relinquished, albeit temporarily, the overlordship which they had held for over 150 years.

Four years later, in 1573, Ralph Tailbois sold the estate to Rowland Johnson of Berwick-on-Tweed for £660 [2]. Rowland died ten years later, and in his will dated 16 October 1583 he bequeathed to his eldest son, also Rowland, and then at school at Chester-le-Street, "my principall hall house at the said Myddleton-St. George with all my lands thereunto belonging viz.-all my arable grounds, medows, pastures commones, croftes, toftes, hedges, ditches houses garths, orchards and whatsoever as in as large and simple manner as his father have occupied the same heartofore and do occupy the same at this present" [3]. Rowland also had property in Yorkshire, but clearly Middleton St. George was a substantial seat, and he would appear to have lived in the manor house. There is some contradiction as to the succession after his death. His will, quoted above, refers to his son Rowland, whereas Surtees names Cuthbert as son and heir. The Victoria County History states that Cuthbert Johnson appears to have sold the estate in parcels. Ninian Girlington bought one part, together with the manor house called the "Grange". He also took over the manorial rights. Richard Maddock acquired the "Red House". John Gaines purchased a capital messuage and various closes - the Foggfield, the Banckes, Bambrough Close, Featon Close, Conyngham Close, Bulkens Close, Dent's Close and Old Close. In 1596 Thomas Bank acquired from Richard Maddock four closes called Whinney Houses, and the Red House or New Hall, "lately builded by Cuthbert Johnson, gent". In 1599 the manorial rights were bought by Richard Heighington [4].

The multiplicity of land and estate transactions in the second half of the sixteenth century reflects the burgeoning trade in assets based on land and greater commercialism in farm ownership and management. No longer was the accent mainly on subsistence, and business profit was increasingly becoming the objective, with owners not necessarily resident in the parish. Richard Maddock, for instance, was a London goldsmith, who had married Cuthbert Johnson's sister [5]. His Middleton interests extended to more than just the Red House, and at some stage encompassed the manorial title, another saleable asset. The flourishing market in land was accompanied by and made possible by changes in the physical make-up of estates and farms, as dealt with later in this chapter.

Francis Killinghall's sale of the manor in 1569 did not mean that the Killinghall family had lost all their interests in Middleton. Robert Killinghall, uncle of the aforementioned Hugh, with lands in Darlington and probably also in Sadberge, had married Elizabeth Surtees, of the Dinsdale family, who were also lords of Middleton One Row. After her husband's death in 1507, she showed enterprise in purchasing in 1523 the second and lesser part (one third) of the manor of Low Middleton [6]. She bought it from Thomas Cambe, who had inherited from his father in 1511, and whose family had owned it for many generations, including a period in conjunction with Elizabeth's own Surtees family. The Cambe line of owners had held the right of presentation to the working rectory, and Elizabeth Killinghall was their successor in this. As noted in the last chapter, she was responsible for presenting James Orpyn, before his institution as rector in 1531.

Elizabeth had a brother, Ralph Surtees, who was described as being of Middleton St. George when he died around 1549. An interesting sidelight in his will is the bequest of salmon to numerous beneficiaries, including "to my sister Killinghall vi puderd salmon" [7]. This reflects the abundance of salmon in the Tees at this time, and indeed for long afterwards. The term "powdered" stems from the fact that they were commonly salted, for eating out of season.

Elizabeth's purchase of one third of the manor not only maintained the Killinghall interest when Francis Killinghall sold the larger portion, but also paved the way for the subsequent uniting of the manor. Her son John had early business aspirations, having leases of coal mines at Windlestone in central Durham and at Ryton on the Tyne. When he died in 1574, he left to his sister-in-law Anne Parkinson "his three chests in his chamber that he lived in at Mydleton" [8]. His estate went to his son Henry, who around 1606 was successful in bringing together the Killinghall's Middleton estate, acquiring from Richard Heighington and Richard Maddock the main part of the manor which Francis Killinghall had sold in 1569 [9]. He did, however, relinquish his West Hartburn land, selling it to Edward Blakiston in 1595 [10].

Thus the Killinghalls were reinstated as lords of the manor of Low Middleton, or Middleton St. George as it was becoming known. Moreover, they had managed to bring together the two constituent parts of the manor, which had existed separately throughout the Middle Ages. Their position as lords of the manor had, however, changed in character. The feudal connotations had largely disappeared, and the title had become increasingly one more of status and patronage, rather than of all-powerful control over the lives of all who lived and worked on the manor. Moreover, the newly united manor had lost some of its land, by virtue of the sale of various parcels in the period between Francis Killinghall's disposal of his estate and the re-acquisition by Henry Killinghall. As noted above, the West Hartburn lands had also been relinquished.

While not showing all the complexity of ownership changes, the accompanying chart in Fig.15 may help to clarify the somewhat confusing lines of descent of the manor, and the eventual unification under Killinghall control.

At West Hartburn, the end of the sixteenth century saw Sir Charles Wrenn and Edward Blakiston holding principal estates, with another estate at Goosepool in the hands of the Paul family. Ralph Paul had died in possession of the latter in 1568, when the estate was curiously said to belong to the manor of Dinsdale. Later the estate adopted from the family the name Paul Hartburn [11].

The separate manor of Over Middleton or Middleton One Row continued to be held by the Surtees lords of Dinsdale until the middle of the sixteenth century. Then, as a result of a family dispute and a settlement of 1552, Marmaduke Surtees gave up his inherited rights in Dinsdale, but was confirmed in his ownership of Over Middleton [12]. Thomas Surtees, grandson of Marmaduke, brought the long succession of Surtees lordship at Middleton to an end, when he sold the manor of Over Middleton to Anthony Felton of Jarrow in 1598, as noted in the previous chapter [13].

Under the Tudors, a critical and continuing issue was the relationship between church and state. One event symptomatic of the changes taking place in the 16th.century was the Rising in the North. As an insurrection it was relatively mild, but it was of great national significance, and caused widespread turmoil and suffering in the northern counties, with Middleton included in the record of involvement.

Before William Killinghall died in 1521, he laid down in his will that his estate was to provide "for the sustentacon of an honest preste which I will shall syng for the sowles of me, myn auncestors and heires in the parishe churche of Midilton George by the space of seven yeres next after my death perceyving yerly for his salary vii marks" [14].

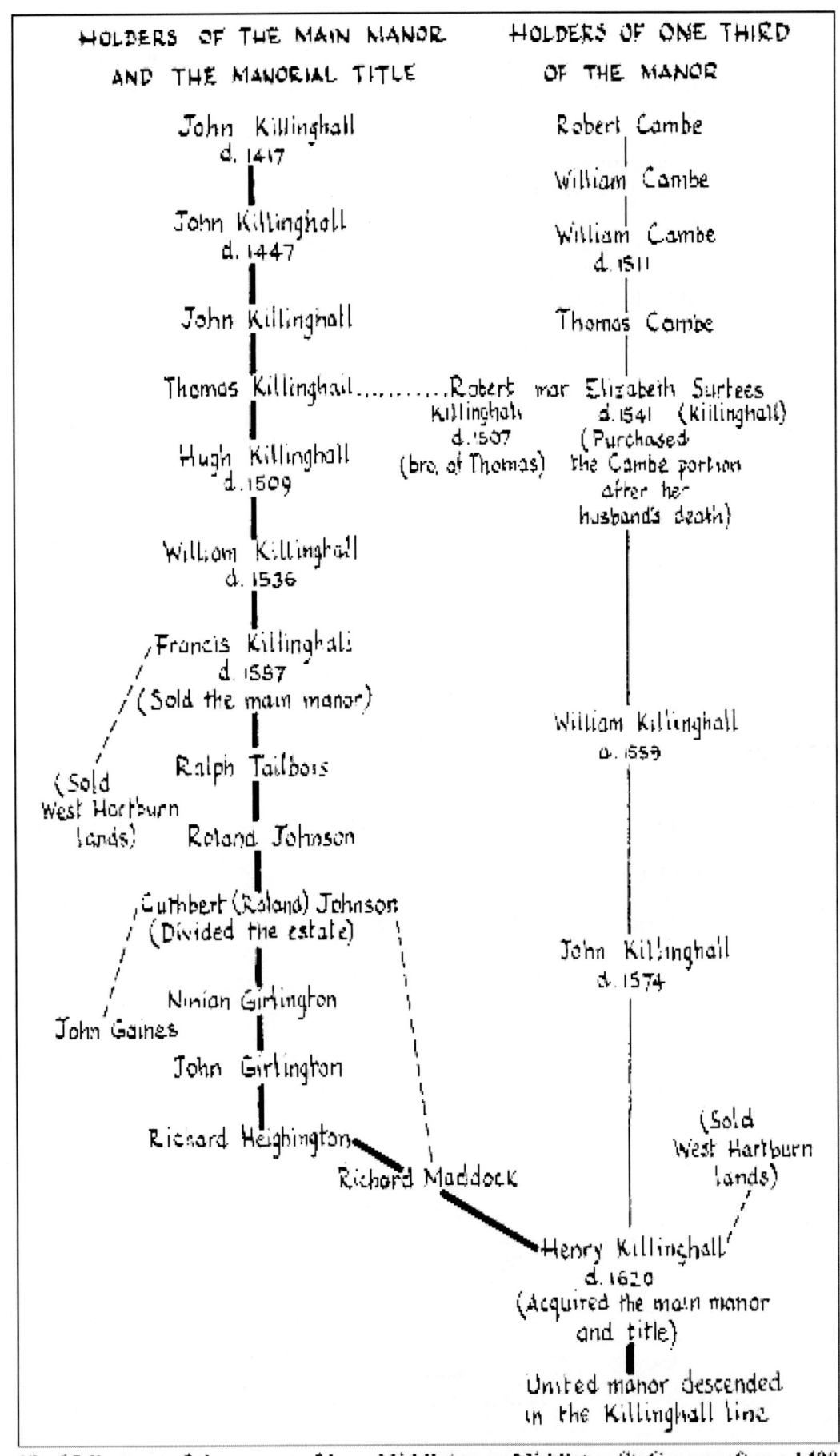

```
HOLDERS OF THE MAIN MANOR          HOLDERS OF ONE THIRD
   AND THE MANORIAL TITLE              OF THE MANOR

      John Killinghall                  Robert Cambe
         d. 1417                             |
           |                            William Cambe
      John Killinghall                       |
         d. 1447                        William Cambe
           |                               d. 1511
      John Killinghall                       |
           |                            Thomas Combe
      Thomas Killinghall........Robert  mar Elizabeth Surtees
                              Killinghall    d. 1541 (Killinghall)
      Hugh Killinghall         d. 1507       (Purchased
         d. 1509           (bro. of Thomas)  the Cambe portion
           |                                 after her
      William Killinghall                    husband's death)
         d. 1536
           |
      Francis Killinghall
         d. 1587
       (Sold the main manor)
                                        William Killinghall
      Ralph Tailbois                        d. 1559
(Sold
 West Hartburn
 lands)   Roland Johnson

      Cuthbert (Roland) Johnson
        (Divided the estate)
                                        John Killinghall
      Ninian Girlington                     d. 1574
John Gaines   |
      John Girlington
           |                                 (Sold
      Richard Heighington                   West Hartburn
                                             lands)
           Richard Maddock
                                        Henry Killinghall
                                            d. 1620
                                        (Acquired the main manor
                                           and title)

                                        United manor descended
                                         in the Killinghall line
```

Fig. 15 Descent of the manor of Low Middleton or Middleton St. George after c.1400

Such provision was common practice for those with the wherewithal to pay for it and was consistent with the dogma of the church. However, before the middle of the century, the situation had changed dramatically, and what had been a sign of strong faith had become in some minds a practice of superstitious ceremony.

The Reformation initiated during the reign of Henry VIII had replaced Roman Catholicism with protestantism as the state faith, with Henry himself as head of the church. Great bitterness and conflict resulted, particularly after Henry's daughter Mary came to the throne as a catholic queen. There was the promise of more stability when Elizabeth, staunchly protestant, became queen in 1558. However, clandestine catholicism continued strongly, and nowhere more so than in the north of England, where support for Rome was still widespread.

The arrival in England of Mary Queen of Scots, when she fled Scotland and crossed the Solway in 1568, caused great alarm to the English establishment. Mary was catholic and had a claim to the English throne. To Elizabeth she was an obvious danger. Although kept closely confined, she was nevertheless seen as a rallying point for the northern catholic sympathisers.

In this uneasy situation, steps were taken to protect against insurrection. Apart from catholic support at home, any move towards putting Mary on the throne of England would have immediately gained the support of France, with the associated risk of invasion from that quarter. The Spanish Netherlands were also a danger. One defensive measure was a muster of what could be termed the "home guard", all able-bodied men who could be called upon to resist invasion. Commissioners were appointed to oversee the muster, and to compile a list of all who turned out and were available to fight.

The muster for the Stockton Ward of the county, in which lay Middleton, was taken on 4 June 1569 at Sedgefield [15]. The abstracted entries from the list relating to Middleton St. George and Middleton One Row, as recorded at the time, are as follows.

Able men furnished wth stele cappes Jacks Bowes and arrowes

        Over midleton   marmaduke wetherilt

Able men wthout armor & wth billes only

        midleton george   Roberte thornbrough
                                    John Cunnyngham
                                    marmaduke andrewe

Able men wthout armor & wepon

        middleton george   henry killinghall
                                    Robarte Alande
                                    Rauff Jameson
                                    Thomas Braskewe
                                    Robarte Bankes
                                    John Applebye
                                    Richard Raynarte
                                    willm Laifeilde
                                    John Parrette
                                    John Cottam
                                    Francis harrison
                                    James Tomson
                                    willm andrewe
                                    George wilson
                                    myles blenkisoppe

Over myddleton	John Dun
	John Andrew
	George myres
	Roberte blaiclocke
	Rauff Arther
	Cuthbert neasmith
	Rauff cacheside
	Rowlly Lamson

It can be seen that there was a total turn-out of 18 men from Middleton St. George and 9 from Middleton One Row. As for the array in general, most were poorly armed and equipped. Only Marmaduke Wetherall from Middleton One Row was able to boast a steel helmet, a jack, and a bow and arrows. (A jack was a sleeveless leather jacket, offering some degree of protection to a soldier.) Three Middleton St. George men had bills (long-handled steel bladed weapons). All the others, including Henry Killinghall, were classified as "without armour and weapons". The absence of anyone listed as being from West Hartburn is probably because by that time it no longer existed as a separate village, and any who still lived there would be included with Middleton St. George. Apart from being part of the record of those troublesome times, the muster roll is the first document to provide the names of ordinary inhabitants of the parish.

The reality of the perceived danger manifested itself in October of 1569, when a complicated series of events culminated in a rising led by the earls of Northumberland and Westmoreland. They rapidly gathered support in the catholic north, and on a wave of catholic enthusiasm, congregations reverted to the old forms of worship. We have no details from Middleton, but at the adjacent Long Newton an altar was set up in the church as an act of defiance, regarded as idolatry in protestant eyes [16]. The rebels crossed the Tees, and marched deep into Yorkshire. There they hesitated, and, in the face of mounting opposition, turned and retreated, before dispersing as best they could. No battles were fought and little blood was shed, but the government had had a considerable shock, and was intent on teaching the rebels a lesson. Over 700 were sentenced to be executed, and it was ordained that at least one should be hanged in each town or village from which rebels had joined the rising.

Elizabeth herself was impatient that retribution should be speedily exacted. On 11 January 1570 she wrote to the Earl of Sussex, president of the Council of the North at York, "We grete you well. Letting you know that we do somewhat marvell that we have hitherto hearde nothing from you of any executions don by marshall law as was appointed to be don upon those of the meaner sorte that have byn rebells there in the north. Requiring you therefore if the same be not already don to procede thereunto for the terrour of other wth all the expeditoion you may and to certfie us of your doings therein" [17].

The Earl of Sussex wrote to Sir George Bowes, to tell him that he had received the queen's letter, and asking him "to use expedytyon (to complete the executions), for I fere that lyngeryng wyll brede dyspleser to us bothe" [18]. This letter appears to have crossed with one from Bowes to Sussex saying," The executions ar done, or will this daye, and to morrow be done throwe all the Byshopricke" [19]. On the same day that the queen expressed her concern, the Earl of Sussex and Sir Ralph Sadler wrote to her, "The martial exequotion is this daye fynished in the Bishoprike and Richmondshire" [20].

Sir George Bowes of Streatlam was the royal representative responsible for the defence of the area during the rebellion, and for the administration of the rough justice afterwards. The lists included in his papers show that three men from Middleton St. George (Midleton George) joined the rebellion, and one of these was executed. Only one man from Middleton One Row (Midleton Rawe) was recorded as having rebelled, and hence was the one to be hanged. West Hartburn is again not mentioned. The published records do not give the names of the victims. The numbers of the rebels and the executions are generally in line with those for other small villages in the area, but differences no doubt reflect the religious allegiances of local families. In the borough of Darlington, the list shows 55 rebels, with 10 of them executed.

The executions took place in the worst of the winter weather, conjuring up the bleak picture of a body dangling from a gibbet on the snow covered bank of the Tees, between the rude houses of Middleton One Row and the river, with a similar wretched corpse hanging a mile downstream at Low Middleton.

Apart from the retribution of the hangings, the population suffered in other ways. As the rebels had retreated northwards they were pursued by the government forces, who "seised all the landes, goodes, leases, and cattells, that appertayned to any man that was between Newcastle and Doncaster" [21]. Clearly Middleton was in the path of that despoliation, and must have suffered accordingly. The Bishop of Durham on 4 January 1570 wrote, "The cuntre is in grete mysere" [22]. The harmful effects persisted long after the rising ended. In September 1570, Thomas Gargrave, Vice-President of the North, writing from Yorkshire to William Cecil, said, "I have not heard the complaint so general of poverty as it now is. They have been much troubled by the late troubles" [23].

A great number of the executions were of the common people. Most of those of higher status were punished otherwise - by imprisonment, fines, and distraint of property and lands. The Killinghalls at Middleton St. George were amongst the catholic supporters. Henry Killinghall was one of those taken into custody at the end of the rising [24], but how active a part he had played and what, if any, retribution was exacted from him is not clear.

The sixteenth century saw great changes in how the land was managed and farmed. A pattern of open fields and pastures has been portrayed in the last chapter as being the traditional manorial arrangement, and the natural outcome of communal settlement and feudal control. However, it has also been stressed that the pattern was by no means precisely or universally followed, and neither was it immune to change. The three manorial units of Low Middleton, West Hartburn and Middleton One Row all exhibited variations from the standard pattern, and also underwent change in the course of time.

The reference in the last chapter to the 1598 sale of lands "in Over Middleton and Stodhow" is significant. Stodhoe, marked by the farm of that name today, lies at the northern end of the parish of Dinsdale, but was clearly regarded as being associated with the adjacent manor of Over Middleton or Middleton One Row in the parish of Middleton St. George. Far away from the common open fields at the south end of Dinsdale, Stodhoe probably developed as a separate farmstead at an early date. With the Surtees family owning the lands on both sides of the parish boundary, it may have been consideration of convenience that linked Stodhoe with the much-nearer Middleton One Row. A feature of recent studies has been the demonstration of the diversity of medieval rural settlement, with many cases of common field patterns intermingled with self-contained farmsteads or small clusters. Stodhoe is an example of this.

A different form of variation has already been remarked on for West Hartburn, where late medieval documents refer to holdings on the east or west sides of the brook. This segregation of holdings could not have applied had there been a standard pattern of common fields for West Hartburn as a whole, with holdings dispersed throughout. The division of lands may have been a feature from the beginning, resulting from the manor extending into two parishes.

There were powerful reasons of convenience for having one's arable land in an integrated block, rather than dispersed throughout the fields. Ultimately, such considerations over-rode the philosophy of the original settlement pattern, and there was a continuous movement towards grouping tenurial strips together by agreed interchange between tenants. When this process was sufficiently advanced, it was possible to move on a further stage to separately fenced closes. This transformation of the agrarian arrangements was accelerated by economic factors and the weakening of the feudal system, as outlined in the last chapter.

At the beginning of the sixteenth century Middleton still had a common field system at the heart of each of its three villages, but with the regularity of layout significantly distorted and modified by influences such as those noted here. By the end of the century two of the village communities and their open fields had gone, and within another three decades the surviving village had lost its common fields.

Depopulation and desertion of villages is often linked with enclosure of the associated open fields. Enclosure could be carried out by the unilateral action of an all-powerful landlord, by agreement, or later by act of parliament. At neighbouring Long Newton, the open fields were enclosed and replaced by separate farms in 1658/9, and this process is well documented [25]. In contrast, no direct evidence is available for enclosure at Middleton. This is not unusual in an area where enclosure was comparatively early, with an associated dearth of records.

West Hartburn has archaeological evidence with a bearing on enclosure. The pottery and other finds from excavations there point to a terminal date for the village of around 1550. It is probable that the desertion of the village was at least in part a consequence of enclosure of the open fields, in whatever form they had taken by that time.

For Low Middleton the archaeological evidence is less secure. No excavations have been carried out, and the only evidence is a scatter of pottery fragments over the subsequently ploughed fields. All that can be said is that these indicate that habitation of the village ceased no later than at West Hartburn, and possibly somewhat earlier. The records of ownership also help to throw a little light on the demise of the village, and the end of the medieval pattern of manor. The breaking up of the estate by Cuthbert Johnson, referred to earlier, points to a disintegration of the old open field arrangement, and the references in the later sixteenth century transactions to numerous closes is clear evidence of earlier enclosure, either piecemeal or as a concerted action, with the eventual dispersal of the village community.

For Middleton One Row, where the village survived the agrarian changes, the dating for final enclosure can be established rather more accurately. However, it would appear that enclosure within the manor took place in two phases.

A document of 1594 sets out the boundaries between the parishes of Middleton St. George and Dinsdale [26]. The significant part relating to enclosure reads,".....a parcell of ground lying towards Morton-fielde, betwixt ye ox-close and Sadbury-field, containing about forty acres, and was about fifty-four years ago in tillage, and about that time laid to pasture, with Middleton-moor adjoyninge to it on the east side of ye said highway,......." The line of parish division is the old Roman road, and the lands in question are at the northern end of the parishes. Conversion to grass therefore took place about 1540, and it is reasonable to assume that this corresponded with enclosure of that area and of the so-called Middleton Moor. Further evidence, quoting from the 1598 document cited earlier, refers to "the severall closes of Stodoo, wherein the tenants and inhabitants of Over-Myddleton hath used to have entercommon". This implies that enclosure had already taken place there, but in the not-too-distant past. This and the conversion of Middleton Moor to pasture probably took place at about the same time around the middle of the sixteenth century.

These references are interesting as being indicative of two phases of land use change. Middleton Moor was well away from the manorial village of Middleton One Row, and, by its very name, originally formed part of the rough grazing land of the manor. Its conversion to tillage probably took place at the time of greatest expansion and land hunger. However, being marginal land, it was an early target for returning to grass under changed economic conditions.

This was, however, a case outside the normal pattern, on a peripheral part of the manor. It was not until the next century that the enclosure of the main area of open field adjacent to the village eventually took place. This comes to light from a case heard at the Durham Chancery court in 1632. The rector, William Casse, and John Killinghall, the lay proprietor of the rectory, alleged that the Middleton One Row farmers had enclosed the common fields without their consent and to their disadvantage. The following is an excerpt from the record of the proceedings [27].

".....The township of Middleton one Row.........was anciently an husbandtowne consisting of tillage, and did maintain tenn or xi plowes for the good of the comon Weal and did yield a great pfit in tithes.....the deffts (defendants) wthout the Compts (complainants) premits or consents not only devided the same & so decayed the tillage thereof converting the same to pasture and medow ....

.....and by the sayd devision have also barred up the ancient wayes & altered the same wthout setting fourth any new ones convenient for cariadge of the sayd tithes......"

The defendants were named as Marmaduke Wilson, Thomas Scrogges, James Conningham and others. They had clearly decided amongst themselves that their interests were best served by enclosing the open arable fields and partitioning them between themselves. Thomas Scrogges gave his name to the farm which was established on his share of the land, and which still exists today. The family of James Conningham had been involved in enclosure at Low Middleton, as witness the earlier reference to Conyngham Close there.

The complainants, John Killinghall and the rector, were not in a position to protest about the enclosure itself, as Middleton One Row was a separate manor over which they had no territorial jurisdiction. However, Middleton One Row was in the parish of Middleton St. George, and their bone of contention was the loss of corn tithes, of which they were the beneficiaries, and the associated difficulty in collecting them. This is clear evidence that the tithes were still being paid in kind, and had not been replaced by money payments, as was sometimes the case.

The court did not proceed to a judgement, but the case provides the evidence for the enclosure which had taken place shortly before, probably around 1630. After this, there was no open common field remaining in the parish.

In the case of Middleton One Row, enclosure did not result in depopulation of the village, which assumed the role of parish nucleus when the other two villages disappeared. The substantial crofts or closes which remained attached to each tenement would contribute significantly to the livelihood of the tenants, making it less necessary for them all to move out to the new dispersed farms, in contrast to the situation elsewhere.

In the course of the sixteenth century Tudor administration resulted in better documentary evidence for the population, their work and their life styles. Instead of an anonymous body of villagers, it becomes possible to identify individuals and families, and to look into their homes and their lives. The practice of compiling an inventory of a person's possessions after his or her death provides a valuable source of information. William Mitchell of Middleton One Row, who died in 1576, was a substantial farmer, with about 80 acres of nominally arable land, and associated grazing rights on the common pasture. An inventory taken on 30 June, shortly after his death, lists his possessions as follows [28].

Livestock

	£.	s.	d.
6 - oxen	10.	0.	0.
1 - steer } 2 - stirks }	3.	0.	0.
7 - milk cows }	10.	0.	0.
3 - calves	1.	13.	0.
4 - mares } 1 - gelding }	6.	0.	0.
17 - ewes with lambs } 11 - wethers }	6.	12.	0.
2 - pigs		7.	0
1 - cock } 6 - hens } 1 - goose } 3 - ducks }		3.	4.
Total Livestock	**37.**	**15.**	**4.**

Household

	£.	s.	d.
cupboard	1.	3.	4.
……….		3.	4.
5 - brass pots	1.	0.	0.
3 - kettles 2 - little pans }		19.	8.
2 - candlesticks 1 - old candlestick }			
1 - reckon croke 1 - pair of tongs 1 - pair of shears 1 - spit 1 - pair of codds 1 - pair of pewter pots 1 – salt 3 - boards }		13.	10.

Crops in ground

Corn and Hay	22.	0.	0.
Hay at Morton		16.	0.

Crops in store

3 - bushels wheat
5 - bushels malt
5 - bushels peas
1 - peck oats   1.   8.   0.

        Total Crops   24.   4.   0

Purse and Apparel

4 – jackets
4 – pair of hose
1 – leather doublet
1 – cloak   1.   1.   0.
1 – cap
2 sheets
2 - towels

        Total Apparel   1.   1.   0.

Farm Gear

3 - ploughs
1 - coulter
2 - forks
2 - pair of harrows
1 - pair of iron wheels
2 – plough beams
1 – ox harrow
1 – coupe wain   2.   1.   4.
1 - wain
4 - axletrees
30 - ….. nails
2 – lynch pins
1 - yoke
3 -
1 - ……   0.   6.
Dung about the house   5.   0.
2 - Axletrees   0.   9.

        Total in Farm Gear   2.   7.   7.

2 - skills, 2 - pots
1 - churn
1 - spinning wheel & stool for it   12.   6.
4 - baskets
3 - chests

1 - bedstead
1 - old almonry
2 - sieves
2.-. riddles   7.   0.
5 – sacks, 3 – pokes
3 – painted clothes

2 – saddles
The wool of three sheep-skins and a piece of one   7.   6.

10 yards of
3 – pair of sheets
3 – old blankets
3 – happens   14.   0.
1 – window cloth
3 – cods
4 - cushioms

        Total Household   6.   11.   2.

Leases		£.	s.	d.
Lease of parcel of ground called the Alms Close		5.	0.	0.
Lease of tenament and two oxgangs of land		2.	3.	4.
Lease of one oxgang of land		2.	6.	8.
Lease of two oxgangs of land taken of Marmaduke Wetherall for 13 years to come		(No entry)		
	Total Leases	9.	10.	0.
Debts		£.	s.	d.
Debts owing to him		5.	12.	5.
Debts owed by testator		26.	6.	8.
	Net debt	20.	14.	3.
	Overall total	60.	14.	10.
	(Doc. shows:	**60.**	**6.**	**6.)**

William Mitchell's leases covered in total five oxgangs of arable land in the open fields. He also leased enclosed land of unspecified extent, attesting to the fact that there had already been some erosion of the traditional pattern of common fields. The relatively high value placed on Alms Close indicates that it was a substantial area, and probably more highly valued simply because it was enclosed.

He practised mixed farming, but with the value of his livestock substantially more than the value of his crops. His holding in the open fields entitled him to a specific extent of grazing on the common pasture. It appears that some of the common field land, and also probably his enclosed field, were being used for producing hay for fodder. Even so, the demand for winter feed caused him to go outside the parish, some of his hay crop being said to be at Morton. Now in Sadberge parish, Morton was then in the parish of Haughton-le-Skerne, about a mile west of the northern end of the parish of Middleton St. George and the manor of Middleton One Row. The number of his draught animals (six oxen and four horses) was commensurate with the size of his common field holding, and the inventory includes three ploughs and three harrows.

The fact that the inventory does not list household possessions under separate room headings is a sign of the modest nature of his house, which would have lain within the village. There was a considerable amount of kitchen and dairy equipment, but a surprising lack of furniture. Living conditions at the time did not require very much, but one bed, three chests and a cupboard still seems rather sparse. A spinning wheel is listed, with a stool for the spinner. There was a dung hill outside the house, this valuable and presumably sizable manuring commodity being reckoned to be worth five shillings.

William's wardrobe was of modest value, but he did have four jackets and four pairs of hose, besides his leather doublet, a cloak and cap. He is not credited with having any cash in his pocket or purse.

William Mitchell was in most respects a typical farmer of substance in the parish in the second half of the century, with land in the common fields of Middleton One Row. However, the earlier incidence of enclosure elsewhere in the parish meant that his contemporaries at Low Middleton and West Hartburn were further advanced in the transition between the old open field farming and the new self-contained farmsteads. In the next chapter comparable inventories from early in the seventeenth century illustrate the progression of this change.

CHAPTER FOUR - THE SEVENTEENTH CENTURY

NO ESCAPE FROM CIVIL STRIFE

From the last chapter, it is apparent that changing conditions were associated with changes of ownership and a new pattern of estates. Rowland Johnson was the last to keep the main Low Middleton manorial estate substantially intact. His sons were responsible for the break up into separate parcels, attracting diverse commercial interests.

With the disintegration of the feudal manor and the disappearance of the villages of Low Middleton and West Hartburn, came a requirement for new farmhouses to serve the new estates, as witnessed by the late sixteenth century transactions noted in the last chapter. From the name, the Grange was presumably the existing manor house, and the Red House or New Hall was built to fit in with the new agrarian layout and farm management arrangements. The Red House later became known as Oak Tree House Farm, and is an early example of the building of new farmsteads outside the old manorial centres after enclosure. John Gaines' messuage was presumably another farmhouse built as part of the same movement.

The inventory of William Mitchell in Chapter 3 illustrates a Middleton One Row farmer in the second half of the sixteenth century, in the declining years of open fields at Middleton. Moving into the next century, there is a comparable inventory made in 1611 for the just-deceased Marmaduke Andrew "yeoman of Meddelton one Rowe in Middleton George parish" [1]. The particulars of his estate are as follows, maintaining the original spellings.

		£.	s.	d.	
13	kine - milk	34.	13.	4.	
12	calves	8.	0.	0.	
3	calves - suckling	1.	0.	0.	
14	oxen	47.	17.	4.	Also 4 oxen sold to John Addey, to be paid as-sencyon day next - commonly called Hallow Thursday £16
2	bulls	5.	0.	0.	
9	cows - fat	25.	7.	8.	
3	young cattle	6.	0.	0.	
20	fat key	47.	17.	8.	
7	fat key	20.	5.	7.	
1	nag "gray paste"	4.	0.	0.	
4	score - ewes	28.	0.	0.	
29	ewes	6.	0.	0.	
20	hogs	3.	0.	0.	
	hay	4.	0.	0.	Hay & etages of Mydlseones Close
		4.	0.	0.	Etages of the same close and that about it, and the hay there
		2.	5.	0.	Hay and etages of the Myle field
		1.	13.	4.	Etages of West Whinesfill Lady Day
		2.	0.	0.	Hay in the closes of the Grest
			13.	4.	The leces of the Bancke Closse - appraised - all the interest

7	cheeses		6.	0.	
	yarn wool		10.	0.	6 score lyne yarn & some other yarn
	gear... plow				
		harrows	1.	0.	0.
		wins			
	Apparel & purse		2.	0.	0.
	Total value of goods Being declared in inventory		302.	6.	0. (total of items above £271. 9s. 3d., the difference largely accounted for by his separately listed household possessions)

Taken some thirty five years later, the inventory of Marmaduke Andrew differs in several significant respects from that of William Mitchell.

Marmaduke Andrew had a much bigger estate, in terms of the value of his farming operations. There was an almost complete concentration on cattle, this element accounting for fully three quarters of the total value of his possessions. He had 49 cows worth between £2. 8s. 0d. and £2.18s.0d. each, two bulls worth £2.10s. 0d. each, and 14 oxen valued at £3. 8s. 5d. each. In addition he had 129 sheep worth between 3s. 0d. and 7s. 0d.

No mention is made of any arable land or crops, other than hay. He only had one horse (called "Grey Paste") and only one plough. His plough gear, including harrows, was reckoned to be worth no more than one pound. The fourteen oxen were clearly not draught animals. The inventory was taken soon after harvest time. If he had had arable land, there would have been an entry for grain in store, but there was none. His land was obviously devoted to grazing or providing feed for his stock. The other significant feature is that all the hay is situated within various named closes, apart from one parcel said to be in the Millfield, which was probably also an enclosed field.

The move towards cattle rearing was general over the area. Enclosure of the open fields facilitated the transition. What may seem puzzling from Marmaduke Andrew's inventory is that the changeover for him seems to have occurred before the enclosure of the main open fields of Middleton One Row. The explanation probably lies in the fact that the c.1630 enclosure was only the final act in the process. Even before then, accumulation of open field strips could have made possible their use for grazing. Another possibility is that Andrew's land could have been concentrated in the Stodhoe grasslands to the north, where enclosure had taken place earlier. Although Andrew is named as being of Middleton One Row, he may also have had land in the Low Middleton or Middleton St. George part of the parish, where again enclosure had taken place earlier. When, some forty years earlier, Andrew had turned out as a young man at the Sedgefield muster, he was listed with Middleton St. George.

Whatever the details of the case, decay of the open fields was associated with the general movement from arable farming to cattle raising, and enclosure greatly accelerated the transition, with individually managed farms. Marmaduke Andrew was obviously a cattle breeder on a substantial scale. A note attached to his probate papers is revealing. It records the sale at Wakefield of 14 oxen and 9 cows listed in the inventory, and at Rotherham of another 27 of the cows. The moving of the cattle and the sales were carried out by Richard Mawer, himself a farmer at Long Newton, who probably also used the flourishing West Yorkshire markets on his own account. This is indicative of an established cattle business, with well set-up marketing arrangements.

Reverting to Marmaduke Andrew's inventory, his household possessions were worth an assessed £23.15s. 8d., suggesting that he was of respectable social status. His house had five rooms, the high parlour, the low parlour, the high chamber, the kitchen and buttery. Most, if not all, of the other houses in the village would have been more basic and less well equipped. The descriptions "high" and "low" may imply a house of two storeys, but could be applied simply as nominal distinctions for one end of the house or the other, or to signify distinction of usage.

The high chamber contained three beds, and there was a truckle (push-away) bed in the low parlour. The low parlour was obviously the living room, containing a long table, a form, five stools and two chairs. There was a cupboard and shelves. The high parlour was probably a smaller room, containing only "household stuff" worth 20s. The kitchen had a considerable amount of equipment, including two spits for cooking, and numerous pots, pans and kettles. The contents of the buttery, used mainly for food and drink storage, are not separately noted.

In 1606 Thomas Bank sold the Red House or New Hall, together with Winnie Closes, to William Allonson [2]. He died in possession in 1619, leaving a substantial estate worth about £550 [3]. The agrarian picture revealed by William Allonson's inventory is the same as that for Marmaduke Andrew at Middleton One Row in 1611. His business was the raising of cattle and sheep, with no indication of any arable cropping. He had livestock worth a total of £203. 2.10, against a value of crops amounting to £51. 0. 0, this being entirely hay for cattle fodder. He leased grazing and meadow at West Hartburn, and owed money to Sir Charles Wrenn on that account. He also had grazing "on the Moor", showing that some common ground still existed, despite enclosure of the former open field arable lands. A lease of land at Norton worth £80 implies a substantial holding there. (This may be a scribe's error, as Morton in the adjacent parish is more likely than Norton some ten miles away.) At West Hartburn, where Allonson had some of his grazing and meadow, the manorial lands had been broken up, and the village had been abandoned.

Eight years prior to William Allonson's death, he had been one of the witnesses to the will of Lawrence Langley, who described himself as a tailor, living at the White House. (Pl.15) This can be identified with the White House Farm of today, at the extreme north of the parish. Apart from the name, this identification is supported by the fact that the farm adjoins Long Newton, and the inventory was taken by William Allonson in conjunction with three Long Newton men. Previously in the manor of West Hartburn, it is an early example of the move out of the old village and onto the new farms created after enclosure.

Lawrence Langley's will, dated 22 December 1610 [4], is a splendid example of testamentary style, in the full religious fervour of the times. It reads, in the original wording, as follows: [4]

"In the name of god: Amen: I Lawrence Langley of the White house wthin the prese of meddelton george in the countie of Durham Tayler: Being at this p'sent by reason of infirmitie of sickness somwhat weakend and feable in my bodie but yett of good & pfett memorey (thanks be unto almightie god) and wearinge wth my self the mortalitie, frailtie and incertenty of this life, in this vale of missery, and howe subject the same ys to infinite calamities & unto death itself: by diveres and sundrey means wherby the lyfe of man ys most aptly applied to a shadowe that shortly vanisheth or flower that quickley fadeth: and intendinge wth my selfe the remembrance of my frends wth that small abilitie of my goods wch almightie god haith bestowed upon me in this life & how & in what manr to dispose of the same: I do make & ordeine this my last will and Testament in manr & forme followinge: first & principallie trhroughe the marcifull grace and goodness of almightie god I do comitt & comend my soule into the hands of my savior & Redemor Jesus christ, trustinge throughe his meritte death & passion to obteine Remission of my sinnes, & life everlastinge in that celestiall kingdome ordeined for elect & saints of god: and my body to be buried att the pishe church of middelton george afforsaid: And towchinge the disposition of my goods: First y geve and bequeth unto Betteres browne of Trimdon my sister & hir childer £3. 6s. 8d. Itn y geve to Richard collinge sonne of Robert collinge of Lonngnewton 10s. Itn. Y geve to margrett Langley my wiffe a bay mayer: and my debts being payrd & buryall descharged of all the rest of my goods wch doth reman behinde y do by this my will make my wyffe full & solle executor In witnes therof y have to this my last will & testment sette my hand & seale the 22 day of December in the eight of the reigrn of our soufferinge lorde James by the grace of god kinge of england france & yerland, defender of the faith etc & of Scotland the fowere & fortey etc 1610"

There are no tools of trade in the inventory which accompanied his will, but they would in any case be few. He did not rely entirely on his craft, as he had five cows, some sheep and a horse, but no corn. His possessions were meagre, and his total estate was worth only £30. 8. 4. People owing him money included Henry Killinghall, lord of the manor, and William Casse, the parson, probably for his tailoring services.

His house was very modest, with two main rooms, the forehouse for living and eating, and the parlour which served also as the sleeping area, together with a milkhouse.

Two other residents of the old West Hartburn area around this time were Agnes Hutchinson and Dorothy Pinkney.

There is an inventory of the possessions of Agnes Hutchinson at the time of her death, but of greater interest is her will itself, made on 11 July 1606, listing her bequests to the poor, the parson, her godchildren, and members of her family [5]. She was seemingly a single woman, as there is no mention of being a widow or of any offspring. [5]

Anno Domi 1606 July the eleventh

I Agnes hucheson seck in boddy but in good & pfyet remembrance praysed be god, Doo mack and ordayne this my last will and testament in manner and forme as foloweth, fyrst I bequethe my soule and me boddy to be buryed in the psishe church of Middleton georg Itm I bequethe unto the powr peopl of the same psishe 6s. 8d. Itm to our mynster 2s. Itm to every child yt I ame godmother unto you 12d. Itm to Tho.hutcherson and Richard other of them 12d. Itm I geve unto Anne Stelling my nice 11 piecs of pewtier; a great caldering a pare of my best shets a pillow boare & two silver spones, Itm I geve unto his Daughter Anne Stelling a cettel a coverlet a cupbord & pewther Dishes 3 candilsticks 2 pewther potts 2 salts a chyst wth all the clothes therin mw best gowne, & 2 silver spones Itm I geve unto constance Stelling a brasse pott & piec of pewther a coverlet a chyst wth all therin, my gryne gowne, and a silver spone, Itm I geve unto franchis Stelling a brasse pott, a pice of pewther, a coverlet, a coffer wth all therin, a worset cyrtell a read pott.....& a silver spone. Itm I geve unto Wm.Stelling a meare and a fole and a silvr spone; Itm I forgeve to my nephew Jacbu 20s. wch he oweth me; Itm after my Debts payed And funerall expenses Discharged the rest of all goods movable and unmovable I geve unto my brother Robart hutchensu who I mak executor of this my last will.

Her house was of two rooms; the parlour, which included her sleeping accommodation, and a kitchen. Its location is unknown, probably on one of the holdings which emerged after enclosure, but just possibly a last housing remnant of the old village.

Once again, her farming scope was concentrated on livestock. Her inventory lists 6 cows, an ox, 4 stotts, 2 quys, 3 calves, a mare and foal, a filly and 41 sheep. Her livestock was valued at £42. 0. 4d. out of a total estate worth £53.13s.10d. Her bequests show an interesting list of personal possessions. She owed rent to Mr.Wrenn, of the family who had acquired West Hartburn from Francis Killinghall in the middle of the previous century.

Dorothy Pinkney, described as a gentlewoman, and also of West Hartburn, died in 1610. Her inventory [6]. shows a form of house and goods broadly parallel to those of Agnes Hutchinson. She had livestock worth £18. 0. 0. out of a total estate value of £55.10. 6., which had a surprisingly high element of £34. 3. 0. for purse and apparel.

From the particulars of the wills and inventories and the other information available, it is clear that the medieval manors of Low Middleton and West Hartburn, with their villages and open fields, had by 1600 been replaced by enclosed farms and estates. Associated with this change, which was under way by at least the first half of the sixteenth century, was a move towards pastoralisation, motivated by commercial considerations. All the evidence shows cattle and sheep rearing as the strongly dominant, and perhaps almost exclusive farming objective. The change to a strong emphasis on stock occurred also at Middleton One Row, although, as noted in the last chapter, enclosure of the open fields there was not completed until about 1630.

The religious strife of the sixteenth century had given way to a tenuous balance between the various parties within the protestant church. However, Catholics continued to be treated with suspicion, and were penally taxed on their estates. A list of recusants within the Archdiocese of York includes in 1595 Christopher Ewbank, gent. of Middleton St. George, his wife Isabel, and their servant Jane Fawcett [7].

The Killinghalls, although not nominally a catholic family, were strong supporters of the old church. Anne, the wife of Henry Killinghall, was herself a catholic, and is shown, with some trepidation, as such in the 1595 list. "She is a most notorious recusant & a dangerous pson." The entry goes on to say, "Hir husband hath latelie bought a ship of some CXL tonne wcth he purposeth to dispose of is not knowne but would be thought of siriouslie & tymelie." [8]. Henry Killinghall's sister Isobel was also a catholic, and William Killinghall, Henry's son, is recorded as discharging his aunt's tax arrears in the period 1629-32 [9].

After the accession of Charles I in 1625, the situation deteriorated again, fuelled by the ever-widening division between King and Parliament, and leading ultimately to the Civil War and the associated disruptions of the mid-seventeenth century. No major Civil War battles were fought in the locality of Middleton, but the area did not escape the disturbing effects. The Scots involvement was a particular source of woe.

The dispute between Charles and the Scottish covenanters led to a hostile Scots move across the border in August 1640. The royal forces attempted to stop the Scots from crossing the Tyne, but were easily defeated at Newburn, leaving the Scots free to occupy the strategic town of Newcastle. The Earl of Strafford, in charge of the king's army, was at Darlington, intending to join the fight, but, on hearing of the defeat, had to content himself with organising the retreat. He issued the following ordinance:

" The Earl of Strafford, Lord Lieutenant-General of his Majesties army, to all Sheriffs, Constables of the Peace, High Constables, and other his Majesties officers:- Whereas his Majesties army is now marching from Newcastle to Darlington, and the villages thereunto adjacent. These are specially to require you, and the rest of the High Constables, to use your utmost diligence in causing to be brought hither, by four a clock this afternoon at the farthest, all such quantities of butter, bread, cheese, and milk, as you can possibly furnish, for the victualling of his Majesties said army, which, being brought hither by the several owners, I shall take special care to see them justly satisfied the price of their commodities; it being his Majesties gracious intention there shall be no burthen nor oppression to his Majesties good and loving subjects. These are likewise to farther to require you, that with the assistance of the Justice of Peace adjoyning, you give order for the taking away of all the upper millstones in all the mills in that your ward, and to bury or otherwise to break them, that the said mills may not be of any use to the army of the Scotch rebels. You are likewise to require all his majesties subjects to remove all their cattle and other goods, as soon as possibly they can, out of their countrey into places more remote and of greater safety for them, until the return of his Majesty, which will be very shortly, by the help of God, that his good subjects may be powerfully secured from the fears and dangers threatned by the said rebels. Given under my Hand and Seal, at Darlington, Aug.30 1640, - Strafford" [10].

It can be seen that the countryside, including the rural communities like Middleton, had the burden of supporting the retreating force, albeit with the promise of payment. There could be no such alleviation to the depredations of the pursuing Scots, as witness the charge to remove cattle and goods, and even to render mills useless by removing millstones.

A treaty made at Ripon represented the best deal the English could negotiate with the Scots. The boundary between English and Scots jurisdiction was fixed at the Tees, and the English were to be responsible for the costs of the Scots army of occupation. Middleton fell within the occupied area, and had to share the consequent burdens, financial and otherwise.

The political involvement of the Killinghalls was evidenced by a curious incident which occurred during the negotiations at Ripon. Objection was taken to the manner and words of the secretary of General Leslie, the Scots commander. John Killinghall and his brother-in-law Nicholas Chaytor were foremost in testifying as to the offence. It was proposed that they should go to the Scots camp to give evidence accordingly, but were refused safe conduct. The Scots denied the accusation, and the affair eventually fizzled out [11].

The Scots finally withdrew in August 1641. The king followed them in the misguided hope of soliciting their support in his struggle against the parliamentarians. In this he failed, and returned to act his part in the deteriorating situation, which led to the beginning of the Civil War the following year.

In the spring of 1642, before the actual outbreak of hostilities, efforts were made to secure adherence to parliamentary policy and the reformed church. To this end, Parliament enacted a measure requiring all males of eighteen years of age and over to put their names, in the presence of witnesses, to a statement, promising "to maintain and defend……the Doctrine of the Church of England, against all Popery, and Popish Innovations…..And further…..to preserve the Union and Peace betwixt the Three Kingdoms of England, Scotland, and Ireland….."

The Protestation, as it was called, was taken for the parish of Middleton St. George on 3 March 1642, under the surveillance of the parson, churchwardens and parish constables, all of whom had to signify their own acceptance. The record of the Protestation [12] kept at the Houses of Parliament, provides for the first time a list of the inhabitants of the parish, or at least of all the males eighteen years old or over. This is a valuable source of information, and is given in full below, retaining the spelling of the original.

> A note or Shedull of their names that haue taken the Protestation in the parish of Middleton George this prsente 3 of March, Anno Dom, 1641. Chrstofer Hall, gent., James Dale, John Wetherelt, sen., Thomas Scrogges, Anthony Dale, Roberte Mawer, George Warde, Willia Dale, Bartholomew Richardson, Edwarde Renny, Cuthbert Bellanby, George Greauson, Thomas Wetherelt, John Stockton, Christofer Gibson, Willia Allen, Thomas Wilknson, Thomas Isackson, Reonald Copeman, Henry Andrew, Owin Horsley, John Wetherelt, jun., John Jonsonn, James Bales, gent., Christofer Raine, Georg andell, Cuthbert Spooner, Christofer Freare, Francis Readman, Roberte Marley, John Chipchase, John Gowlande, Francis Moorye, Willia Savill, Roberte Seamer, Richarde Iton, Raiph Batmeson, James Elstobbe, Thomas Marley, Willia Herryson, Thomas Culley, Christofer Allonson, Thomas Middleton, Willia Casse, Marmaduke Wilsonn, Mr. Willia Killinghall is at London otherwise we doe verily think he would haue taken the protestation.

> The names of such protestants as haue refused to come and take the protestation; Willia Lodge, Richard Brasse, Richard Story, Christofer Copman. The names of the popish recusants within the saide parish: James Aislough, gent., Steaphen Hick, John Sadlerre, Thomas Dawson. Signed. Curate ibid, Marmaduk Wetherelt; Churchwardens, Thomas Lickley, Thomas Hutchinson; Constables, Francis Newton, Roberte Marton.

59 names are listed. 50 of these assented to the Protestation by signing or having their names entered as conformers. Four Roman Catholics were named as recusants, and four protestants also refused to sign. In view of the family support for the old form of religion and their catholic sympathies, it was perhaps convenient for William Killinghall to be away in London. His son John signed the Protestation at Haughton, being described as being of Haughton Field. William's brother Francis was also included in the Haughton return as having refused to take the Protestation [13].

The returns were submitted as required, but it appears that no action was taken against those refusing to sign. The war which was about to break out, provided a more positive indication of loyalties.

The war continued through 1642 and 1643, with neither side gaining clear supremacy. The situation changed when the Scots again entered the fray, the services of the covenanting army being provided as allies of parliament, in return for an agreement to bring the English and Scots churches into Presbyterian style alignment, as witnessed by the Solemn League and Covenant. The support of the Scots helped turn the tide in favour of Parliament, and, with the Royalist defeat at Marston Moor in July 1644, the outcome was virtually decided, although the war was to drag on for another two and a half years.

William Killinghall, conspicuous for his absence from the Protestations, died during the conflict in 1644. His son John continued to support the Royalist cause. He was branded a delinquent for bearing arms against Parliament, and in 1644 his lands were sequestered [14]. He surrendered in

November 1645, and petitioned for pardon. The petition was granted after he had compounded for the return of his estate. A fine of £60 was recorded in 1645 [15] and one of £48 in 1646 [16], but the amount he eventually had to pay was said to be £440 [17]. John died in 1652, but suspicion of the family remained, and, a year later, his widow Margaret had to appear before the justices to signify her allegiance, in the form, "I doe declare and promise to be true and faithfull to the Common Wealth of England as it is now established without a king or house of lords". [18]

Christopher Hall of West Hartburn was another strong Royalist supporter and a very intransigent opponent of Parliament. When money was subsequently being raised from offenders, it was recorded that "in 1642 Hall sent a horse into Col. Errington's troop", and a later hearing registered a further catalogue of charges. "That he hired Hen.Lawson to carry a pike three months under Capt.Eden, in Col.Hilton's regiment. That he lent Sir Thos. Ridell, jun., Governor of Tynemouth Castle for the King £140. That he compelled Geo. Hodson of Long Newton, by threats, to fight against Parlt. under Capt.Chris.Wray, which he did till he was killed at Bradford. That he paid assessments and afforded billets to the King's party, but bade the Parlt. party eat the ground if they could, for he would pay them no assessment." Still later, another charge was added, "that he hired two butchers to drive eleven of his beasts to Newcastle for the Earl of Newcastle's army." [19]

Hall protested his innocence, saying that he was a bed-ridden 87 year old. His pleas fell on deaf ears, and on 13 March 1650 he was declared a delinquent, and his estates were to be sequestered [20]. On 25 March he asked to be allowed to compound for his estates, but died in August of the same year. His brother Thomas and Margery Pinkney, acting as executors, repeated the request exactly a year later. Christopher Hall had had landed interests in many places apart from West Hartburn, and his affairs were very complicated. These complications were used as a defence against the imposition of penalties. Margery Pinkney claimed that she and Hall were joint purchasers of properties, and that when he died they were all hers, and hence not liable to sequestration. The investigating committee alleged that she feigned illness to avoid being cross-examined, but this would appear to have been somewhat unfair, as she did die very soon thereafter [21]. On 14 January 1652, Thomas Hall, the other executor, committed himself to pay a fine of £394. 2s. 8d., reckoned as one sixth of the estate valuation, and the sequestration was suspended [22].

The Parliamentary Commissioners, meeting at Sadberge on 23 August 1644, published a list of the "Names of such persons as have been in arms against the King and Parliament, having lands within the parish of Middleton George, viz. Mr. Jas. Ascough, a papist; Mich. Pudsey of Pikton in Yorkshire, Mr. John Killinghall, John Sadler, a papist; Katherin Mainchforth, widow, papist." A warrant was issued for sequestering the estates of those named. Christopher Hall was not included at that stage [23]. Two weeks later, on 7 September 1644, at a similar meeting at Great Stainton, it was recorded that Captain Robert Ellis of Rudston in Yorkshire had lands sequestered in West Hartburn, which had been let to Richard Wilkinson [24]. The lands in question were within the Goosepool estate which had become known as Paul Hartburn,

One of the sequestrators was John Husband, and a further warrant, issued at Durham and dated 17 September 1644, authorised him to let the lands of William Killinghall, Michael Pudsey, and James Ayscough of Middleton St. George and Middleton One Row, and to sell the possessions of Killinghall and Ayscough [25].

The settlement of the Killinghall estate has already been noted. On 28 February 1646 it was recorded that the Pudsey farm at Middleton St. George was let to John Wetherel and his son of the same name for a rent of 100 marks [26].

In a letter dated 20 May 1647, the Durham County Committee for Compounding claimed that they themselves were still suffering, with the county as a whole, for the burdens of the war, stating "Our county has been so exhausted with great and sad oppressions that we have had to spend ourselves and our estates in the service with no allowances and to engage our credits to procure supplies both before and since the departure of the Scottish army, for payment of our ministers and associated forces above what could be raised by rents or sequestrations" [27].

On 30 March 1652, the commissioners prepared a list of all who had their lands sequestered between 1 April 1644 and 1 December 1651, and who had not been discharged by compounding for their estates. This list of those still resisting or unable to pay included "Jas. Aiscough of Middleton one Row, gent, Rec, Del, Michael Pudsey of Middleton George, gent, Rec, Del and John Sadler of Middleton-one-Row, yeoman. Rec" [28].

The Ascough estate was included in a list of such lands put up for sale on 18 November 1652 [29]. On 1 July 1653 Ascough paid a fine for a property he had in Dinsdale, and his estate was discharged. Shortly afterwards, on 22 August, the manor of Middleton One Row was also discharged from sequestration [30]. It was bought from the Treason Trustees by Gilbert Crouch, as were many other properties. He would appear to have acted as an intermediary, often for the return of lands to their dispossessed owners.

The estate of Michael Pudsey, included in the same Act for Sale, was described as "The mansion or farmhouse called Middleton George, with the lands, etc., as the same are returned by the Surveyors." They were said to be worth £119.11s. 5d per annum. He asked leave to compound for the return of his estate, and this was confirmed when he paid a fine of 5 times the yearly value, amounting to £656. 5s. 0d. on 6 June 1653 [31]. This is the farm which later became known as Church House Farm. The house was a substantial one for the period, consisting of hall, parlour, kitchen, buttery and milkhouse on the ground floor, with two chambers and a storehouse above. The parcels of land specified in the survey are all pasture and meadow, with no mention of any arable land.

Three years later, a list of papists and delinquents who were still under sequestration included among the papists John Sadler of Middleton One Row, yeoman [32].

Even before the strife of the Civil War, security in the northern counties was far from assured. At the beginning of the seventeenth century the crowns of England and Scotland were united. However, this did not bring an end to cross-border strife and fear of continental invasion, and the population was still called upon to act as a security force when required. At a muster of able-bodied men taken in 1618 before Sir Ralph Conyers, deputy lieutenant for the Stockton Ward of the county, Middleton St. George managed to produce a man with a musket, but who was said to be lacking a sword. Three men were listed for Middleton One Row, two with muskets and the other with a corselet. It is significant that the latter was Alan Aiscough of the catholic lord of the manor family. A note against his name says, "His armour taken from him", no doubt reflecting the suspicion with which he was held [33].

It has been shown that by about 1630 the parish of Middleton St. George had lost the last of its ancient common fields at Middleton One Row, those at Low Middleton and West Hartburn having disappeared during the previous century. New self-contained farms had been established, although it probably took many years for a stable pattern to appear. The villages of Low Middleton and West Hartburn had disappeared, leaving Middleton One Row as the only village community in the parish. Most of the population lived on the farms, and in cottages associated with them or with the carrying on of rural trades.

The independent farms gave more scope for commercial farming, but agrarian practices remained relatively primitive. Cattle raising was the principal business, but the big improvements from selective breeding were yet to come. The enclosed fields provided opportunity for better management, but, where corn was still grown, crop improvements were limited, and it is likely that three or four course rotations continued, with wasteful fallow years.

In the seventeenth century much more information becomes available about the individuals and families making up the population. The surviving records provide a deeper insight into their lives.

The Protestation of 1642 affords the first opportunity for a demographic assessment of the parish. As noted in the previous section, 59 men aged 18 and over were listed. Based on the assumption that 60% of the population were aged 18 and over, and 40% were children and adolescents, the total population of the parish at that time can be estimated to have been about 200. The names listed in the schedule are themselves interesting, as again this is the first time all the families are represented, except for any rare cases of a family without an adult male. Some of the names are recognisable from other sources, such as land and property transactions, but others have not previously appeared.

The parish registers provide the other early source for names of the population. A statute of Elizabeth I decreed that registers should be kept with effect from 1558, the first year of her reign. Unfortunately, the early registers of Middleton St. George have been long lost, and the surviving registers date from 1616 for marriages and burials, and from 1652 for baptisms [34].

Adding to the woes of the population in the Civil War strife there were outbreaks of plague, at Middleton St. George and elsewhere in the area. In the conditions of warfare and death from the pestilence, the Middleton St. George registers, like many others, were neglected, but the following retrospective entries give some indication of the toll from the disease.

A note of such as died in tym of the sicknes forgotten to be set downe in their prop. place

1645

Dec.24	Thomas Lickley
25	John Jonson
	Mary, Ann, and Thomas, children of Thomas Culley, bur. in Easter week in the same yeare.
	three children of Willa Daile died thereabouts.
	Isabell, wife of Xpofer Allonson, at the sa tyme.
	(blank) s. Marmaduke wetherelt
Oct.10	Matthew Wetherelt
Dec.25	Thomas, s. of the said Marmaduke.

1647

Aug.1	An, d. of the said Marmaduke.
Sept.25	Elizabeth, wife of Willa Daile
6	Thomas, son of Robert Richinson

Thomas Lickley, as churchwarden, had been one of those overlooking the signing of the Protestation three years earlier.

Children were especially vulnerable. Three, if not all four, of the Wetherell deaths were children of the rector Marmaduke Wetherell. Other entries in the register bear witness to the fact that infant mortality was very high, even outside the plague periods.

The assignment of the plague entries to years extending from 1645 to 1647 seems surprising. The plague may have lasted for a long time, but that would be unusual. There may have been more than one outbreak, but more likely the dates of the 'afterthought' entries may simply have been confused. Whatever the explanation, it is almost certain that there were others who perished but were not recorded, and there is no doubt of the seriousness of the ravages of disease.

In the parish register is an interesting list showing how the population were put in their places for church attendance. It reads as follows;

<u>An Order for the seatinge of the Parishioners made by Commission for the Arch-deacon of Durham.</u>

On the South side	
In the first seate	Mr. Killinghall
In the 2d	Marmaduke Willson
In the 3d	Jo: Sadler James Dale Tho: Scroggs
The 4th is assigned to the Parson, and the 5th to the Clarke	

In the 6th	R. Marley, Jo. Witherell, Th:Lickley
In the 7th	Cut. Spooner, & Mr. Ascoughs Men

On the North side

In the first seate	Mr. Ascough
In the 2d	Mrs. Pinkenay
In the 3d	Mr. Foster
In the 4th	Sr. Coiners Darcy's tenants
In the 5th	The red house, Fr. Newton, Cut. Middleton
In the 5th & 6th	Mr. Killinghall's Tenants of Middleton
(6th & 7th?)	and Anthony Dale, during his father's life onely
	File
	Davies Duncan
	Raphe Tunstall
	Tho Thomson
	John Band

This list is misleadingly included next to baptisms of 1753, but it certainly does not belong to that time. Based on the names assigned to the pews, it must date from the first half of the seventeenth century. This is supported by the fact that one of the signatories was probably the Ralph Tunstall who was rector of Long Newton in that period, and who died in 1659. Mrs Pinkney in the second seat on the north side was doubtless Margaret Pinkney who took land at West Hartburn in 1607 and died in 1651. Thomas Lickley in the sixth row on the south was probably the churchwarden who died in the plague year 1645.

The front rows were occupied by the two lords of the manor, the Killinghalls of Low Middleton on the south side, and the Ascoughs of Middleton One Row on the north side (despite their openly catholic front). Moving back from them, there seems to have been no attempt to segregate the people of the two manors.

It has already been noted that by this time the Killinghalls had lost the feudal element of their role as lords of the manor of Low Middleton, but they remained the major landowner in the parish and did retain a position of authority, as well as the patronage of the church, including a share of the tithes. The diminution of the powers of the lords of the manor of Middleton One Row was even more pronounced. They never had a part in the control of the church, and any remnant of feudal authority was much reduced when the medieval style manor was transformed into commercial farms and estates. Little more than the title remained to the Ascoughs in the seventeenth century, and even this seems to have disappeared after 1720 [35].

With the restoration of the monarchy in 1660, parliament had to look afresh at the means of raising money for government expenditure. One measure enacted in 1662 was the hearth tax, the amount payable being calculated from the number of fire hearths in a person's house, and hence was generally in proportion to the size of the house and the substance of the householder.

The following enumeration of hearths is taken from the 1666 return for the parish [36].

Middleton St. George		Middleton One Row	
Will. Killinghall, Gent.	10	James Askew Gent.	5
Leonard Browne	2	Ralp. Wilson	2
Marmaduke Wetherall	4	Rodger Wilson	2
Marmaduke Horsley	1	Margrett Frear	1
Jno. Allinson	1	Robert Marley	2
Geo. Emmonson	1	Jno. Daile	1

Henry Wilkinson	1		Tho. Cunningham	3
Will. Wilkison	1		Robert Martin	2
Robert Gates	2		Jno. Smart	1
Matt. Woar Gent.	2		(Total)	19
Francis Ffoster	1			
Jno. Thompson	1			
Christ Scarlet	1			
Will. Wetherall	1			
(Total)	29			

As lords of the manor of Low Middleton or Middleton St. George, the Killinghalls possessed by far the grandest house, their mansion having 10 hearths. The parson, Marmaduke Wetherall, had a four hearth property. William Wetherall, possibly his brother, and with a family of at least four children, had a house with only one hearth, as did Francis Foster's farm on the site of the former village of West Hartburn.

At Middleton One Row, James Askew, the lord of the manor there, had a substantial house with 5 hearths, Thomas Cuningham had three hearths, and four other properties were two hearth houses.

These bare statistics do not give a comprehensive picture of the population, as there were evasions and exemptions were allowed for those too poor to pay. The latter class were numerous, as evidenced by a list of such appended to the Middleton One Row return, naming a further 23 people, each with a single hearth. Strangely, only two non-payers were noted for Middleton St. George.

Overall, there were 14 tax paying properties listed for Middleton St. George with a total of 29 hearths, and the 9 tax paying Middleton One Row houses had 19 hearths between them. About half of the tax paying properties had only one hearth, as did those housing the exempted poor, indicating that a substantial part of the population lived in one or two-roomed cottages. They would generally be single-storied, with walls probably still of wattle and daub, and with thatched roofs. The multi-hearthed houses would have various degrees of additional accommodation, and the more pretentious would have upper storeys. In 1698 the blacksmith, Thomas Robinson, sold to Robert Hilton "the east end of his cottage (at Middleton One Row) comprising one low room and a chamber over it". No houses from this period recognisably survive in the parish, but it is likely that brick was becoming more generally available as a building material for the new farmhouses. The manor house at Low Middleton stood in a class above the others, and is dealt with later in the chapter.

There are twenty two family names listed as being liable to pay the tax in the parish. Fourteen of these families are represented in the Protestation twenty two years earlier, but eight do not appear there. This is a sign of considerable fluidity of movement in the turbulent times of the mid-seventeenth century.

It is interesting that the benefices of Middleton St. George and Dinsdale were held in plurality by Marmaduke Wetherell. In 1654, at the time of the baptism at Middleton St. George of his son Christopher, he was designated "clerk", the term commonly used for a lay assistant in the church, but also sometimes used to signify a clergyman. When he died in 1690 and was buried at Middleton St. George, he was described as rector of Dinsdale and Middleton St. George. Richard Scruton succeeded him in both parishes.

Three acts were passed between 1667 and 1681, to help support home woollen manufacture, ordaining that all burials must be in woollen shrouds [37]. The relatives of the deceased, or other persons responsible for the burial, had to produce an affidavit confirming this within eight days. The penalty for non-compliance was a fine of £5, to be divided equally between the poor of the parish and the person notifying the default. The burial registers recorded compliance, as in typical Middleton St. George examples.

   Dec.10 1678 Francis Killinghall, gent. According to the Act.
   Apr.18 1680 Willia Freare. In sheeps wool only.

However, not everyone was prepared to comply, and some took an active dislike to the act, as they anticipated their own deaths. Pope's "Moral Essays" echo that feeling, when his dying lady voices her repugnance.

> 'Odious. in woollen. Twould a saint provoke',
> (Were the last words that poor Narcissa spoke)
> 'No, let a charming chintz, and Brussels lace
> Wrap my cold limbs, and shield my lifeless face'.

Elizabeth Killinghall, the lady of the manor of Middleton St. George, who died in 1678 after only six years of marriage, seems to have been of a similar unconforming mind, her burial entry being endorsed, "Buried in Linnen contrary to ye Act".

Although the act remained in force for over a century, it had lost its effectiveness before the end of the century, and penalties ceased to be applied long before it was eventually repealed.

When Elizabeth's mother-in-law Margaret Killinghall died in 1692, her burial place was stated in the register to be "in ye chancell of Middleton St. George". This shows the continuation of customary burial in the church reserved for the manorial lords and their families. Elizabeth's husband William Killinghall died in 1694, and in his will ordained that he was to be buried "in my parish church of Middleton" [38]. An earlier William, who died in 1644, wrote in his will, "If it please God to call me in his mercie nere home to be buryed amongst my ancestors at Middleton" [39]. It is not known how this worked out in even earlier times, with the complication of the divided manor, but it is clear that, once Elizabeth Killinghall had secured the advowson in 1523, it was the Killinghalls and their successors as lords of the united manor who had the right to be buried in the church. Not all availed themselves of the privilege, as some were buried away from Middleton.

The responsibility of the churchwardens for maintenance of the church was demonstrated in 1697 when the archdeacon visited the parish and admonished them, with instructions to deal with certain specific shortcomings [40]. A carpet was to be bought for the communion table, and an altar rail was to be set up. The interior of the church was to be whitewashed, and lamps were to be provided. Repairs were necessary to the porch. The churchwardens were to see that all this work was carried out before the next visitation.

The cost of repairs and maintenance had to be borne by the parish, and an earlier example is recorded in 1662, when the churchyard wall was in need of repair [41]. The cost was divided between the landowners, and the apportionment set down in the parish register.

After the complicated series of property deals in the second half of the sixteenth century, Henry Killinghall's recovery of the main part of the manor around 1606 meant that the Killinghalls were again undisputed lords of the manor of Middleton St. George, a position they held throughout the rest of the seventeenth century. It was this Henry who had caused concern by buying a ship for unknown but suspicious purposes around 1595, and whose wife Anne was regarded as a notorious catholic recusant.

Their son William appears in church court proceedings in 1611. It was said that he kept a kitchen wench with illegitimate twins, and when the churchwarden called to collect an 8s.4d. assessment he was beaten off by Killinghall. William responded to the proceedings that he was acting out of charity in keeping the woman, and only "struck the churchwarden lightly with a small gold-headed cane which he used to walk with ordinarily". Francis Killinghall, assumed to be a younger brother of William, was also in trouble with the church court over the irregularity of his marriage to Margery "his pretended wife" [42].

Henry Killinghall died in 1620, and was succeeded by William, who continued the family's catholic sympathies, and was notable for his absence from the signing of the Protestation. William's son John has already been mentioned as joining with the parson in legal proceedings in 1632 against the enclosers of land at Middleton One Row. He, as we have seen, took an active part as a Royalist in the Civil War, and suffered the consequences. Nevertheless he was able to negotiate a pardon, and pay for the restitution of his estate. John died in 1652, to be succeeded by his son William, who died in 1695. His eldest son, also William survived him by only a few years into the next century, dying in 1703.

The hearth tax returns confirm William Killinghall as having a substantial house, with ten hearths. This house was probably that called "The Grange" in transfers of the manor around the beginning of the century. Valuable information on the size and arrangement of the Killinghall manor house can be deduced from inventories taken when William died in 1644 [43], and when his son John died in 1652 [44].

Both the inventories list the possessions of the deceased against the various rooms of the house. There are some small differences in the names given to rooms, but it is clearly the same house. Taking John's 1652 inventory as the basis, 17 rooms were listed, as follows:

Living and service rooms	Bed chambers
Hall	Chamber over hall
Parlour	Chamber over parlour
Kitchen	Kitchen chamber
Little buttery	Little storehouse over buttery
Old buttery	Little chamber adjoining hall chamber
Larder	Chamber at the stair head
Brewhouse	Chamber over milk house
Milk house	Closet
Room within the stable	

The Killinghalls were not great magnates, but could be classed as middle gentry. Their modest wealth gave them a lifestyle substantially better than anyone else in the parish. This is apparent from comparison of the Killinghall inventories with those already seen from local farmers.

Their house at this time was of two storeys, with the living and service rooms below and the bedchambers generally above. Also at ground floor level were the brewhouse and milkhouse, both of which may have been separate from the main house. Obviously there were other outbuildings, and the inventory lists a room within the stable.

A conjectural reconstruction of the house is shown in Fig.16. The layout is based on the inventory information, interpreted in conjunction with the arrangement of surviving examples of houses elsewhere of similar period and status. A T-shape arrangement of the main living and service ranges has been adopted, on the assumption that the arrangement which can be seen today is a survival of the old alignment when the house was extensively rebuilt in the eighteenth century. The main walls were likely to have been of the locally available red sandstone. The roof would probably have been stone tiled. Multiple chimney stacks would have been necessary to serve the ten fireplaces noted in the hearth tax returns.

The following schedule of contents as listed in the 1652 inventory sheds some light on how the house was used, how it was furnished, and how the occupants lived:

A true and pfect inventorie of all such goods and chattells as were and did belonge to John Killinghall of Midleton George in the Countie of Durham Esqr. dyed seized off praysed by us whose names are undr. written the xix day of february 1651 (1652 by our present calendar)

   His purse & apparel   £13. 6s. 8d.

In the parlour
One Table wth. drawe leaves, one livery table, one litle table, two furmis, three chayrs, fower joynt stools, two Carpetts, one cupboard cloath, six setworke Quishons, one high chare for A child, one payre of And Irons, one payre of tonges, one fyre shovell, one stand Bed, one fether Bed, one down

Bedd, one bolster, one payre of pillowes, two payre of blanquetts, one sute of cloath cerurtaines wth coverings of the same, wth iron rodds, one sute of variucks hangings
Total   £8. 0s. 0d.

In the Chamber over the Hall
Two bedsteeds, one mattarice, two feather beds, two bolsters, two payre of pillowes, three payre of blanquetts, one yeallowe rugg & curtains wth rodds, one sute of wrought curtains wth covering sutable, and iron rodds, one square table, one little livery table, three imbroidered chayrs, six quishons one oversea coveringe, one happen, one Carpett
Total   £13. 6s. 8d.

In the litle chamber adioyninge the hall chamber
One lowe bedsteed, one mattarice, one feather bedd, one payre of pillowes, one bolster, one payre of blanckquettes, two coverings, one Chist, one payre of blankequetts, one happine
Total   £1. 0s. 0d.

In the Chamber at the staire head
One stanbedd, two feather bedds, one boulster, two paire of pillowes, thre blanckquetts, one oversea coveringe, one sute of greene curtains wth iron rodds, one lowe bedsteed, one featherbedd, one payre of blanckequetts, one boulster, one payre of pillowes, one cloath coveringe, one livery cupboard, two litle ioynt stooles, one desk, Curtains and vallanss for a Canapbedd
Total   £2.10s. 0d.

In the little butterye
One chayre table, one litle cupboard, two hogsheads, two flaggons, one quart pott, fower pewther candlesticks, one wanded woyder, one bason & Ewer, 12 peece of pewthr
Total   £5. 0s. 0d.

In the old Buttery
One Cupboard, one old table, two hogsheads, two stands, one Tubb wth salt, one spinniwheele
Total   £1.10s. 0d.

In the Hall
One leefe table, one table wth a frame, one livery cupboard, one chayre, one styll
Total   £1. 0s. 0d.

In the larther
Two hogsheads, one beife lead
Total   £1. 0s. 0d.

In the Kitchin
One Cupboard, two tables, one longesetle, three brass kettles, three iron potts, three brass potts, six pans, three drippin pans, two frying pans two payer of Racks, six spitts two ladles, one bayster, two scumers, one beife forke, one toastinge Iron, two covers for dishees, two smoothinge irons
Total   £10. 0s. 0d.

In the Milkehouse
One cheesepriss, two Cherns, three milchskeels, one dozen & a halfe of milchbouls, halfe a dozen of cheespotts, one cheestrough, one press, one safe, one tubb
Total   £4. 0s. 0d.

In the rome wthin the stable
One bedsteed, one chafe bedd, one boulster, one payer of blanckquetts & two happens, one Otetunn
Total   £1. 0s. 0d.

In the Brewhouse
One Chest, one kneedinge trough
Total   £0.10s. 0d.

In the Kitchin chamber
One stanbedd, one flockbedd, one featherbedd, one bolster, one payre of pillowes, three blanckquetts, one sute of stript curtanes & coveringe, wth iron rodds, one lowe bedsteed, one featherbed, one bolster, one payr of pillowes, one payre of blanckquetts, one rugg, one chest, one liverye cupboard, two chayres, three druncks, two boxes, one cupboard cloath, one paire of tonges & fyer shovell
Total   £6. 0s. 0d.

In the Chamber over the Milkhouse
One stand bedd, one featherbedd, one bolster, one payr of blanckquetts, one greene rugg, one low bedsteed, one chafebedd, one payer of blanckquetts, one white rugg, one longe chest, wth twelve payre of course sheets, five payre of pillowbores, six table-cloaths, two dozen of napkins, fower towels
Total   £5. 0s. 0d.

In the Closett
One truncke, one ioynt stoole, one litle cupboard, one table basquett, one voyder & knife, six dozen of plane tree trenchers, two selleers, one silver pothanger, six silver spoons, one litle silver botle, one silver taister, one lyne wheele, one doble guilt bear boull, one doble guilt wyne boule, one silver pothanger, one silver bote, fourteene payre of lyn sheetes, twelve payre of pillowborrs, one damask table cloth, one dozen of damask napkins, one damask drinking napkine, six lyn table cloaths, five dozen & a halfe of lyn napkins, one dozen of dyaper napkins, three large towells, five lyn towells, six cupboard cloaths, two drinking napkins, fower payer of new harden sheets, one score of harden, two dozen & a halfe of harden napkins, fower harden towells, one harden tablecloath

Total   £26. 6s. 8d.

In the Chamber over the Parlour
One Canabye bedsteed, one featherbedd, one bolster, one payer of pillowes, one payer of blanckquetts, one livery cupboard, one chayre
Total   £2. 0s. 0d.

In the litle storehouse over the butterye
One foldinge table, one chist
Total   £1. 0s. 0d.

The parlour seems to have been a large room, where most of the daily activity took place. It was furnished with three tables, and seating was on forms, chairs stools, and even a high chair for a child. Normal family meals were probably taken there. However, its usage was not confined to the daytime, as it also contained a bed. The windows were curtained, and there were wall hangings. William Killinghall's inventory eighteen years earlier showed similar furnishings, but also noted carpets and a desk. William's close sight had probably deteriorated, as a magnifying glass was listed amongst his possessions. Very impressively, he also had a clock in the parlour, which was quite unusual in this period before pendulum clocks had been introduced into England.

The size of the hall cannot be judged from the inventory, as it contained little in the way of furnishings - two tables, a cupboard, two chairs and a stool, worth only £1 in total. In William Killinghall's time it was similarly sparsely furnished, but did boast a carpet. It was probably a spacious room for affairs other than those of family and domestic routine. It would be used for business and estate management transactions. In earlier times it may have accommodated the manor court, but this had probably disappeared as an institution by this time. With extra seating brought in, the hall could also have been used for formal meals when visitors were being entertained, as the provision of a separate dining room was not a normal feature at this time and in this level of society.

The kitchen naturally contained all the cooking equipment, together with two tables, a longsettle and a cupboard, there were a number of hogsheads, presumably containers for ale, in the two butteries and the larder. Amongst the contents of the Little Buttery were a number of items of pewter, including four candlesticks. There was a spinning wheel in the old buttery.

Each of the bedchambers contained one or two beds. The better bedrooms had the luxury of curtains, carpets and rugs. At least one of the beds had a canopy, and must have been a four-poster or tester. Others were called "standbeds". "Low bedsteads" were noted in some of the rooms. These corresponded to what were called "truckle beds" in William's earlier inventory. When not in use, these could be pushed out of the way under the main beds. Mattresses were mostly of the feather bed variety, but there were also mattresses filled with down, flock and chaff. Beds seem to have been well provided with blankets, pillows and bolsters. No sheets were listed in the chambers, but they were clearly used by those qualifying for the luxury, as a large quantity was available in store and listed separately. Most of the bedchambers would have had fireplaces, contributing to the total of ten declared in the hearth tax returns. One of the better bedrooms housed a desk, which had been in the parlour in William's time. The room within the stable would have accommodated one or more servants, and had a chaff mattress on the bed.

One of the bedrooms and a closet housed a large amount of household linen and other domestic items. Despite the fact that there was no dining room, the possession of a damask table cloth and napkins indicates the ability to entertain in some style. Food appears to have been eaten from wooden plates, no less than 72 plane trenchers being listed in the closet store. There were unidentified items of pewter elsewhere, and William's earlier list included 54 pewter flagons. John's inventory had a few items of silver, including six spoons, but his father William apparently possessed much more, silver plate being listed to the considerable value of £36.14s. 0d. Perhaps the financial exactions in the aftermath of the Civil War had resulted in some depletion. Cutlery does not appear to any significant extent, and there is no mention of any glassware.

The inventory particulars give an impression of a household living in relative comfort, in a house designed and arranged for living and working, without undue ostentation. Nevertheless, it did provide the facility for a modest degree of luxury and social graces when occasion demanded.

The inventories can only tell us what was listed at the time, and some things, for one reason or another, escaped the scheduling. For example, not a single book is listed, but this does not indicate a lack of literacy. William Killinghall left in his will to Robert, one of his sons, "all my school books and law books with desire he may make good use of them and follow that profession". (William's widow was the daughter of a York lawyer.)

Like the books, some items, mainly of a personal nature, were named as specific bequests in the will, and were not necessarily individually identified in the inventory. William willed to "my loving wife all her jewells, my silver cann, six spoones,, my lesser salt", and bequests to his eldest son John included "my evidence chist" and "my painted desk".

The remainder of John Killinghall's 1652 inventory deals with his stock and crops from his farming activities, as set out below.

Six Oxen, twelve Kye, one Bull, one fower yeare old Quy, two three yeare old stotts, six two yeare old styrks, six yeare old Calves, seaven halfe yeare old Calves: £114. 0s. 0d.

three Swyn hoggs, two Sowes, one Brawne, two litle pigs   £ 3.10s. 0d.

Twentie Sheep hoggs, fortie Ewes, two tupps   £ 24. 3s. 4d.

two Mayers. two Geldings, one stoned Coalt   £ 20. 0s. 0d.

twentie thrave of Wheat, fiftie thrave of Otts   £ 12. 6s. 8d.

In the Garner

six bushells of Wheat, thirtie bushells of Rye, six and twentie bushells of Otts, three bushells of Pease, nyne and twentie bushells of Bigg malt, one and twentie bushells of Ote malt. £18. 3s. 4d
Seaven acres of Hard Corne £20. 0s. 0d.
three fflitches of Bacon £ 2.15s. 0d.

John Killinghall clearly had a substantial farm in his own hands, with six working oxen, three young oxen, twelve cows and a heifer, six stirks, thirteen calves, a bull, five horses, sixty two sheep and eight pigs.

His inventory was taken in February and there were only seven acres of hard corn (wheat and rye) in the ground, leaving his other arable crops to be sown in the spring. The yield from the previous season's crops remaining in the barn included a large proportion of rye and oats, but not very much wheat. There was in addition a quantity of big (barley) malt and of oats malt, presumably for brewing ale. Some peas were also grown.

In 1644, the just deceased William Killinghall had had a similar mixed farm. As his inventory was made in June, most of the corn listed was still growing. Some of the previous year's crops, however, remained in store, including malt in the barns and kilns. The growing corn was said to be in fields called Parson Close and the Corn Close.

John Killinghall's farm stock and crops were worth a total of £194.18s. 4d., and his household goods and personal possessions £102. 9s. 4d. The corresponding valuations for his father William were £366. 7s. 8d. and £120. 0s.10d. respectively. William also had debts owing to him amounting to over £100, which effectively added to the value of his estate. The reduction in the family assets between 1644 and 1652 may be explained by the depredations of the war and the need to pay for the restitution of the estate.

After about half a century of turmoil and change, the restoration of the monarchy led to more settled times. Like many other landed families on the wrong side in the Civil War, the Killinghalls continued in their estate, still dominant as lords of the manor, but not unscathed by the events and the associated financial retribution. Others who kept on the right side no doubt took advantage of the eventual settlements to reinforce their position or to step up and take the place of those who had fallen by the wayside.

The catholic cause made a brief come-back during the reign of James II, but after the Glorious Revolution of 1688 the established church was generally unchallenged, and its form of worship accepted by most of the population. Catholics, like the Ayscoughs of Middleton One Row, continued openly in their faith, but were still regarded with suspicion, and their toleration was seriously tempered by the deprivation of significant civil rights.

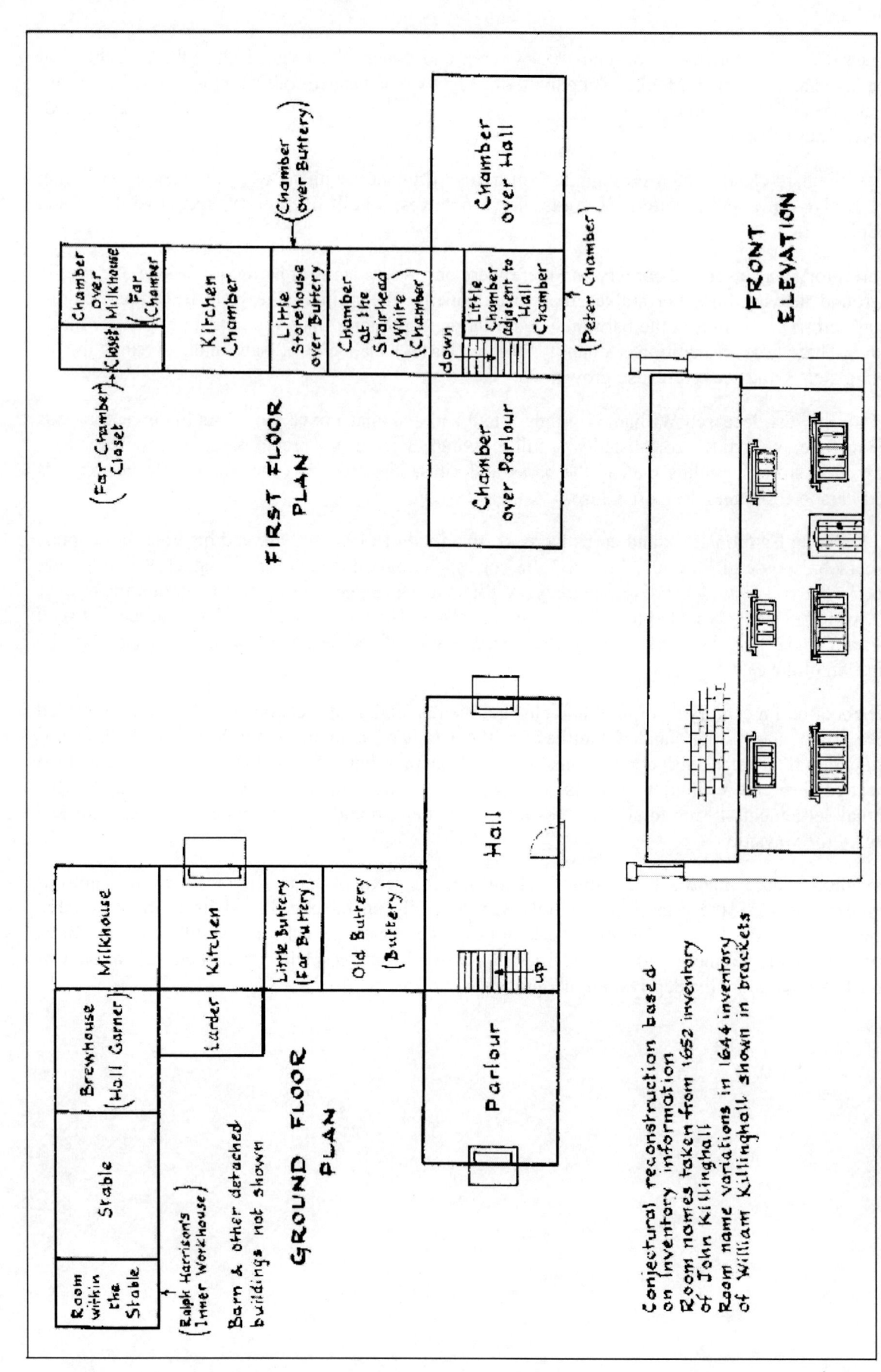

Fig.16 Conjectural reconstruction of the Killinghall manor house in the seventeenth century

CHAPTER FIVE - THE EIGHTEENTH CENTURY

SLOW RURAL PROGRESSION

Compared with the turbulent times of the previous century, the greater stability of the eighteenth century results in a paucity of evidence for development within the parish. However, the church registers record in greater detail the passage of many of the individuals and families making up the population, and afford some insight into their lives.

Agriculture remained the sole occupation of the parish. The estates established in the late sixteenth and early seventeenth centuries developed over the period, but the indications are that before 1700 a pattern of farms had been established much as exists today. The village of Middleton One Row continued as the only substantial assemblage of houses within the parish, although a few cottages by this time made up a separate hamlet at Oak Tree.

In the course of the century, the name of Killinghall disappeared from the scene, but the family connection continued in the manorial descent. John Killinghall, who participated in the Civil War, died in 1652, and the previous chapter looked at his manor house and possessions. His widow Margaret effectively took over from him until their son William came of age. He had a long tenure as lord of the manor, dying in 1695. In contrast, his eldest son, also William, did not survive for long, dying in 1703. Being unmarried, his estate passed to his cousin Robert. On Robert's death in 1758, his son and successor John was the last of the Killinghalls of Middleton St. George [1].

John's aunt Elizabeth had married William Pemberton, a merchant of Darlington. The Pemberton family emanated from Stanhope in Weardale, and by the seventeenth century were established at Aislaby in the parish of Egglescliffe. When John Killinghall died in 1762, unmarried and childless, he left the family estate to his cousin (once removed) William Pemberton, grandson of William Pemberton and Elizabeth Killinghall. The manor continued in his hands until he died in 1778. His son and heir, again a William, carried the Pemberton lordship of the manor into the next century, his death occurring in 1801 [2].

One component of the estate was Red Hall Farm, established in the sixteenth century after enclosure of the open fields. The layout of the farm and its fields is shown on the 1726 plan reproduced here as Fig.17 - the earliest extant farm plan for Middleton [3]. Red Hall eventually became Oak Tree House Farm, now surrounded by airfield developments.

From 1759, land tax assessments begin to give information about landowners and farmers and the extent of their holdings. The earliest assessment in 1759 [4], however, is of limited value, as it does not distinguish between owners and occupiers. 26 holdings are listed, but some were very small, consisting only of a cottage and garden. Mr. Killinghall is named as the holder of only one farm of low value, but he was the main landowner. His other farms were leased out, including the largest, which was farmed by William Kay. The Kay family had been established in the parish for some time, William himself having been born there in 1693, the eldest son of Francis Kay, gentleman. The next son, called Francis after his father, was evidently destined for business, being apprenticed to the Newcastle-upon-Tyne Company of Hostmen in 1708 [5].

Based on subsequent connections, the farm listed against the name of George Middleton was Church House. Thomas Wilkinson had three holdings, as did the Bamlet family. The Richardson family had two, and the Wrightsons had one farm, plus one other very small holding. Mr. Whaley, named as holding a substantial farm, was the rector at the time. One of the Richardson holdings was the farm which became known as Middleton One Row East Farm. This was surveyed as part of the Killinghall estate in 1757, and is the subject of the very fine plan reproduced here as Pl.2. Fig.18 shows Palm Tree House Farm, surveyed and planned at the same time [6].

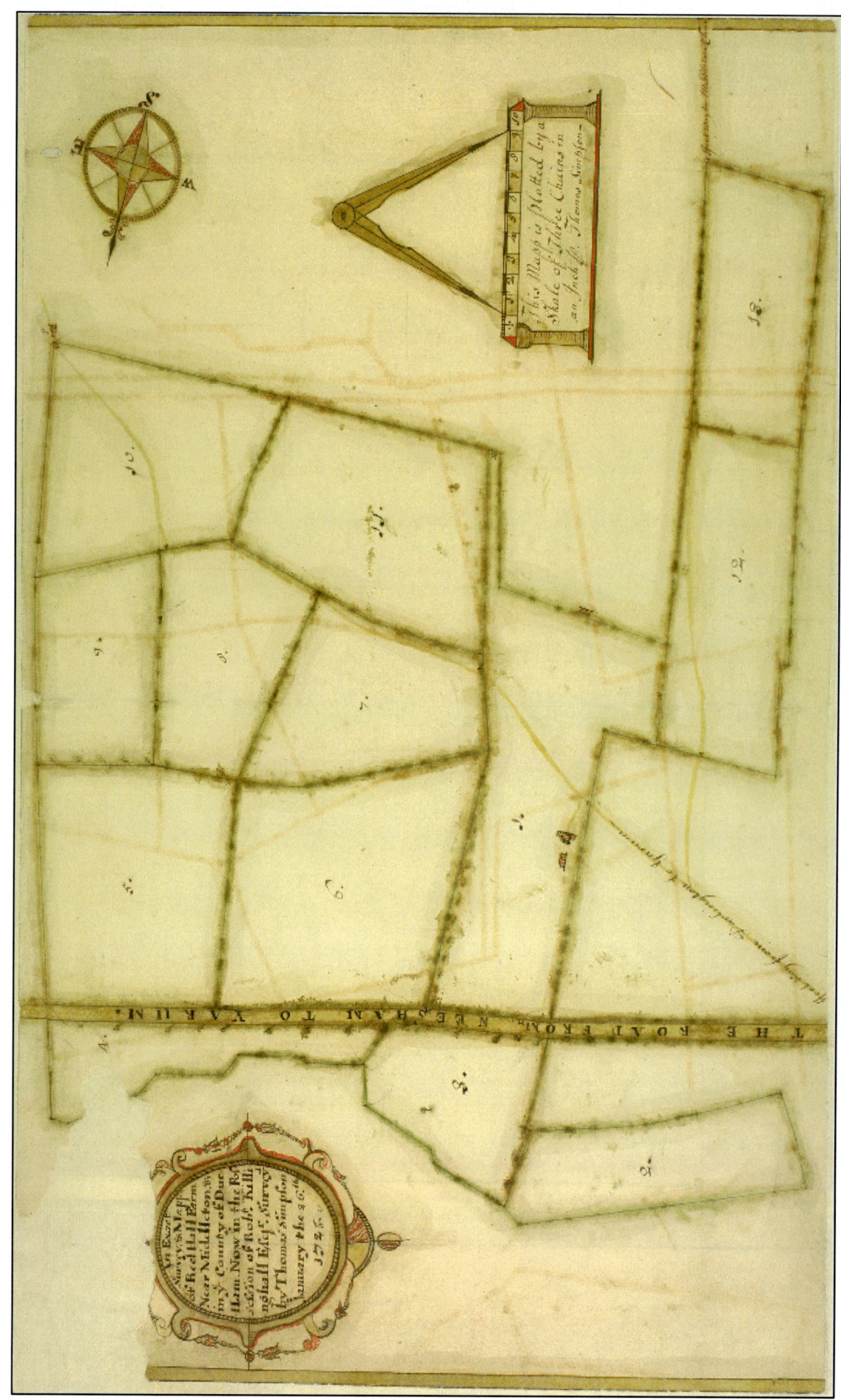

Fig.17 Red Hall Farm, in 1726 – part of Killinghall estate and later becoming known as Oak Tree House Farm

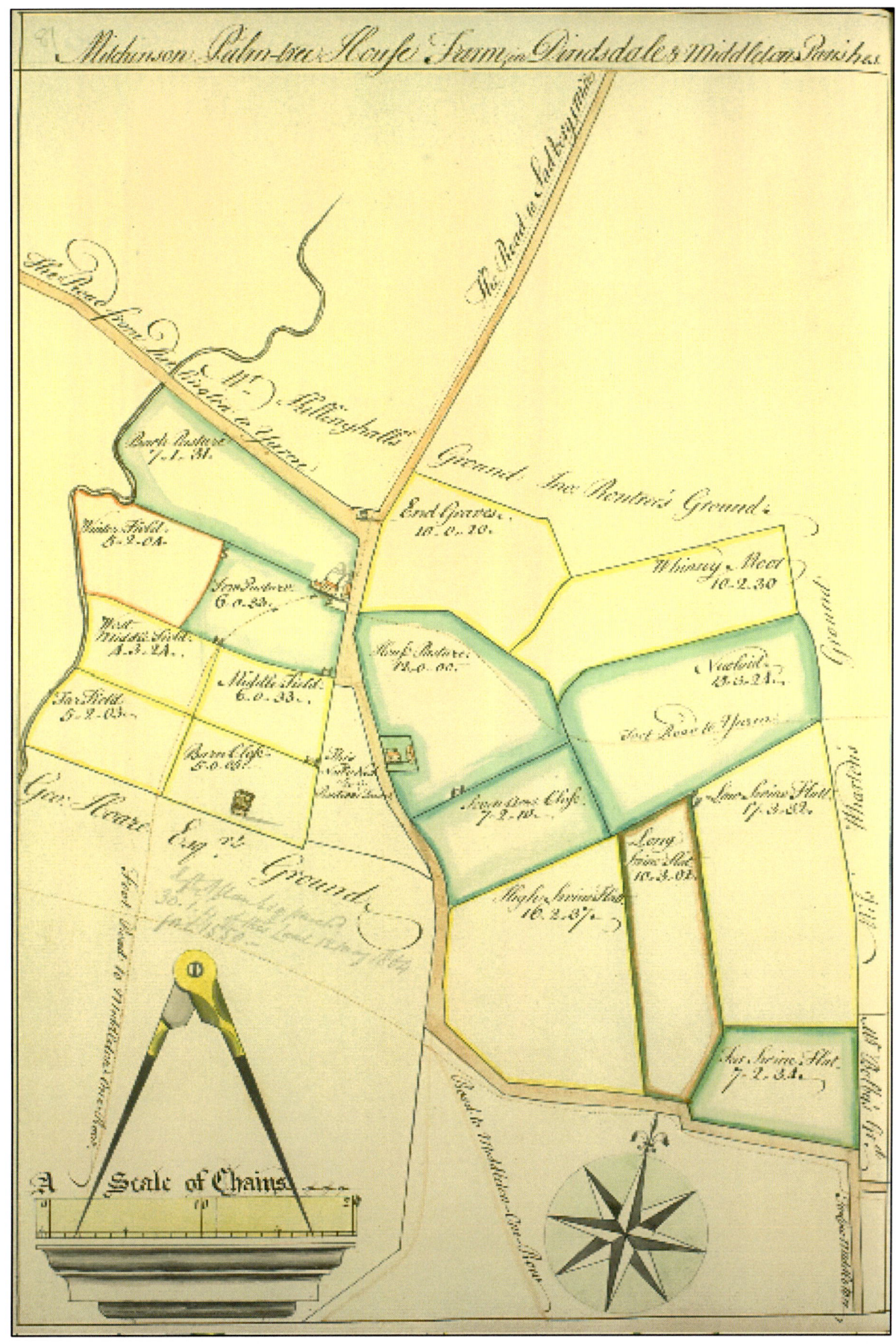

Fig. 18 Palm Tree House Farm in 1757, belonging to Killinghall Estate, extending into Middleton St. George and Dinsdale Parishes

In the tax assessment for 1789 [7], owners and occupiers are shown separately for each property, which is much more revealing. The names of farms are still not given, but in the list below have been added in brackets, where known or reasonably inferred.

Proprietor	Occupier	£.	s.	d.	Farm or Property
Lady Wharton	Wm. Smith	3.	7.	11	(West Hartburn)
Mr. Masterman	Self	3.	11.	$5^{3/4}$	(Foster House)
Mr. Wrightson jun.	Self	2.	2.	$10^{3/4}$	
Mr. Geo. Hoar sen.	Jonathon Dryden	0.	10.	0	
Mr. Geo. Hoar sen.	John Burton	2.	4.	4	
Wm. Hoar	John Burton	0.	3.	7	
Geo. Hoar jun.	John Bell	2.	14.	4	
Geo. Hoar jun.	Robt. Pattison	2.	3.	$7^{1/4}$	
Geo. Hoar jun.	John Bruce	2.	4.	$3^{3/4}$	
Geo. Chambers	Self	1.	0.	$0^{1/4}$	
Thos. Clavering	Th. Downs	4.	12.	11	(Middleton St.George)
Thos. Clavering	Ann Middleton	4.	12.	11	(Church House)
Mr. Pemberton	Watson Balmer	3.	15.	$8^{1/4}$	(Low Middleton)
Mr. Pemberton	Ely Middleton	3.	15.	$8^{1/4}$	
Mr. Pemberton	Self	2.	2.	11	
Mr. Pemberton	Self	1.	10.	$0^{1/4}$	
Mr. Pemberton	Geo. Chambers	1.	5.	$8^{1/2}$	
Christopher Richardson	Self	1.	1.	$5^{1/2}$	
Margaret Richardson	Tho. Richardson	1.	1.	$5^{1/2}$	
Rev. Mr. Whaley	Wm. Oliver		5.	0	(Oak Tree)
Tho. Richardson	Self	1.	5.	$8^{3/4}$	
Mr. Pemberton	Robt. Harrison	3.	11.	$5^{3/4}$	
Mr. Wrightson sen.	Ralph Wright	1.	17.	$10^{1/2}$	
Mr. Pemberton	Wm. Oliver	3.	4.	4	
Mr. Wrightson sen.	Mary Christelow		5.	$8^{3/4}$	
Ninian Gascoigne	Self		1.	$5^{1/4}$	
Mr. Pemberton	Ed. Gascoigne		2.	$1^{1/4}$	
Ann Middleton	Self		1.	$5^{1/4}$	
Total		**57.**	**0.**	**0**	

At this date there were 28 properties assessed. The listing shows that the Killinghalls had been replaced by their Pemberton successors to the manor. They owned four substantial farms, as well as the Hall land in their own hands, and two lesser holdings. Watson Balmer had taken over from the Kays as farmer at Low Middleton.

Sir Thomas Clavering of Axwell Park owned the two highest-rated farms in the parish. One was Middleton St. George Farm, in the tenure of Thomas Downs, and the other was Church House Farm, occupied by Ann Middleton, whose husband Michael had died five years previously. The Hoar family of Durham were substantial landowners in the parish, owning four farms and two houses, including Middleton One Row Farm. The farm owned by Lady Wharton, of Skelton Castle, was West Hartburn, and was farmed by William Smith. A Mr. Masterman owned and occupied Foster House Farm.

The Richardson family, present in 1759, were still there in 1789 with three holdings, owned and occupied by themselves. Scroggs Farm was probably one of those in their possession. The Wrightsons, who also appeared in 1759, were in 1789 holders of two farms, including White House.

A notable feature from these returns is the extent to which farms were owned by interests outside the parish. Stimulated by the pioneering work of agrarian improvers, farming had by the second half of the eighteenth. century become a fashionable pursuit for county gentry, and an investment for those reaping profits from trade, commerce and industry.

In 1798, when a new tax assessment was made [8], property ownership remained much the same, although there were some tenancy changes. The main Pemberton farms carried on in the hands of Watson Balmer, Ely Middleton, Robert Harrison and William Oliver, with a smaller holding farmed by George Chambers. Three of the Hoar farms continued to be farmed by John Bell, Robert Pattison and John Burton, but William Preacher had replaced John Bruce as farmer of the fourth. The Richardson family continued in their three properties. In 1798 both the Wrightson farms were let out. Masterman still owned Foster House, but it was occupied by Michael Middleton.

The land tax assessments do not give acreages, but farm sizes can be roughly assessed from the valuations. The large farms would appear to have each extended to between 100 and 200 and more acres, and there were numerous smaller holdings, down to cottages with only their immediate surrounds.

While it is possible from the land tax assessments to see something of the eighteenth century structure of farms within the parish, there is little specific information on their working. Enclosure in the sixteenth and seventeenth centuries had brought the immediate benefits of being able to decide how to use one's own land and how to order one's own working methods and routine, besides the great convenience of integrated rather than dispersed holdings. However, beyond this, progress in agricultural methods was slow, and wasteful three-course rotations, with one fallow year in three, continued long after enclosure. With no effective drainage, much of the heavy land was difficult to work and of low productivity.

Nevertheless, as the eighteenth century progressed, the teaching of agricultural reformers, such as Jethro Tull and Lord Townshend, began to have effect, albeit very slowly. The use of turnips as a field crop allowed the introduction of a four-course rotation, without the need for a fallow year, and also provided winter feed for cattle. Improvements were often resented by traditionalists, but their undoubted benefits resulted in their spread northwards from their demonstrated success in the south and in East Anglia. An example of this was the new practice of spring sowing of wheat, which was being introduced into this part of the country by the mid-eighteenth century [9].

The incentive to improve productivity received additional impetus after about 1750, by which time the Industrial Revolution was well under way. Between 1700 and 1800 the population of England increased from about six million to about ten million, many now divorced from the countryside, and greater agricultural efficiency was necessary in order to feed the extra mouths, without vastly increasing imports of grain. Under these pressures, the price of wheat rose from an average of around 33 shillings a quarter in 1764 to a corresponding average of some 90 shillings a quarter around 1800 [10]. The new or expanded landowning class was receptive to changes based on scientific advances, and which were commercially advantageous.

As demonstrated earlier, the agricultural efforts of the parish in the early seventeenth century tended very strongly to cattle raising. The balance between cattle and corn was inevitably susceptible to economic pressures, and the need for bread for the growing population had probably resulted in the second half of the eighteenth century in a more even balance between arable and grazing land.

Cattle, however, remained very important, and cattle breeding was one aspect where the north-east took a leading part at the end of the eighteenth century. Charles and Robert Colling of Ketton, on the north side of Darlington and no more than six miles from Middleton, used selective breeding to such effect that their shorthorn bulls of impressively increased weight brought prices many times greater than had previously been achieved [11]. Such demonstrable success so near home was bound to have had related progressive effects at Middleton, as elsewhere.

The farmers, whether owner-occupiers or tenants, had their houses on their properties. Farm workers either lived with the farmhouse family or occupied their own cottages nearby. It is not known how far, if at all, the farmhouses had advanced beyond those postulated from the seventeenth century inventories. They would have still been of simple and relatively crude construction, and, with one or two possible exceptions, did not survive the age of farmhouse re-building which followed in the nineteenth century.

A later commentator referred to the village of Middleton One Row in this period as comprising "a few mud-walled cottages" [12]. Although this may have been a somewhat slanted description, it does indicate the general primitiveness of the housing. At least two of the farms had their farmhouses in the village, and the houses of farm labourers and various craftsmen and tradesmen were also situated there, together with one or more ale-houses.

The outstanding piece of building in the course of the century was the manor house itself, which was substantially replaced by a new "Hall". On 10 October 1719 Robert Killinghall, lord of the manor, married Jane Allan, the eldest daughter of George Allan of Blackwell Grange, Darlington [13]. This coming together of two gentry families was the occasion for the creation of the new mansion, which still stands today (Pl.16), with some Victorian additions. The building date is generally reckoned as 1721, as original rainwater lead work bears that year, together with the entwined initials of Robert and Jane. Their life together in the new house was woefully short, Jane dying in 1727, presumably as a result of childbirth. She was buried just two days after the baptism of their son John, the last of the male line of Killinghalls [14]. Interred in the chancel of St. George's Church, her grave slab is the only Killinghall memorial to be seen in the church.

As may be expected from its building date, the house is of Queen Anne style and of brick and red sandstone construction. It is of three storeys, heightened from the two storeys of its predecessor. Its simple aesthetic design is of pleasing appearance, and would have been very impressive when it appeared around 1721. Although there has been no architectural survey of the building, it would seem likely that part at least of the old structure was retained behind the new facade and was incorporated in a rearrangement and possibly extension of the living range [15]. The substantial status of the new house is illustrated by the fact that in 1798 the house and its contents were insured for £3000 [16].

In the field south of the Hall stands an octagonal dovecote, also of brick construction. This is likely to have been built around the same time as the Hall. The dovecote stands at a corner of a rectangular level area, artificially raised above the low riverside land to the south. This area was probably created by levelling out part of the old medieval village site, along with general landscaping of the Hall grounds.

Turning from homes to people, the parish registers supplement the land tax returns in providing information about individuals, families and the community as a whole [17]. Figure 19 charts the number of baptisms, marriages and burials for Middleton St. George from 1650 to 1800 in ten yearly intervals. (Figures for ten year periods minimise the effects of short term variations.)

The register particulars are by no means a precise basis for statistical deductions, being subject to random factors, human shortcomings and other register irregularities. Nevertheless, some demographic conclusions can be drawn from them. The fact that the number of births or baptisms is broadly proportional to the population level does provide a very rough means of estimating population. Assuming a birth rate of 30 per year for every 1000 of population, and applying an adjustment factor for register irregularities, the population of Middleton St. George parish can be calculated to have been about 220 over most of the eighteenth century. This fairly closely matches the figure of around 200, estimated from the Protestations information in 1642, and would seem to indicate a generally stable population.

However, this has to be qualified by a noticeable feature of the register statistics, namely the relatively low level of baptisms, and presumably births, in the period around the beginning of the century. Projecting backwards, the figures show a decline in the number of baptisms in the second half of the seventeenth century, reaching a low point around 1700, and coming back to its former level before the middle of the eighteenth century. If this is taken at face value, it would indicate a

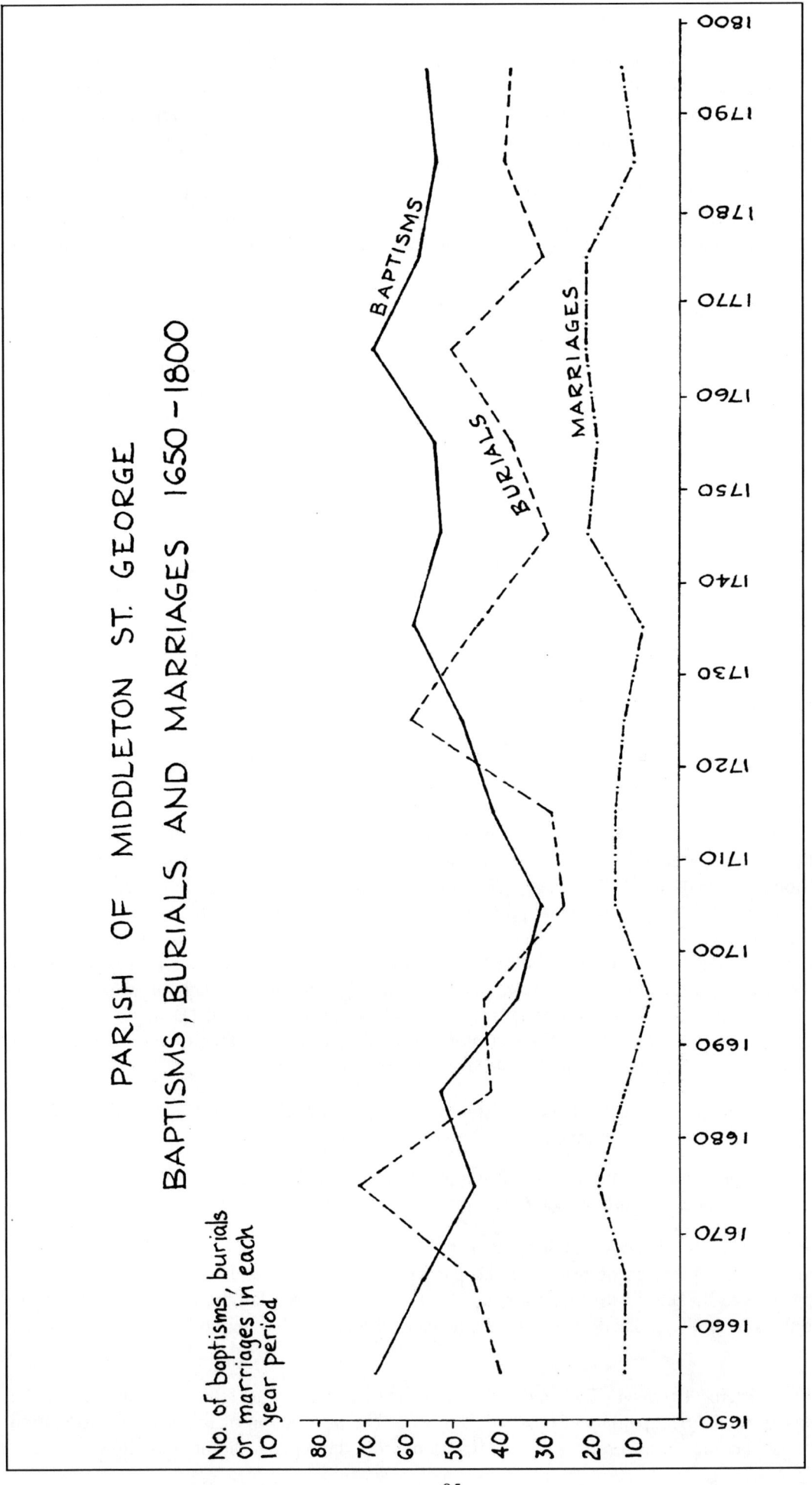

Fig.19 Baptisms, burials and marriages in the parish of Middleton St. George 1650-1800

population "trough" with a lowest level of about 160 around the turn of the century. Assuming this to be a true reflection of the population level, it has an interesting correlation with national trends, for which the pattern is a slow increase of population throughout the seventeenth and eighteenth centuries with a flattening-off between about 1650 and 1750 [18]. Middleton exhibits a lagging image of this, with a generally steady population throughout the period, but an actual decline between about 1650 and 1750. One reason offered for this trend interruption is declining fertility, as a result of later marriage. However, no similar trend is discernible from the registers of adjoining parishes, and purely random factors may have played a part, including the possibility of careless keeping of the registers in that period.

Another interesting feature is the relationship between baptisms and burials. Up to about 1730, births and deaths seem to have generally matched each other, in some decades the number of baptisms being greater than the number of burials, and in others burials exceeding baptisms. Thereafter, the pattern of births is very similar to the pattern of deaths, but the number of births consistently outnumbers the number of deaths. This would appear to reflect either a modest rise in health standards, or at least the end of the outbreaks of plague which had debilitated the population in the previous centuries. The excess of births suggests a population increase, but this may have been offset by a drift to employment elsewhere.

Out of a population of some 220, about half could be accounted for by those listed as occupiers of properties in the land tax assessments and their families. The remainder were mostly farm workers and domestic servants, who "lived-in" at the farms on which they worked, or occupied untaxed cottages.

Most of the families named in the tax valuations can also be identified in the parish registers. Some are long-term residents, while others appear for only a short time. The Wilkinson and Richardson families were in the former category, and have a continuous series of entries from the beginning of the registers. In contrast, the Wetherill family were prolific in the early eighteenth century, but the name had disappeared from the registers by the end of the century.

Over a twenty year period from 1690 to 1710 baptisms and burials were recorded under 51 family names. A hundred years later, over a similar time span from 1790 to 1810, similar events were recorded under 65 family names. It is remarkable that only 11 of these family names occur in both periods. These were Christelow, Jackson, Middleton, Pemberton, Pincher (Pinchard), Richardson, Robinson, Thompson, Wilkinson, Wilson and Wright. The ultimate fate of families to die out, or to continue in the female line only, is no doubt partly responsible for this, but other factors were marriage alliances and a surprising degree of mobility of the population. Movement over the short range must always have been a feature - to and from adjoining parishes, and also to the nearby towns of Darlington, Yarm and Stockton. This is apparent from register entries such as when George Woodhouse was baptised in 1798, with parents Thomas Woodhouse, native of Darlington, and Jane Chambers, of Middleton St. George. What is more surprising is the number of more widespread origins within County Durham and north Yorkshire, exemplified by other entries.

> 17 Mar. 1799 (Bap.) Thomas Chambers, 2nd.son of Thomas Chambers, farmer, native of Gilling, Yorks, by his wife, Isobel Hull, native of Middleton St. George.

> 10 April 1803 (Bap.) George Cummings, 4th.son of Thomas Cummings, native of Church Merrington, by his wife Margaret Naseby, native of Witton Gilbert, both in County Durham.

This situation is strikingly illustrated by looking at the entries for the first ten years after the baptism register started to state parishes of origin of the parents. In this period, between 1798 and 1807, children were born to 25 sets of married parents. Of these, only three fathers had been born in the parish, and only four mothers. There was not a single case of a family having both parents born in the parish.

The baptisms registered between 1755 and 1776 state in most cases the father's occupation. The burials register gives the occupations of most adult males. The abstraction of this sort of information cannot be precise, because of uncertainty of identifications from the register, but it does allow a general view of the make-up of this entirely agricultural parish. It should be emphasised that not all those listed were necessarily active at the same time.

Out of a total of 91 men appearing in the baptism and burial registers over the 21 year period, 21 claimed to be farmers or yeomen. 34 others were described as labourers, all presumably working on the land. There was clearly sometimes a thin distinction between farmer and labourer, with some people wearing both labels at different times. In support of the farming operations and the local population were 23 craftsmen and tradesmen. There were three blacksmiths, one "wright". two carpenters and a sadler. Four people were named as "innholders", one being classed also as a labourer, and another as a brewer. There were three shoemakers and two tailors. One of the two butchers was said to be from Yarm. John and Thomas Christelow were hand-loom weavers, and Edward Wright was a basket maker. John and William Smith, were the millers. The 1783 entry for the burial of William Allan describes him as a fisherman of Middleton One Row. Five men, like John Killinghall and William Pemberton, were described as gentry, and the occupations of seven others were not distinguishable from the register entries.

In this century the first mention is made of education in the parish, which at the same time provides an example of concern for the needy. The notice of this comes from an entry in the parish register of Dinsdale.

> August 1st 1727 Payd to the school Master of Middleton for Mary Pinchard's two daughters and Margaret Allen's boy, 00.07.06
>
> Payd at the same for a spelling book, 00.01.00

The baptism of James, the illegitimate son of Margaret Allen is recorded in the Middleton St. George register on 9 November 1721.

In 1768 a new school was built by public subscription, for the purpose of instructing children to read and write. Thomas Davison, the schoolmaster, had a son baptised in 1773. When another son was baptised in 1777, his address was given as School House, almost certainly at Middleton One Row. In 1782 a trust deed was set up to regularise the administration of the school charity. The rector and churchwardens of Middleton St. George and the rector of Dinsdale were trustees. They had the responsibility for appointing or dismissing the master. The deed confirmed the provision of a house for the master, who was also to have the use of the school garth [19].

Relief of the poor was the responsibility of the parish, and the church was also the guardian of public morals. A church court case in 1732 laid down how a woman from Middleton St. George had to do penance, presumably having been found guilty of immoral behaviour. She was to "present herself in the Parish Church on Sunday, April 21, 1732, where, being in her penetential habit, viz., bare-headed, barefoot and bare legged, having a white sheet on and a Rodd in her hand, and standing upon some Forme or other high place so as the whole Congregation may see her, immediately after the Nicene Creed, shall, with a distinct and audible voice, say after the minister her penance" [20].

Around the middle of the eighteenth century, the registers also give a little detail on location within the parish. As might be expected, a number of families are described as being of Middleton One Row, including the Christelow weavers and the shoemaker Thomas Hull. The number of entries of people from Oak Tree show this to have been a significant hamlet by the second half of the eighteenth century. Thomas Ianson was blacksmith there in 1761.

The identification of farmers with their properties is shown in some of the entries. George Middleton was at Low Middleton in the 1770s. At The Mill House (now East Middleton Farm) in 1761 was Christopher Jackson, a tailor, but by 1775 the occupant was Ninian Gascoyne, a butcher. The two Smith millers were not given a location in the register. The Wilkinson family occupied Foster House between 1761 and 1775, but appear to have moved to Palm Tree House Farm at Fighting Cocks by 1778, by which time the Middletons had replaced them at Foster House.

William Smith was the farmer at West Hartburn Farm "commonly called Gingerbread House". Michael Middleton, farmer at Church House, was buried in 1784. By 1779 the farmer at White House in the north of the parish was William Robinson.

Showing that the parish boundary was not sacrosanct, Thomas Huddart of Low Moor Bottom, just across the river from Low Middleton, was buried in 1794 at Middleton St. George, instead of at his home parish of Sockburn. Earlier, in 1726, William Robinson was baptised at Middleton St. George, where he and his brother John were buried just two years later, despite the fact that Spring House, their father's farm, was in the parish of Haughton-le-Skerne (now Sadberge). With St. George's Church being close to the eastern parish boundary, it is not surprising that some on the west side of the parish of Egglescliffe had their children baptised at Middleton St. George rather than at their much more remote home church.

From 1761 the designation of bastard children begins to be included in the register entries. In the 51 years between then and 1812, 26 baptisms of illegitimate children are recorded, out of a total of 298 baptisms. The 9% rate of illegitimacy calculated from this is probably an under-assessment. In some periods at least there were undoubtedly births outside wedlock which did not find their way into the baptismal register. This must certainly have been the case prior to 1761, when illegitimacy is not mentioned and very few baptisms are noted against the mother's name only. This is hardly likely to be a reflection of the true situation.

The holding of the benefices of Middleton St. George and Dinsdale in plurality, already noted in the seventeenth century, continued in the eighteenth, as attested in the Middleton burial register:

14 Feb. (1747) William Noble, Rector of Midleton and Dinsdale, departed this life February ye 11th.day at 8 at night, and was buryed February ye 14th. in Dinsdale Parrish Church, in the Quire, 1746/7 being Rector of Midleton 24 years 19 weaks and one day.

Another register entry, this time in the baptisms, shows that a curate was employed to perform many of the church and parish duties:

1786 Nov. 9 John, s. of the Revd. James Bradfute, Curate of this P., by Marion his wife.

The lay assistant in the church, the parish clerk, also appears in the registers. John Pinchard, who died in 1795, was said to have been clerk of the parish for 22 years. He had followed his father in the post, who had been clerk for 45 years.

The birth of John Killinghall, the last of the name to occupy the position of lord of the manor, is marked by the register entry of his baptism on 27 February 1727. He was buried at Middleton on 23 February 1762. His cousin, William Pemberton, who succeeded him, was not buried at Middleton when he died in 1778, but William's widow Winifred was interred there eight years later.

The eighteenth century has been portrayed here as a time of stability and consolidation of a settled rural structure. On the broader front, the American colonies were lost and the French Revolution had caused widespread trepidation throughout Europe, but these happenings had little direct impact on the local scene. However, one local event before the end of the century reflected changes in lifestyle and was the first of the factors responsible for transforming the face of the parish in the nineteenth century.

The Dinsdale Estate, on the Tees and adjoining the western boundary of the parish of Middleton St. George, had been acquired by the Lambton family, whose fortunes had prospered on coal, and who were later to become Earls of Durham. In 1789 William Henry Lambton, looking at the possibility of extending the Durham coalfield, was test boring on the north bank of the river, about half a mile west of the village of Middleton One Row. No coal was found, but a sulphurous spring was released. This was effectively the beginning of the Dinsdale Spa [21].

The spring and the spa which developed from it were in the parish of Dinsdale. However, the proximity to Middleton One Row and the powerful influence of the spa on the growth of the village and the parish of Middleton St. George make no excuse necessary for including the story of the spa in this work.

Dr. John Peacock of Darlington was an enthusiastic advocate of the spring, and gave an account of its discovery. "The men had bored to a depth of 72 feet, chiefly through what they called red rock and whinstone, when the spring burst forth, accompanied with a tremendous smoke and sulphurous stench, so that they were obliged to relinquish their operations in that place during several weeks" [22]. This is graphic testimony to the intensity of the "bad eggs" smell of sulphuretted hydrogen released in apparently large quantity. Only when the pressure had reduced sufficiently to make the smell bearable was work able to recommence.

The reputation of sulphur springs was already known in the area, and a spring at Croft had been used medicinally for some time [23]. To take advantage of the new spring, a hole was dug to collect the water and allow bathing. One man was, in the earliest days, said to have been cured of rheumatism after bathing in the water and also drinking it.

Word of the curative powers of the water rapidly spread, and sufferers came in the hope of alleviating their pains and problems. The lack of facilities was however a disincentive, and in 1797 a proper cold bath was constructed to make things easier for bathers. This was soon followed by a warm bath and a suite of dressing rooms. The appeal of the spring was by this time no longer confined to the local people, and by the end of the century visitors were arriving from a much wider area, with an increasing impact on the village and parish.

Pl.3 The residential agglomeration of Middleton St. George as seen from the air. Middleton One Row is prominent in the centre foreground with its long established single row of houses. More recent developments sprawl onwards on three sides. Extending northwards is Middleton Lane, leading to the nineteenth century industrial village. To the right of the reservoir in the centre distance is the line of houses built for the ironworks which stood behind them. Beyond the reservoir is Fighting Cocks, the location of other industrial enterprises.

Pl. 4　The twelfth century motte near Middleton One Row, which overlooked the medieval river crossing. A wooden tower would originally have surmounted the mound and from this the adjacent Victorian house took the name Tower Hill.

Pl. 5　Low Middleton from the Air. The Hall and farm are together in the centre of the picture with the river Tees in the foreground. The superimposed line shows the approximate extent of the medieval village.

Pl. 6 The site of the medieval village of West Hartburn from the air. The Hart Burn, now known as Goosepool Beck, meanders along the bottom of the picture. On the left hand side of the road, in the long narrow field extending from the stream to Foster House Farm, can be seen the earthwork remains of the southern half of the village. The village street runs up the centre of the field, before turning left in the direction of Low Middleton, just short of the present farmhouse. The corresponding area to the right of the road, leading up to West Hartburn Farm, is the site of the northern half of the village, but ploughing has obliterated all traces of it.

Pl. 7 House D at West Hartburn, marked X on the aerial view above. In the foreground is the living area with a central hearth. The far end of the house beyond a cross wall is the animal area.

Pl. 8 Font, possibly of late twelfth century date

Pl. 9 Carved head beneath corbel of thirteenth century

Pl. 10 The Killinghall arms are in the centre flanked by the Cocks emblem on the left and the Pemberton arms on the right, but with their three griffins' heads replaced by the heads of three cockerels

Pl. 11 St. George's Church before the demolition of the tower in 1961

Pl. 12 St. George's Church today, with its thirteenth century nave and chancel rebuilt in the early nineteenth century.

Pl. 13 Interior of St. George's showing the thirteenth century chancel arch and mark on east wall of nave indicating the width before enlargement in the nineteenth century.

Pl. 14 Castle Hill, the oldest house at Middleton One Row. Probably the seventeenth century manor house of the Ayscoughs, and later a farm house.

Pl. 15 White House Farm at the northern edge of the parish, established when the lands of West Hartburn were enclosed in the sixteenth century. Lawrence Langley was living there in 1610 when he made his will. The house is probably a re-building of the early nineteenth century.

Pl. 16 Low Middleton Hall. The old manor house of the Killinghalls in its c. 1721 re-built form.

Pl. 17 Middleton Hall. The original house built by the Rev. William Addison Fountaine around 1820.

Pl. 18 St. Laurence's Church at Middleton One Row, built in 1871 to replace the old parish church in the fields at Low Middleton, over a mile away. The vestry was added in 1926.

Pl. 19 The Weslyan Chapel, built in 1869 between Killinghall and Fighting Cocks

Pl. 20 The former bath house of the spa, in its period of use as the club house of the Dinsdale Spa Golf Club.

Pl. 21 The Dinsdale Spa Hotel, built in 1829, and now adapted for residential use.

Pl. 22 Hodgkin's 1926 painting of the Middleton Ironworks, viewed from the north west, showing graphically the smoke which was a cause for pollution complaint. The fact that only three furnaces are shown suggests that the portrayal may be of the works in its early years, around 1870.

Pl. 23 The blowing engine house just before its demolition in 2004. This was the last remaining ironworks building, having been spared when the furnaces were demolished, which latterly provided the premises for C. N. Hadley's machine shop.

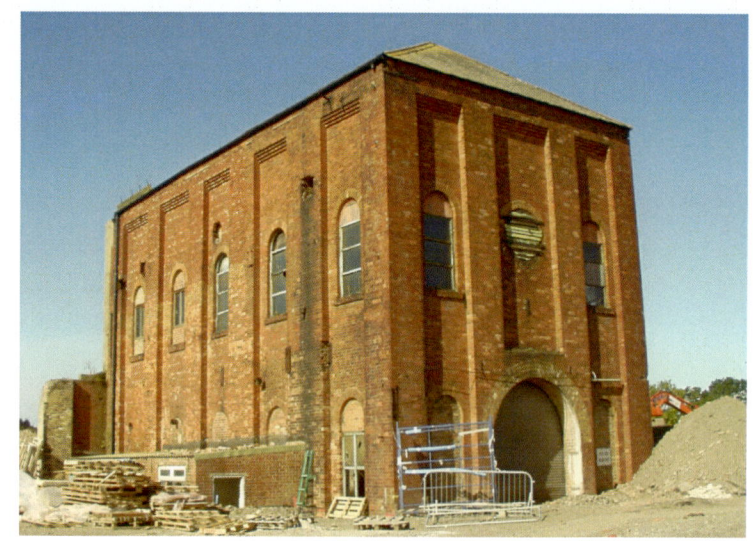

Pl. 24 The ironworks site developed for new housing

Pl. 25 Ironworkers and managers, possibly soon after the re- opening of the works in 1900.

Pl. 26 The works from a similar viewpoint to that for the Hodgkin painting, at the time of demolition in 1947. The furnace which stood to the left of the lift tower had already gone. The engine house and chimney are to the right of the furnaces and the office building is on the left.

Pl. 27 The same view today across the recreation ground

Pl. 28 Two saddle tank shunting engines making their final appearance in front of the rapidly disappearing works they had served.

Pl. 29 Salmon fishing at Low Middleton ferry c. 1880. A poor reproduction, but very evocative of past times.

Pl. 30 Fighting Cocks Station on June 30th 1887, the last day before passenger trains began to run on the re-alignment of the line which took it through the new Dinsdale Station. The bearded man in the foreground is the station master. In the background is the squire's mill, without sails, as by this time it was engine driven

Pl. 31 The new Dinsdale Station on July 1st 1887, the day of the opening of the re-routed line from Darlington.

Pl. 32 Robert Pallister, the wheelwright, with his wife Catherine, outside their house at Fighting Cocks. In the foreground are the blacksmith's and wheelwright's shops, with the blacksmith, Thomas Knott, standing in front of the carts. This photograph was taken around 1880.

Pl. 33 The smithy at Fighting Cocks prior to demolition.

Pl. 34   An early cricket team at the field opposite to Almora Hall.

Pl. 35   Almora Hall, the house of Jonathan Westgarth Wooler, around 1880.

Pl. 36 The Square around 1914, with the drinking trough and lamp in the middle of the roadway provided by the Dinsdale Smelting Company.

Pl. 37 The Lyric Cinema in Station Road after closure, with bill board still displaying one of the final films shown.

Pl. 38 A Lancaster bomber with crew and ground staff at Goosepool c. 1944

Pl. 39 The end of an era on the line which saw its beginning. Steam locomotives awaiting scrapping in sidings by the ironworks site, adjacent to the line on which Stephensons's "Locomotion" ran in 1825 to open the Stockton and Darlington Railway.

CHAPTER SIX - THE FIRST HALF OF THE NINETEENTH CENTURY

SPA AND RAILWAY BRING CHANGES

The nineteenth century was to see great changes for Middleton St. George, including a re-shaping within the parish and the creation of a new village. By 1800 the first of the influences for change, the spa, was already beginning to have effects arising from its growing popularity, but otherwise the parish remained devoted to agriculture, as it had always been. The Napoleonic Wars gave farming a short-term boost, as sea-blockade conditions made home grain production of enhanced importance. A good deal of land which had been pasture was temporarily turned over to the plough, only to revert to grass when peacetime conditions returned.

As already noted, the Pemberton lordship of the manor just survived into the nineteenth century, having lasted only two generations. William Pemberton, who had inherited the title of lord of the manor from his Killinghall cousin, died in 1778. His son and heir, another William, died in 1801, leaving the estate to his mother's two sisters, Elizabeth and Sally Cocks of Plymouth Dock. They changed their name to Pemberton, and came to live on the estate, dying there in 1809 and 1811 respectively. Their successor was their brother Elisha Cocks [1].

The 1806 land tax assessment [2] lists "Mr. Pemberton" as proprietor of the estate farms. Presumably this represents the Cocks inheritors, who held in their own hands a larger farm than previously, rated at £4.17s.9d. against £1.7s.4d. in 1798. The land held by the tenant Balmer had also increased in value from £3.17s.9d. to £7.5s.11d. He probably now had two farms, the one held by him in 1798, together with that previously held by Robert Harrison, worth £3.15s.10d. in 1798. Ely Middleton and William Oliver both retained their farms. It appears that the farm previously worked by George Chambers had been taken over by William Woodhouse.

Sir Thomas Clavering still had his two farms, with tenants Downs and Middleton, as before. The Whartons, with their Smith tenants, remained at West Hartburn, but at Foster House F. Glanville had become the proprietor, keeping the Middleton tenant. The Hoar family estate was greatly diminished. Their small property tenanted by John Dryden remained, but three of their other four farms had been sold, two of them probably to Carr Ibbotson. The Richardsons owned two properties, and occupied one of them. The Wrightsons' two farms were still leased out.

In later land tax assessments between 1814 and 1826 [3], Elisha Cocks, Esq. is listed as the proprietor of the former Killinghall / Pemberton estate. Sir Thomas Clavering also continued as a major landowner. Carr Ibbotson seems to have increased his number of farms from two to three. The Whartons, Hoars, Wrightsons and Richardsons continued as owners of farms.

The Gascoyne family had owned and occupied a small property since at least 1759. Between 1821 and 1826 the valuation jumped from 1s.5d. to 7s.1d. This was the Devonport Inn, or its predecessor, and the 1826 jump in value was probably due to substantial building improvements consequent upon the success of the spa. A Mrs. Garth had acquired a farm by 1814, and still had it in 1826, with Thomas Chambers continuing as tenant. She lived at Cockerton Hall, in the village of Cockerton then just outside Darlington, on a site now occupied by shopping developments. She was the widow of John Garth, organist to the Bishop of Durham and a celebrated musician.

The Reverend William Addison Fountaine, who had replaced Mr. Whaley as rector in 1798, appears in the 1806 land tax assessment as owner of two small properties, one tenanted by the Oliver family and the other let to Thomas Chambers. In almost forty years as rector, he experienced and contributed to the rapidly changing face of the parish. He is memorable as carrying on the eighteenth century tradition of a sporting parson, while at the same time entering with enthusiasm and financial acumen into the nineteenth century industrial age.

William Addison, as he was originally, was a local man, from a family with clerical traditions. His great uncle had been master of the Free Grammar School at Darlington [4], before becoming rector of Dinsdale. His own father had followed in the living, and he himself was born there in 1767. He married Mary Fountaine at Leeds in 1800 [5], by which time he had been rector of Middleton St. George for two years. It seems that the marriage came to a premature end with Mary's early demise. The daughter of a Leeds alderman, she probably brought money to the marriage, and he combined her family name with his own, becoming known as William Addison Fountaine, or sometimes William Fountaine Addison.

Because of his wife's illness, which confined her to their house in Bath, his personal involvement in the parish for a number of years was at best intermittent. It is significant that the rector's name does not appear against any baptisms before the autumn of 1813. Up to 1810 most of the register pages of baptisms were attested by his father "Will. Addison Snr. Rector of Dinsdale, in the absence of William Addison Fountaine Rector of this Parish". The rector did publish banns of marriage in1798 and 1799 and married one couple, but between 1800 and 1813 he only officiated at one marriage (in 1805). The others were celebrated by the curate or by a visiting minister. By 1814 the situation had changed, and after that date the duties at baptisms and marriages were shared by the rector and curate. Clearly by that time the rector had become more firmly established in residence in the parish.

By 1814, when this closer involvement is indicated, he had come into possession of Forster Field Farm or Foster House, valued for land tax at £3.8.0, which was worked and presumably occupied by his tenant Michael Middleton. The situation changed again when he re-married, to Lucy Rattray of Coventry [6], and built himself "a handsome mansion house upon his own estate within the parish" [7]. Where he lived previously is unknown, Surtees around this time saying that the old parsonage house had long been ruinous. The new "mansion" was built in the southern half of his Forster Field Farm, to reflect his status and to provide much better accommodation than the existing farmhouse in the northern part. This is the building (Pl.17) which eventually became known as Middleton Hall (as distinct from Low Middleton Hall, the successor of the old manor house). By 1821 the rector was living there with his wife and family. Their first child, named William after his father, had been born in 1817, and eventually followed his father into the church. A daughter, named Lucy after her mother, was born in 1819, and then a second son David, who died soon after his birth in 1820. Two more daughters Rosamund and Dorothy followed in 1822 and 1824, and finally another son Joseph in 1829 [8].

On establishing his household there, he had clearly taken the management of the farm into his own hands. He employed three farm labourers, and also a gardener and a milkmaid. The farm was mixed in character, with arable land and animals for milk, meat and draught working. Pigs and calves went to the local butcher, and also provided for household consumption. His diary[9] records details of day-to-day farming activities.

24 Feb. 1821	Old farm horse taken ill.
10 Mar.	A stormy day. Pattison the farrier came to see the black mare.
19 Sept.	At Yarm Fair. 3 young horses taken for sale but only disposed of black mare 37 years old for £26. A fine day.
22 Sept.	40 stooks of corn sent to Oliver's thrashing mill.
24 Nov.	The white cow calved. Bull calf.
1 Mar. 1823	The red cow and the Dalia Lucy both taken to Curry's bull.
29 Mar.	Beans sown about Tues. and Weds.

Horses were central to the running of the farm. Apart from ploughing and other arable operations, horses were essential for haulage of coal and timber, and for general carting. Pattison the farrier was a frequent visitor to the farm.

The rector's daily routine and personal activities around the parish were largely carried out on horseback. He sometimes hunted, and noted in his diary the perils of the chase and the river.

19 Jan. 1821	Out with the Hurworth Hounds, had a good run. Mr. Wilkinson of Ditton Castle nearly drown'd in swimming Mr. Maud's horse over the Tees at Newsham.
26 Dec. 1823	Joseph Addison was at home on my return and I first knew from John Wilkinson of poor Marmaduke Theckston being drown'd at Worsall in crossing the river after the hounds. (Joseph Addison was almost certainly William's half-brother, "the eminent barrister at law") [10].

He was proud of his own greyhounds, and hunted hares with them. His diary records the shooting of 37 brace of pheasants and partridge in 1822. He also used nets for catching birds.

His household reflects his comparative affluence. He had his own "man", and there was a domestic servant to assist his wife in the house, besides a nurse and under-nurse to look after the children. On 31 Oct.1822, he had cause to write "Mrs. Fountaine much disturb'd by Betty Robinson the under-maid's ungrateful behaviour".

The entry for that day also includes one of numerous references to family ailments. "I had taken Dr. Peacock's medicine and was much purg'd by it". On 4 Dec. Dr. Peacock called to see him again. This was the same Dr. Peacock who was prominent in promoting the spa. Another entry, on 5 May 1821, reads "The children took each a dose of calomel".

Social calls and correspondence find frequent reference in the diary. They had a carriage for family transport.

11 Feb. 1822	Drove with Mrs. F. to Darlington where dined. Got £30 at bank, paid Juliet. Mr. White of Brenting Moor sent off to Durham Jail for shooting his servant man. A letter from Mrs. Watkins Daventry. Sent to post and a letter from Mrs. Wedderburn received
2 Dec. 1822	With Mrs. A.F. and two elder children and din'd at Darlington.

An interesting connection appears in the diary entry for 1 February 1821, when Mrs. Fountaine was recorded as sitting for a portrait by Mr. Bewick. This was William Bewick, possibly of the same family as the famous wood engraver, Thomas Bewick. Darlington born, he had considerable talent, and a widely acknowledged reputation in the art world. However, financial difficulties around this time caused him to resort to the more mundane painting of portraits for local gentry and their ladies [11].

The duties of a parish incumbent were lightened by the fact that there was a curate to carry out much of the routine work. In the early years of the incumbency, the rector's apparent absence would have put even more responsibility on the curate. The Rev. Charles Cowper was the curate during the first decade of the century, and was succeeded by the Rev. William Clementson around 1810. Nevertheless, the rector does not appear to have been oblivious to his pastoral responsibilities, as witness entries from his diary.

14 Feb. 1821	Sent bacon and flour to poor people.
8 April 1822	Sent for, and attended a poor sick man of the name of Jonathan Fowler.
30 May 1822	Walk'd with Mrs. F. to Middleton, with papers relative to the distressed Irish. (Ireland, suffering from agricultural depression following the end of the Napoleonic Wars, was further afflicted by famine in this year.)
21 April 1823	Called on return home at Anderson and went to Oliver's to baptise his eleventh child call'd Ralph.

> 28 May 1823 At the church to marry James Teesdale and Mary Peverall and from there wt. Mrs. F. and all child'n and sister Ann to Middleton to see the race for the Wedding Favours.

The church of St. George at Low Middleton had been re-built some years previously in his incumbency to cater for the increasing number of visitors, but remained remote and inconvenient for most people. This is reflected in a diary entry for a bad Sunday. "25 May 1823 Very wet. Few people at the church and in consequence the sacrament was deferr'd. Mr. Clementson read prayers. No sermon. He got wet and exchanged part of his dress".

The rector was in the fortunate position of owning land through which passed the planned route of the Stockton and Darlington Railway. He profited from this by selling the appropriate land to the railway company, and also became a shareholder of the company.[12] The planning, setting-out and construction of the line brought him into contact with prominent railway personalities, including Edward Pease, the "Father of Railways", and George Stephenson, as noted later in this chapter. When he executed his will on 1 Feb.1821, this was done at the house of Francis Mewburn, the solicitor for the S. & D.R., who later became what was to be the last Chief Bailiff of Darlington.

The financial benefits from the rector's railway interests clearly greatly increased his affluence, and allowed him to extend his estate. By the time of his death in 1837, he owned five farms, including the two Goosepool farms in Long Newton parish. As detailed later, the total area of his estate exceeded that of the squire.

William Addison Fountaine continued as rector up to the time of his death in 1837, although after August 1836 he did not officiate at any birth, marriage or funeral services. He appears to have spent his last days at his house in Bath. A memorial plaque in the chancel of St. George's church states that he died at Clifton (Bristol). He is buried in the crypt of the church of St. Saviour at Walcot, Bath [13], where his wife joined him fourteen years later [14].

Reference has been made to the rebuilding of the church in this period. The expanding village of Middleton One Row, with its spa visitors, put an excessive demand on the small church of St. George standing in the fields at Low Middleton, which could not accommodate all the potential worshippers. Its greatly inconvenient situation had to be put up with for another half century or more, but a decision was made to increase the capacity of the existing building. We do not know the condition of the old building, but it may well have been in need of substantial repair, and the motivation for rebuilding may have been more than simply increasing the size.

The Victoria County History says that the reconstruction of the building was carried out towards the end of the eighteenth century [15], but it is almost certain that the dating for this was the early part of the nineteenth century, when the growth of the spa was gathering pace. The village history produced by the Women's Institute puts the rebuilding date as 1822, possibly on the strength of a directory description of the village which gives this date, but if this were the case it is very surprising that the surviving abstract from the rector's diary in that period makes no mention of it. The parish register is likewise silent on the matter. The answer undoubtedly lies in notes compiled by a later rector, who recorded that the enlargement was effected in 1805 (the year of the Battle of Trafalgar) during the incumbency of the Rev. Addison Fountaine [16].

The enhanced capacity was achieved by demolishing the north wall of the nave and building a new one some seven feet (about two metres) further out. The chancel was rebuilt at the same time, but fortunately the thirteenth century chancel arch was retained. It is not known to what extent the opportunity may have been taken to enlarge the chancel, or whether it was simply a rebuilding on the old lines.

The chancel is misaligned by one and a half degrees from the nave. It is sometimes said that where this occurs, as it does elsewhere, it is an intentional feature, simulating the drooping head of Christ on the cross. However, other opinion puts it down simply to a lack of accuracy in setting out at a time of rebuilding, and this may well have been the case here.

There is a change of material in the new walling, with a good deal of coursed Aycliffe limestone supplementing re-used sandstone, whereas the earlier walling is mostly of irregularly laid local sandstone. A section of rendering has been removed inside the church, with an arrow marking the line of the previous north wall of the nave. A close inspection of the outside of the west wall also reveals the division between the two periods of building. The re-built chancel is entirely of the dressed limestone.

The VCH refers to "the old mullioned windows" being destroyed. They were presumably in a poor state, or else considered too small for adequate lighting. In any event, they were replaced by brick-arched gothic-style openings and wooden window frames. The building was re-roofed, and the vestry was added, probably at the same time. There was apparently a western bellcote, which was replaced by a tower in 1888. (This was taken down as being unsafe in 1961.)

Any distinctive medieval features, apart from the chancel arch, were largely lost in the reconstruction, and the resulting building was without embellishment. It is basically this building which stands and is used for monthly worship to the present day. Its plan is shown in Fig.20. It is still without electric lighting, and bottled gas heaters provide the only warmth.

A substantial part of the chancel floor is unevenly paved with old slabs, but whether these date from or pre-date the re-building is not clear. There is only one marked tomb, that of Jane Killinghall who died in 1727. Other burials in the chancel are unmarked, but the large cover slabs are there to be seen. The remainder of the chancel and the whole of the nave floor is now concreted, masking anything which may have been there. The few wall monuments all post-date the re-building, as do the memorial windows.

In 1836 an act was passed for the commuting of tithes. By this, the long-outdated payments in kind to the church were replaced by fixed money payments. For every parish covered by the act a map was produced, with an accompanying schedule, showing all the land within the parish, and listing the owners and occupiers. Acreages were given and also categories of land usage. These maps are of the greatest importance to local historians. For Middleton St. George, as for many other parishes, the tithe map provides the first comprehensive and detailed picture of the parish [17].

The layout of farms and other landholdings as shown on the Middleton St .George tithe map is reproduced in Fig.21. Details of all the farms, acreages, owners and occupiers are tabulated below.

Farm	Acres-Roods-Perches	Owner	Occupier
Low Middleton	336-2-10	Henry Andrew William Cocks, Esq.	Himself & Thomas Coke,
Oak Tree House	Incl. above		Joseph Colpitts
			John Eeles
Middleton One Row East	103-3-8		Owner
High Scroggs	57-0-31		Owner
Palm Tree House (part)	105-3-39		Henry Walton
Dinsdale Moor House (part)	35-2-17		Matthew Burn
Forster Field	120-1-10	Rev. William Addison	Thomas Thornton
Home Farm	114-0-7	Fountaine	Francis Wright
White House (part)	110-3-21		Robert Henderson
Church House	210-0-24	Sir Thomas John	Anthony Robinson
Middleton St. George Farm	160-0-33	Clavering, Bart	John Pybron
Scroggs	73-2-10	Christopher Richardson	George Weston
Field House	43-0-25	Esq.	William Carter

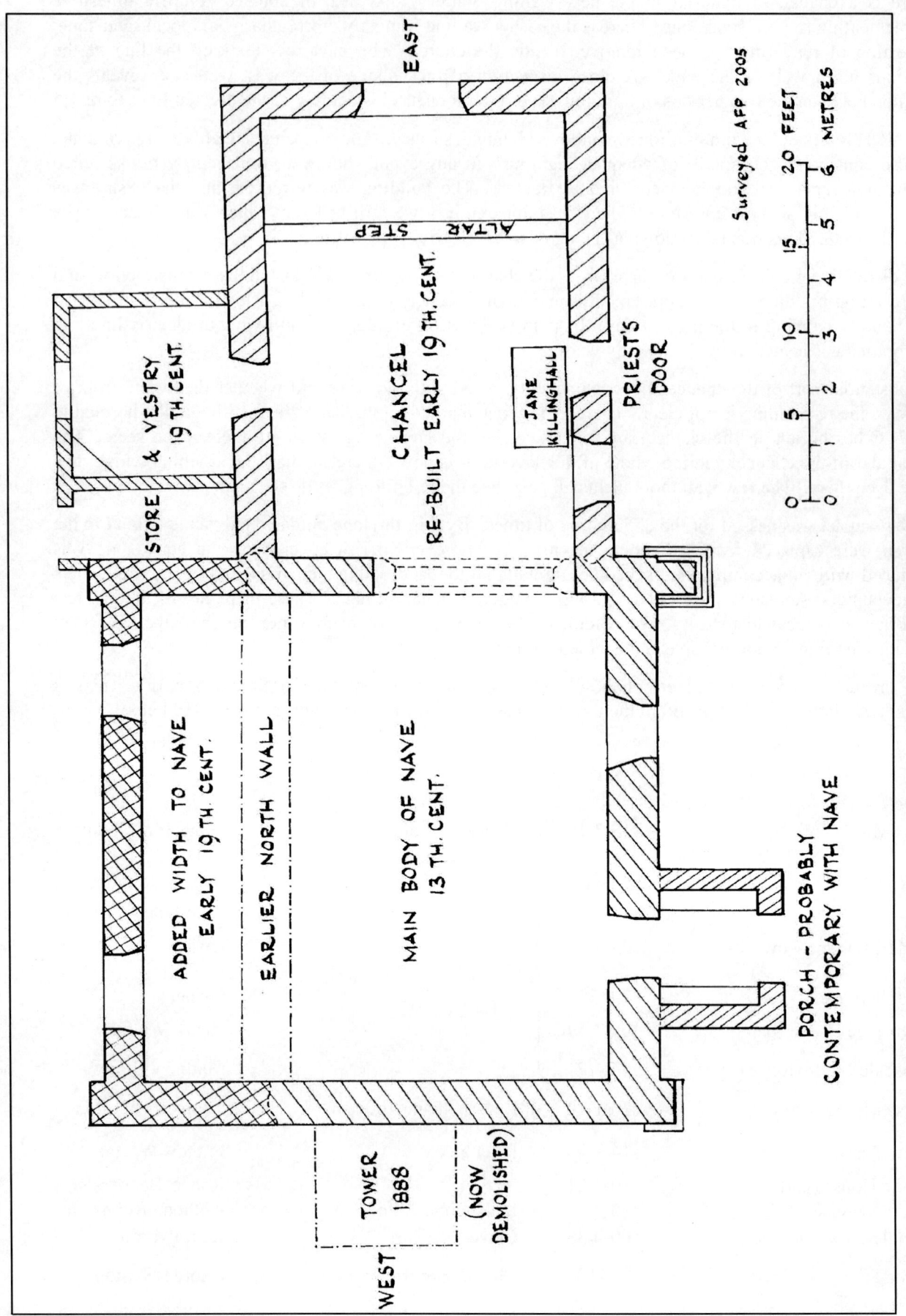

Fig.20 Plan of St.George's Church - the old parish church of Middleton St.George

Middleton One Row Farm	78-0-0	Thomas Wrightson Esq.	William Shield
			William Hunter
			Thomas Adamson
Middleton One Row West	103-3-6	Miss Ann Harland	Thomas Stockdale
Thorn Tree House (part)	38-1-25		Jonathan Dyden
Oak Tree	19-2-32	Mrs. Ann Chambers	Thomas Eeles
Cottage Farm	45-2-22	Trustees of the Cottage Farm	Ann Hanson
West Hartburn	<u>242-0-30</u>	Messrs. Potts & Robson	Matthew Jameson
	2002-0-26		
(In Long Newton Parish)			
West Hartburn (detached)	70-1-15	Rev. William Addison	Robert Elgy
Low Goosepool	138-0-3	Fountaine	Robert Elgy
High Goosepool	<u>144-0-26</u>		George Clarke
	352-2-4		

There were nineteen farms in the parish, with some 2000 acres of land between them. The largest farms had over 200 acres each, while the smallest came down to only 20 acres. In addition two farms of the so-called township were at that time in Long Newton parish, as was a detached part of one of the other farms. The Long Newton properties amounted to another 350 acres approximately.

In terms of land ownership, the whole parish, together with the farms in Long Newton, was in the hands of nine individuals or groupings. These owners did not necessarily farm on their own account, but generally leased their farms to tenants.

Squire Cocks, with his six farms, owned a third of the parish. Low Middleton Farm, extending from the Hall, was listed as being occupied by Cocks himself and Thomas Coke. Coke probably worked the farm for the squire, living in the farmhouse, leaving the squire in the Hall. Middleton One Row East Farm and High Scroggs Farm were being farmed by or for Cocks himself, but Oak Tree House Farm, Palm Tree House Farm and Dinsdale Moor House Farm were all occupied by tenant farmers. Both the latter farms extended westwards into the parish of Dinsdale.

The Reverend William Addison Fountaine, had greatly increased his estate, and had become the second most extensive landowner in the parish. His Forster Field Farm was by this time being farmed by Thomas Thornton. It was however only about half its previous size, and later became known as Foster House Farm. The southern part, in which stood the rector's new house, had been split off to form a new holding called the Home Farm in the tithe papers. White House Farm (extending outside the parish on the north), had been acquired by the rector sometime after 1826, doubtless funded by income from his railway interests. The two Goosepool farms in Long Newton parish had also come into his possession, as had the detached part of West Hartburn. All three were occupied by tenants. When account is taken of the Long Newton properties, the rector's land holding surpassed that of the squire. Apart from Home Farm, the remainder continued as one estate until broken up in 1938.

Sir Thomas Clavering was an absentee landowner, with his two farms, Church House Farm and Middleton St. George Farm, both leased out. Christopher Richardson had tenants in Scroggs Farm and Field House Farm. Miss Ann Harland also owned two tenanted farms, Middleton One Row West Farm and Thorn Tree House Farm, the latter partly in Dinsdale parish. Middleton One Row Farm, owned by Thomas Wrightson, was said to be occupied by three tenants. The small Oak Tree Farm, owned by Mrs. Ann Chambers, was being farmed by Thomas Eeles, who also had a share in the larger Oak Tree House Farm of the squire. Cottage Farm's Trustees had let this modest-sized farm to Ann Hanson. The large West Hartburn Farm, excluding the detached part in Long Newton, was owned by the Potts & Robson partnership, and was occupied and farmed by Matthew Jameson.

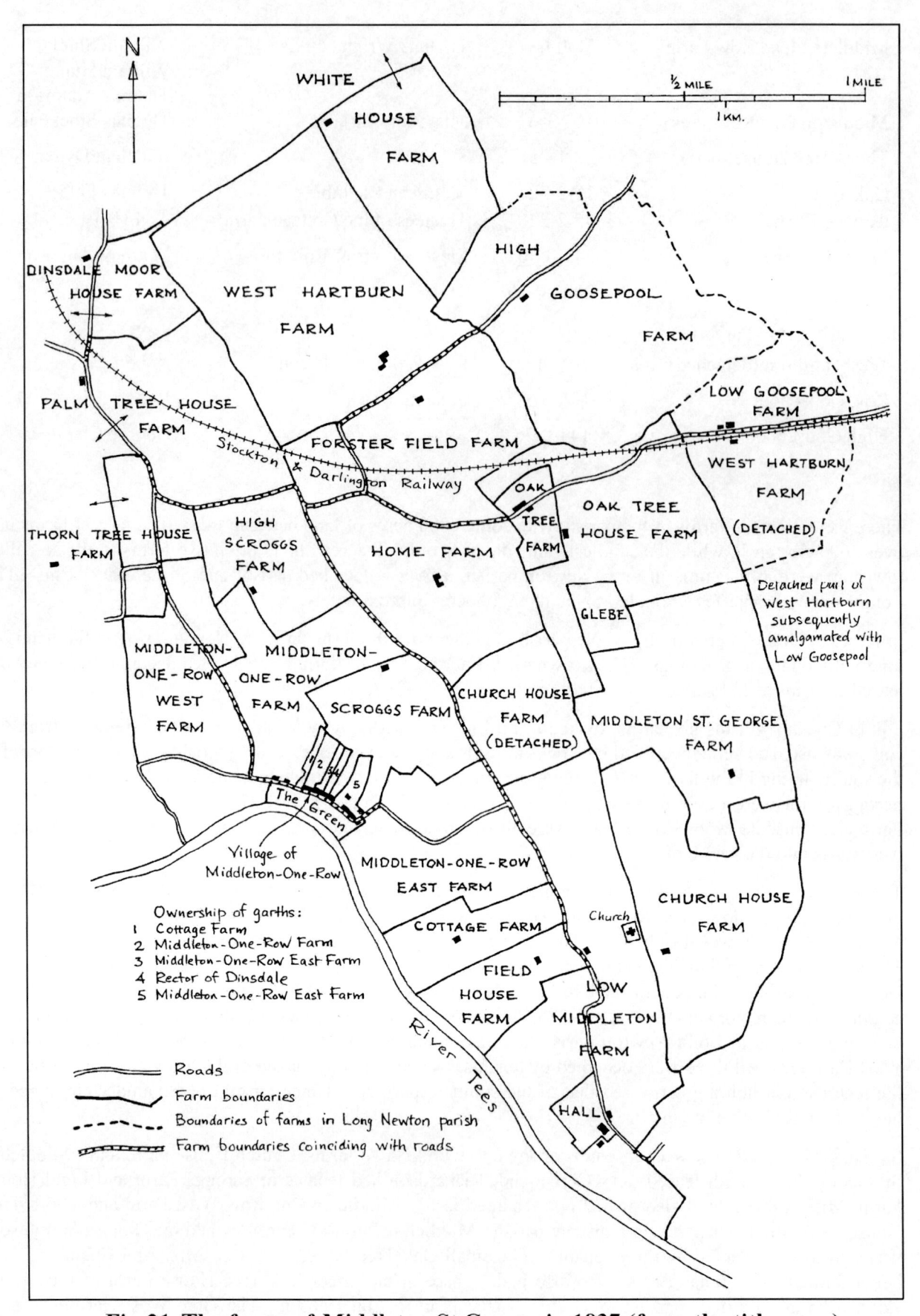

Fig. 21 The farms of Middleton St. George in 1837 (from the tithe map)

The glebe land of Middleton St. George consisted of two adjacent fields. Indicative of the ancient links between the parishes, one of the garths at Middleton One Row was part of the glebe land of the parish of Dinsdale.

Of a total of 2032 titheable acres in the parish, 1352 acres were listed as arable, 662 acres as pasture or meadow, and 18 acres as woodland. Farming in the period was clearly mixed, but with corn growing predominating. The cultivation proportions were not however uniform throughout all the farms. A full half of Low Middleton Farm was under grass, and the grass proportion was even higher on the nearby Field House Farm and Cottage Farm. In contrast, West Hartburn Farm was about 80% arable.

An interesting feature from the schedule accompanying the tithe map is the naming of the individual fields. Most of these field names have now gone out of use and are forgotten. The majority of the names are descriptive of usage, location, shape or size, such as Mill Garth, Kiln Close, Horse Pasture, Rape Field, High Moor, Great Field and Crooked Lands. Others are picturesque and of indeterminate derivation, like Cold Sway, Old Man's Hill and Old Wife's Close.

The rector's 120 acre Forster Field Farm, shown in more detail in Fig.22, was typical as far as its general make-up was concerned. It did have some special features, with the Stockton and Darlington Railway running through it, and with half of the deserted medieval village of West Hartburn lying beneath the rough grassland of the field still known as The Greens. The plan shows the field names and their agricultural status when the tithe map was produced. The fields had clearly had to adapt to the railway, and the westernmost had become divided into Little Chopping Field and Great Chopping Field. Changing usage is exemplified by the fact that the Horse Pasture was given over to arable at the time.

A remnant of medieval tenure continued in respect of the village green on the river bank at Middleton One Row, which served as a sheep pasture. Middleton One Row East Farm had 22 stints there, that is the right to graze 22 sheep. Middleton One Row Farm had 25 stints, the Cottage Farm 4 stints, and the Rector of Dinsdale 4 stints.

The amount of the "rent charge" to replace tithes, and the apportionment of this between farms, was established by agreement between the tithe owners and the landowners and occupiers. Presumably this entailed extensive consideration of tithes paid in the past and the valuation thereof. For Middleton St. George parish, an aggregate rent charge of £152.6s.6d. was determined. Christopher Jackson of Middleton One Row, the appointed valuer, divided this amount between the two people hitherto entitled to the tithes.

To the Revd. William Addison Fountaine, Rector	£78.9s.11d.
To Henry Andrew William Cocks Esq., Lay Impropriator	£73.6s. 7d.

The rent charge from each farm was divided equally between the rector and the lay impropriator, except for £4.13s.4d. due from the latter's own Low Middleton Farm and his Oak Tree House Farm, which sum was included wholly in the rector's total. The payments due from the individual farms bore no consistent relationship to their respective areas, and a variety of factors must have contributed towards determining the agreed amounts.

The amounts recorded as rent charges in the schedule were nominal payments, and not the actual amounts to be paid in any given year. The payments due were adjusted annually by the application of an established formula, taking into account the current prices for wheat, barley and oats.

The apportionment was the subject of a meeting in the school room at Middleton One Row on 1 May 1837, and the agreement to the new arrangement in lieu of tithes was confirmed by the Tithe Commissioners on 17 February 1838, with a supplementary agreement a year later on 19 March 1839.

The French Wars in the early nineteenth century had provided a boost to agriculture, with severe restrictions on food imports resulting in a heavy emphasis on home production. However, with the subsequent reopening of foreign trade farm prices fell, and agriculture entered a period of serious depression, from which it did not begin to recover until the late 1830s. The commutation of tithes was just one factor helping in a small way towards the slow recovery, which continued in a stuttering fashion until mid-century.

It has been appropriate to take the picture of the agrarian parish up to the point in 1837 when the tithe map provides the first comprehensive view of it. However, by this time other influences were at work, one of which was the continued development of the Dinsdale Spa [18].

Dr. John Peacock of Darlington was a strong supporter of the spa, and he provided treatment and advice for visitors. In his booklet of 1805[19], he describes a substantial spring, with a steady flow of 12 gallons a minute at a more or less constant temperature of around 52° F throughout the year.

Another local advocate of the spring was Thomas Dixon Walker of Hurworth [20]. He produced an analysis of the water from the spring, the outstanding feature being the high sulphur content. Dr. Peacock concurred in this, saying that it could only be matched in that respect by the famous spa at Aix-la-Chapelle. The sulphur richness was visually evident from the yellow deposition in the channel leading from the spring and also in the baths themselves, which had to be frequently scraped clean. It was said that sticks left in the channel for a few days, and then dried, could be used as matches.

In a lengthy description of the way the spa cure worked, Dr. Peacock said that the air we breathe is composed of two gases, one being oxygen or "vital air", and the other nitrogen or "azotic gas". He explained that oxygen, if taken into the system in too great a proportion, acidifies the blood and causes numerous diseases. The claim was that the excess oxygen could be neutralised by the sulphur, chiefly in the form of sulphuretted hydrogen held in solution in the spring water.

The complaints for which the spa treatment seemed most commonly and most successfully used were eruptive diseases of the skin and chronic rheumatic troubles. Amongst the first type, many cases of leprosy were treated, always it was said, with success. Gout was prominent amongst the treatable ailments, but it was emphasised that the essential first step in curing this affliction was the giving up of strong drink!

It was also claimed that various internal complaints could be cured or alleviated. These included diabetes, lead poisoning, fever, indigestion, general sickness, depression and debility. The treatment was even said to be beneficial in the first stages of consumption.

The bathing treatment varied with the type of ailment. Cold baths with sudden immersion were used for feverish people, while tepid baths were recommended for those in a debilitated condition. The water was also drunk in large quantities, Dr. Walker reporting on his patients, "Some of whom drink four and others six large tumblers full before breakfast", said that "One slim gentleman in particular informed me that he had twelve tumblers in the course of the morning".

Whatever current medical opinion might think of Dr. Peacock's reasoning, he was certainly in line with modern thinking when he remarked that the regular and healthy life, in the pleasant surroundings of the spa, could well bring about a cure or an improvement, "Let there only be hope at the bottom of the cup."

Advertisements for the spa, and accounts of it, always dwelt on the beauty of its setting. The river bank where it was situated was thickly wooded, and on the opposite side of the river stretched a wide expanse of fertile farming land, with the Cleveland Hills as a backcloth. Shady paths ran through the woods, offering a walk to Middleton One Row in one direction, and to Low Dinsdale in the other. Contemporary illustrations portray an idyllic picture, depicting fashionably dressed ladies and their escorts taking a leisurely stroll, with the spa buildings in the background.

An early visitor to the spa was Robert Surtees, the foremost historian of County Durham. He travelled exhaustively, visiting local gentry and clergy, and obtaining access to their documents in order to compile his monumental work.

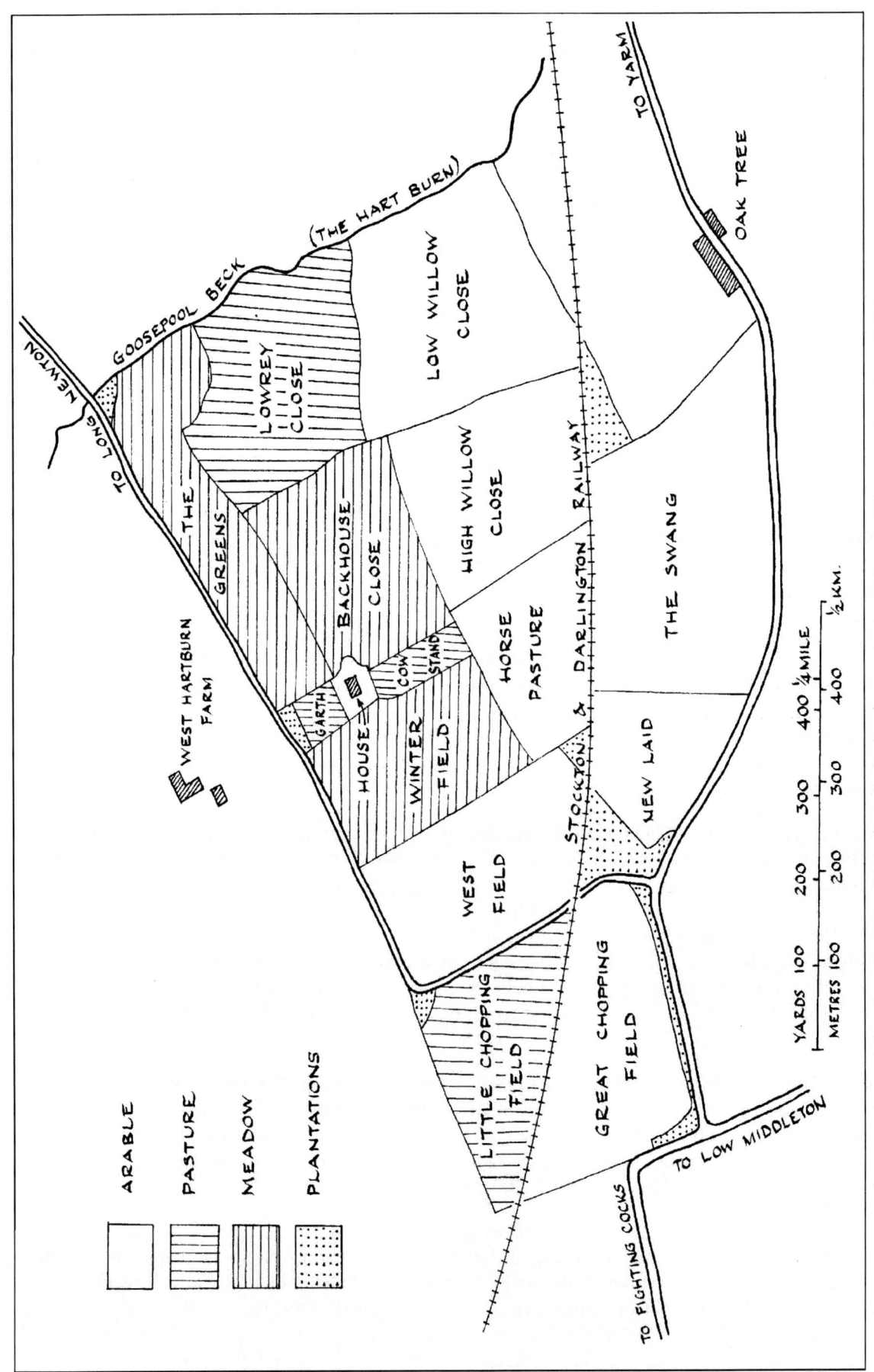

Fig.22 Forster Field Farm in 1837 - now Foster House Farm - showing field names

He was, however, not strong, and took a rest cure at the spa while he was in the area for the purpose of researching the Killinghalls, the Pembertons, the Places of Dinsdale and other local families. Some verses he wrote at the time included the following [21].

Of Buxton to tell,
Compared with this well,
I hold would be nonsense completely;
No water is sure
To perform such a cure,
And none ever tasted so sweetly.

If advice you would seek,
You may see Johnny Pyake,
He'll give you directions that's proper;
He comes here once a week
For patients to seek,
On a trundle a - d meer, with a crupper.

The "Johnny Pyake" in the poem was Dr. John Peacock, the staunch proponent of the spa.

In the early decades of the nineteenth century the spa flourished, but the facilities remained rather primitive. There was a big improvement in that respect, with the aim of enhancing the attraction for visitors, when a new set of baths, both warm and cold, was built in 1824. An engraving of the bath house, as it was around 1835, is shown in Fig.24 [22].

With the increasing patronage of the spa, the demand for accommodation also increased, providing a great stimulus to the hitherto sleepy village of Middleton One Row. Dr. Walker testified to this when writing in 1828 that "The accommodations are now of very superior description, the Inn having lately been rebuilt upon a more extensive scale, and the general convenience and comfort of the place much improved; in fact three-fourths of the village, within the last ten years, has been rebuilt, and many houses added" [23]. This is borne out by an 1834 report of "many new and rebuilt and enlarged houses within the last twelve years" [24].

This, however, was not considered sufficient, and in 1829 a large hotel was opened adjacent to the spa. (Pl.21) This was built by Lord Durham (later the first Earl of Durham), the son of William Lambton, whose men had discovered the spring forty years earlier. The hotel was sited in a commanding position at the top of the high river bank, with the spa building on the brink of the river below. The cost of building the hotel was about £30,000. It contained some seventy well-furnished apartments, together with domestic offices, stables and other amenities appropriate to the times. It was a centre for social life, and balls were held there during the season, attended by the gentry of the neighbourhood, as well as visitors. A stage coach ran every day during the summer from Newcastle to the hotel.

A list of charges for 1835 shown in Fig.23 makes interesting reading. Lodging rooms could be had for 10s.6d. to14s. per week, ordinary board for £1.15s.0d., and board in a private room for £2.5s.6d. Servant's board, including ale, cost 3s.6d. a day. Additional charges were made for private sitting rooms, fires in private rooms, and other extra services. Warm baths were 2s.6d. each, and cold baths 1s.0d.,while the water could be drunk for 1s.0d. a week.

Sir George Head visited the spa in 1837 and commented that, "it possesses attractions as a place of summer resort not to be equalled, I think in all England". He remarked on the large quantity of water drunk by patients, "some of whom drink four and others six large tumblers full before breakfast." He was enthusiastic about the potency of the water, and as evidence of this recounted that silver objects in a person's pockets, such as snuff-boxes and shillings, were turned yellow after a few days of drinking it. The value of exercise did not escape him, and he commented that, "The situation of the bath-house and spring being close to the River Tees, the inmates of the hotel have thereby the additional advantage of accelerating the natural process, by descending and returning by a steep hill, three or four hundred yards in length in order to reach it" [25].

A visitor from the medical profession was A.B. Granville, M.D., F.R.S., who included the Dinsdale Spa in a tour of English spas in 1840. He was impressed by the Spa Hotel and the village of Middleton One Row, but was not so enthusiastic about the water, here and at Croft, especially when he discovered that it was fed through lead pipes. "How such an arrangement could ever have been permitted for a moment, it is not easy to conjecture......I should be sorry indeed to prescribe any such water internally, under ordinary circumstances, without great and minute precaution; but under the circumstances of a large body of lead being constantly present in it - I should prescribe it never" [26].

Despite the attractions of the spa, the viability of the huge hotel must always have been questionable, and it lasted only a few years before being closed as uneconomic, leaving the hostelries and boarding houses of Middleton One Row to cater for the visitors.

The estate, including the spa, changed hands in 1844, the trustees of the second Earl of Durham selling it to Mr. H. G. Surtees, of the family who had been the medieval owners, for £40,000.

The second great stimulus to the parish was the coming of the railway. Middleton St. George has the distinction of being one of the places on the Stockton and Darlington Railway, the first railway constructed with parliamentary authority to carry passengers, and the first public railway to use steam locomotives [27].

The opening of the railway in 1825 was the culmination of many years of planning and the investigation of alternative schemes. The primary objective was to provide a link between the Auckland coalfield and the main centres of demand and distribution between the collieries and the coast. As early as 1767 a canal was proposed between Winston and Stockton, with Darlington on the route. As shown in the plan in Fig.25, this would have passed through the site where the present village of Middleton St .George now stands, between Fighting Cocks and the Square, proceeding by Goosepool and onwards to Urlay Nook and Stockton. The scheme failed to materialise, due to lack of financial backing and other reasons. Further canal projects in the next thirty years met a similar fate.

In 1810 a "cut" was constructed between Portrack and Stockton to improve the navigability of the river Tees. During a dinner at Stockton to celebrate the occasion, the subject of a link between the coalfield and Stockton was again discussed, and for the first time a railway was suggested as an alternative to a canal. More surveys followed, with canals generally preferred, until George Overton reported in favour of a railway. This was the turning point at which the advocates of a railway gained the initiative.

The name "Stockton and Darlington Railway" was first used in 1818, in which year it was decided to apply for an act of parliament to authorise its construction. Legislative problems followed, and the bill was not passed until 1821. A meeting was held in the King's Head in Darlington on 12 May 1821 to form a new committee. Amongst the members appointed was Edward Pease of the prominent Quaker family of businessmen, who later became known as "The Father of Railways". Another member was the Reverend W. A. Fountaine, the rector of Middleton St. George. As already noted, he had a strong vested interest beyond his incumbency, being the owner of Foster House Farm on the proposed route of the line. He later became a shareholder of the company.

Having approached Edward Pease to offer his services, George Stephenson was appointed Engineer. His colliery experience made him a strong advocate of steam locomotives, contrary to the views of Pease, who was an adherent of horse traction. The act which had been passed envisaged only horses, and made no mention of locomotives. The committee instructed Stephenson to ascertain whether he considered the proposed route of the line to be entirely satisfactory, or whether he thought any alterations to be necessary.

Accordingly in October 1821, when the harvest had been cleared, Stephenson commenced a new survey of the line originally planned by Overton. A local man, John Dixon, was appointed to assist him, and Stephenson's eighteen year old son Robert also helped with the survey.

DINSDALE SPA HOTEL.

Terms.

	£	s	d
Board p.r Week	1	15	0
Ditto, in a Private Room	2	5	6
Lodging Rooms from 10s. 6d. to 14s. p.r Week			
Double Bedded Rooms from 14s. to 21s. p.r Week			
Private Sitting Rooms from 14s. to 25s. p.r Week			
Fires in Sitting and Bed Rooms, p.r Week	0	3	6
Waiter, 3s. Chamber Maid, 2s. 6d. Boots, 1s. p.r Week			
Servants Board and Ale, p.r day	0	3	6

SOUPS EVERY DAY.

Charges for Bathing.

Vapour Baths	0. 2. 6 each
Warm Baths	0. 2. 6 do
Cold Baths	0. 1. 0 do
Shower Baths	0. 1. 0 do

for Drinking the Water.

Grown-up Persons, p.r Week	0. 1. 0 do
Children, under fifteen years of age	0. 0. 6 do
Day Visitors	0. 0. 6 do

N.B. Persons will not be charged for drinking the Water during the time they shall use the warm Baths twice a Week. Towels and Glasses will be provided by the person attending the Spa, and no charge will be made for the use of them or attendance.

Fig.23 Tariff for the Dinsdale Spa Hotel 1835

Fig. 24 The bath house of the Dinsdale Spa about 1835

Several workmen were engaged to handle the survey staffs and chains. The plan in Fig.25 shows how Stephenson's proposals differed from those of Overton.

According to all accounts, George and Robert enjoyed their task of measuring, recording and planning. It involved long days tramping over the route, and it is said that after a session's work they would call at any convenient cottage or farmhouse for a meal of bread, butter, milk and potatoes. At the end of the day they would put up at a nearby inn. One of their stopping places was very likely to have been the Hartburn Tavern, now Low Goosepool Farm.

On the 18th.of January 1822 Stephenson presented his report and estimates. Although confirming that a line could be constructed on the route planned by Overton, he strongly recommended that several alterations should be made. These alterations, he said, would result in a better railway, and a shorter route, with reduced building and maintenance costs.

Considering the part of the line near Middleton, difficulties were caused by the "hill and valley" nature of the land across which the line was to pass. The following quotations from Stephenson's report are interesting.

"At Haughton the old Line Crosses the Skerne and Main Post Road between Darlington and Stockton on a level with the surface of the turnpike, and proceeds along the river on the opposite side as far as Haughton Mill and from thence to the Wheat Sheaf.

Here the line becomes extremely unfavourable as well by reason of its circuitous course as its ascent, which will occasion a diminution of nearly one third in a horse's power, being 25 feet in about two miles.

In pointing out the new line from the Skerne at Darlington towards Yarm, Stockton. etc., I endeavoured to avoid ascending to the Wheat Sheaf. I succeeded in getting a line almost direct to the Fighting Cocks with a little descent towards Stockton.

The old line may seem to possess an advantage by crossing the Skerne at a narrower part of the vale than at Darlington, but this objection certainly vanishes when compared with that part of the line from Haughton to the Wheat Sheaf.

From the Wheat Sheaf the old line proceeds nearly direct to the Oak Tree, in which distance there are heavy cuttings and embankments.

The new line from the Fighting Cocks to the Oak Tree is not at all a favourable Line, but will contain less cutting than the old Line, and is, therefore, preferable.

Near the Oak Tree the two Lines form a junction from which place the surface of the ground or country is remarkably regular, so that little or no cutting will be necessary in the present Line, which goes within the Main Post Road very near Stockton.

This seems to be as beautiful a Line as could have been chosen."

The Wheat Sheaf Inn on the road between Middleton and Darlington eventually became just a farm, but has now regained its status as a hostelry under the name "The Old Farmhouse". The other inns to which reference is made, the Fighting Cocks and the Oak Tree still continue in the same capacity.

The committee accepted Stephenson's estimate and recommendations, and he was instructed to go ahead with the work. The first rails were ceremonially laid on 13 May 1822 at St. John's Crossing at Stockton.

Negotiations on the line were seemingly still proceeding and the Reverend Addison Fountaine recorded in his diary on 30 May 1822, "Mr Stephenson called about the line of the railroad through my farm". Six months later, on 2 December 1822, he noted the correspondence between himself and Edward Pease about compensation for allowing the line through his land.

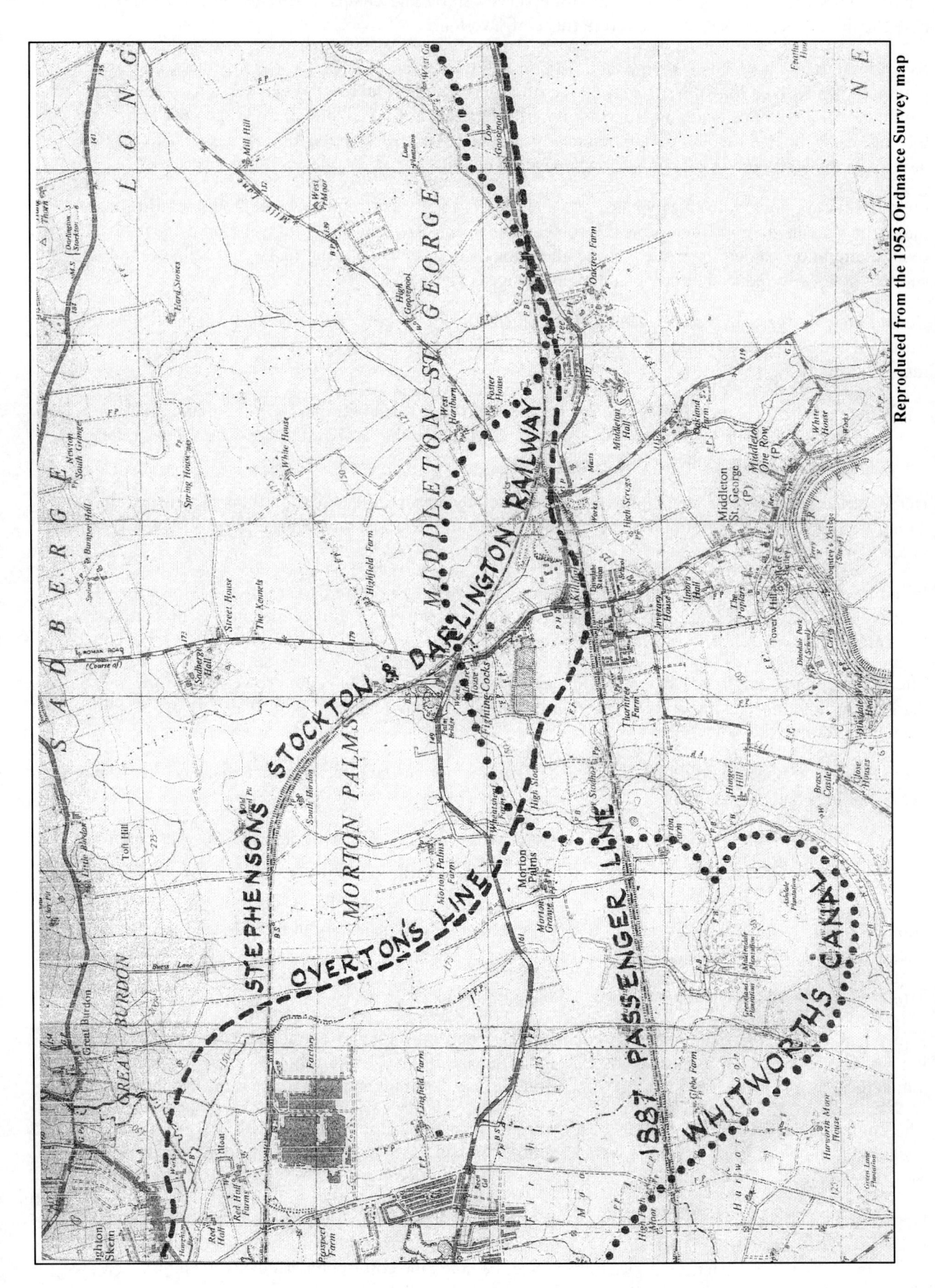

Fig. 25 Coal to the coast– proposed routes by water and rail between Darlington and Stockton.

Work on the local section of the line must have started soon afterwards, and the rector wrote in his diary, "The ladies walk'd and I rode to Fighting Cocks to see the commencement of the railroad". On 21 April Mr. Coates, the S & DR agent paid him £200 in respect of Foster House land taken over by the railway.

By this time, the Hetton Colliery Railway had opened, using steam locomotion. The practical demonstration of this form of traction was influential in the railway committee. A new bill was in progress to take account of Stephenson's line changes, and the opportunity was taken to insert amendments covering the use of locomotives and also the carrying of passengers.

In the meantime, work proceeded in the forming of cuttings and embankments and on the laying down of rails. The line was single track, with passing places at quarter mile intervals.

The opening of the railway, commemorated by John Dobbin's famous painting, took place on Tuesday 27 September 1825, when vast crowds gathered along the route to see the inaugural run. After rope haulage at the Shildon end of the line, the steam locomotive "Locomotion" took over and hauled the train to Stockton. There was only one closed carriage, the other so-called carriages being merely open trucks. At Darlington, six wagons of coal were uncoupled, and in their place wagons carrying the Yarm Band were added. The journey recommenced, and the historic train proceeded past Fighting Cocks, Oak Tree and Goosepool, towards Stockton. The engine took on water at Goosepool, and probably made an earlier stop at Fighting Cocks.

By Low Goosepool and beyond, the railway ran beside the road to Yarm, allowing a contest of speed with the traditional modes of transport. "Numerous horses, carriages, gigs, carts and other vehicles travelled along with the engine and her immense train of carriages, in some places within a few yards, without being the least frightened. And at one time the passengers by the engine had the pleasure of accompanying and cheering their brother passengers by the stage coach which passed alongside, and observing the striking contrast exhibited by the power of the engine and the horse - the engine with her 600 passengers and load and the coach with four horses and 16 passengers."

At the opening of the line, the company possessed only one locomotive, and most of the traffic on the line was horse-drawn. Few passengers were carried at that time, but special provision was made for them. On 10 October 1825, just two weeks after the opening, a horse-drawn coach called the "Experiment" made its first run between Darlington and Stockton. Thereafter, "Experiment" ran daily, and the first ever railway timetable was published, setting out its times of departure and arrival. The single journey was scheduled to take two hours, and the fare was one shilling.

After a while, when the extent of the demand became appreciated, the company sub-let the passenger traffic to various coach proprietors, who paid a toll for the use of the railway. There were no stations, and passengers were taken up and set down at any point. The drivers frequently stopped at the lineside inns for refreshment, and it is said that sometimes pressure had to be put on them to get them on their way again! Fighting Cocks, Goosepool and Urlay Nook are quoted as being three of the inns offering such delaying attractions.

In 1833 it was decided that locomotives could profitably be used for the haulage of trains specifically for passengers, the Manchester and Liverpool Railway having done so from its opening in 1830. The horse coach proprietors were bought out, and steam-hauled passenger trains commenced to run on 7 September 1833. The public obviously made good use of the new facilities, as in April 1834 a six times a day service, for passengers and goods, was announced.

As already mentioned, the S. & D. R. started with "Locomotion" as their sole engine. Another, named "Hope", was delivered two months later, and three or four more in the following year. "Locomotion" seems to have had a fairly rough life, as it is recorded as having had several mishaps, including a boiler burst in 1828, when one person was killed. In 1833 it collided with an ass, straying on the line near Goosepool. The engine had yet another incident when it ran into some stationary wagons, again at Goosepool.

The first stations did not appear until after the company took over the passenger traffic from the private operators. The Middleton St. George tithe map of 1837 shows the railway running across the north of the parish, with "Depots" marked at Fighting Cocks. Not a station in the sense we know it, this was where coal and other goods were unloaded from the train for onward despatch by horse-drawn vehicles. However, it did also serve as an alighting and boarding point for passengers. The proximity of the spa made the availability of rail transport particularly significant. Sir George Head, when he visited the spa in 1837, wrote of being "speedily consigned to a steam-carriage on the Darlington railroad", which deposited him at the Fighting Cocks [28], from where he was taken by horse-drawn transport to the spa.

By 1839 between 20 and 50 coal trains were passing through Middleton every day on their way to Stockton. Dr. Granville on his visit to the spa in 1840 lamented this activity, saying that, "It is to be regretted that, of late years, the intrusion of the noise of approaching and passing railroad-trains between Darlington and Stockton, in the rear of Middleton One Row, has somewhat interrupted the tranquillity of this charming retreat" [29]. This criticism would appear to have little real justification, as the peace of the place could have been little disturbed by trains a mile and a half away.

Despite any such reservations, the railway was here to stay, and was in little more than two decades to have even more impact on the parish, when it provided the supply line for the setting up of the ironworks.

Under the beneficial influence of first the spa and then the railway, the village of Middleton One Row grew and prospered. In 1821, before this growth had gathered much momentum, there were 46 families in the whole parish, and about half of these lived in Middleton One Row. A further small nucleus of population was at Oak Tree, where six families were living. The remainder of the inhabitants, were on the farms or in scattered houses elsewhere. A directory of 1827 lists most of the residents at that time [30].

William Blenkiron was the grocer and draper in Middleton One Row, and also ran a circulating library. Elizabeth Ditchburn kept another shop, of undefined business. Jane Pincher was a glover. Christopher Jackson was the village tailor, and his son, also Christopher, was master at the school. Thomas Hull was a boot and shoe maker. Another directory [31], a year or so later, adds a butcher, Nicholas Hanson, to the list of tradespeople. Matthew Brewster kept the Devenport Hotel, which also served as the posting house. Most of the houses in the village offered lodgings to visitors to the spa.

The local farms and other horse owners were served by Robert Moore, the blacksmith and farrier in the village. William Palmer, the joiner, also had his premises there, as did Anthony Fortune, the cartwright.

At the hamlet of Oak Tree, Thomas Baxter was landlord of the Oak Tree Inn, and Thomas Ellis was brewer and malster. James Ingledew was a shoemaker. The parish had a second cartwright, Matthew James, at Oak Tree - a measure of the demand for their services.

For a parish with a population of only 209 in 1821, there would appear to have been ample provision of supplies and services for the inhabitants. This reflects the fact that communities had to be largely self-contained. Account has also to be taken of the effect of spa visitors, especially in the season, temporarily boosting the population and the demands to be met by tradespeople.

The needs of most people continued to be served locally for a long time after this. Nevertheless, the communications revolution was having its effects, and the coming of the railway age was particularly significant for Middleton.

Just two years after the opening of the S&DR, there were two companies (Pickersgill & Langstaff and Scott & Co.) running horse-drawn coaches on the railway between Darlington and Stockton. The coaches had individual names, like the Defiance and the Defence. The directory notes that these coaches conveyed passengers and parcels to Middleton One Row, baths and spa. The coaches were timed to leave Darlington and Stockton simultaneously at eight in the morning and at four in the afternoon.

The journey time from Darlington to the Fighting Cocks stopping point was half an hour, and from Stockton one hour. From Fighting Cocks, a horse-drawn carriage was available to take visitors on to the spa. The opening of the Yarm Branch of the railway provided a direct link between there and Darlington, and served visitors to the spa coming from that direction.

Visitors from north or south, travelling by stage coach on the Great North Road, if they were uncertain of the railway, had the option of taking a traditional horse-drawn carriage connection directly from Darlington to Middleton One Row and the spa.

Stepping across the boundary into Dinsdale Parish, Nicholas Hanson was in 1827 the superintendent of the spa and baths, and also provided lodgings.

The village appeared to have a good mail service. In 1827 there was a horse post from Darlington to Middleton One Row daily, leaving at 5am, arriving at Middleton One Row at 8am, and leaving to return at 4pm. Surprisingly, there was also what was termed a foot post, which left Darlington at 7a.m. There was a morning delivery to Darlington in the summer, provided by John Teasdale, who left at 8am and returned at noon.

Twenty years later, in 1848, Middleton One Row was described as follows.

"The village which has no particular trade, is composed of one row of well-built houses, extending nearly half a mile, principally built for the accommodation of visitors to Dinsdale Spa - and from the vicinity of which the inhabitants of Middleton derive no little advantage. The "Devonport Hotel", which stands near the centre of the village is a remarkably well regulated establishment, judiciously fitted up for the reception of visitors; and an omnibus runs between the hotel and the railway station, according to the time that trains arrive and depart......" [32].

At that time the Devonport was kept by Thomas Ellis. A short distance along the row, William Hunter was landlord of the Queen's Head, as well as being a farmer. At Oak Tree the blacksmith, Thomas Moore, kept the Oak Tree Inn. Thomas Ellis remained at Oak Tree as brewer and malster, while his son of the same name did the same job at Middleton One Row.

By 1848 Harriet Jackson was postmistress at Middleton One Row. The mail was delivered from Darlington at 9.50a.m. and despatched to Darlington at 2p.m.

The main shop was run by John Magoris, described as grocer, tea dealer and stationer. A circulating library was still attached to the business, but in that respect he had competition from another, run by William Palmer. There were two butchers, Thomas Adamson and James Harrison. Betsy Shipman appears as a milliner and dressmaker. William Johnson was listed under "gardeners and seedsmen".

There were still blacksmiths at both Middleton One Row and Oak Tree, Anthony Dobbing and Robert Moore respectively. Shoemakers appeared in profusion, Thomas Hull and Isaac and Robert Teasdale being listed as such at Middleton One Row, and Thomas Garrett and James Ingledew at Oak Tree.

Margaret Usher was lessee of the Dinsdale Spa wells and baths. Mr. Thomas Forsyth had for some years been running the hotel, but this was in serious decline. In 1841 they had employed a staff of fifteen, but by 1851 the hotel was closed, and visitors taking the waters were all accommodated in Middleton One Row.

The census of 1851 provides a comprehensive review of the parish before the next major influence was to change it beyond recognition [33]. The population had risen from 209 in 1821 to 332 in 1851. There were a number of factors contributing to the increase. Firstly, there were the enhanced demands to meet the accommodation and other requirements of visitors to the spa. Secondly, the coming of the railway brought associated employment opportunities. Thirdly, the census included Goosepool, whereas this had previously been excluded as being part of Long Newton parish.

Lastly, there was at this time a boarding school in the parish, with the resident pupils swelling the population total. The direct influence of visitors to the spa was relatively insignificant, the qualifying time for the census being the night of the 30th March, which was out of season for most visitors.

The broad split of population between the various parts of the parish was as follows.

	Houses	People	
Village of Middleton One Row	35	130	Incl. 4 visitors
Hamlet of Oak Tree	12	43	
Hamlet of Goosepool	5	22	
Scattered parts of parish	21	137	Incl. 3 visitors and 24 boarding scholars
	73	332	

Neglecting boarding scholars and some empty houses, there were on average between 4 and 5 persons in each household.

A summary of the occupations listed in the census is given below.

Landed proprietor	1
Farm bailiff	1
Farmers	14 (incl. 1 farmer/schoolmaster & 1 farmer/innkeeper)
Farm labourers	24
Miller	1
Miller-journeyman	1
Cowkeepers	2
Retired farmers	3
Blacksmiths	4
Joiners & carpenters	4
Carpenter's apprentice	1
Cartwrights	2 (incl. 1 joiner/cartwright)
Groom	1
Gardener	1
Shoemakers	5
Cordwainer	1
Tailors	3
Glover	1
Dressmakers	3
Butchers	3
Baker	1
Housepainter	1
Laundresses	2
Innkeepers	3 (excl. 1 farmer/innkeeper)
Common brewer	1
Lodging house keepers	8
House servants	18
Errand boy	1
Lodger (annuitant)	1
Lodgers (unspecified)	3
Visitors	17
Station house keeper	1
Railway labourers	2

Labourers (unspecified)	2
Commission agent	1
Annuitant	1
Schoolmasters	2 (excl. 1 farmer/schoolmaster)
Schoolmistresses	2
Boarding scholars	24
Dependants (no occupation)	165

"Visitor" is taken to imply a person not making a home in the parish, and probably staying only a short while, e.g. on holiday, visiting relatives or visiting the spa. "Lodger" is assumed to a rather more permanent resident, probably following his or her occupation in the parish.

In a wide range of occupations, including the services to meet the needs of the community, the absence of a resident doctor is perhaps the most obvious omission.

In Middleton One Row the recorded population was 130, including 14 visitors, living in 30 dwellings. There were five empty houses. Most of the households in the village were named as tradespeople or lodging house keepers. Six houses had one or more visitors each, and the heads of nine other households were also listed as lodging house keepers, although they had no visitors at the time of the census. As already noted, the census was taken outside the main visitor season. The 14 visitors comprised six with places of birth within five miles of the parish, and six others born elsewhere in Durham, Yorkshire or Northumberland. One had a London birthplace and the other was Irish. Four of the visitors appeared to have been relatives of householders.

Outside Middleton One Row, most of the working inhabitants of the parish were employed in agriculture, either as farmers or farm labourers. The farms and farmers, as identified in the census, were as below.

Name	Area (acres)	Farmer	Notes
High Scroggs Farm	80	Thomas Pallister	
White House	110	George Clarke	
West Hartburn	243	William Smith	
Foster House	110	Thomas Thornton	
Goosepool Farm	135	George Thornton	High Goosepool
High House	not stated	Elizabeth Pyburn	Prev. Middleton St.George Farm
Church House	200	Anthony Robinson	
Middleton St. George	105	Michael Darling	Also boarding school Prev. Home Farm
Scroggs Farm	70	William Moore	
Cottage Farm	45	Richard Dawson	
Goosepool	110	Ann Carter	Low Goosepool
Hartburn Tavern	75	John Thornton	Also inn
Oak Tree	118	John Fortune	Oak Tree House
Middleton One Row	106	Thomas Stockdale	Middleton One Row West
In census for Dinsdale Parish:			
Dinsdale Moor House	100	John Donking	
Thorntree House	204	Catherine Dryden	
Palm Tree House	not stated	no farmer noted	

The farm attached to the manor at Low Middleton is not separately identified, and the census only makes specific note of one of the Middleton One Row farms. Those farms whose houses lay on the Dinsdale side of the parish boundary were included in the Dinsdale census.

Farm tenancies were clearly subject to short or medium term changes, only four of the sixteen farms where comparison is possible were in 1851 in the same hands as they had been in 1836, with another one being farmed by the widow of the 1836 farmer. The remaining eleven farms had all changed hands by 1851, including George Clarke's move from High Goosepool to White House.

At the time of the census, agriculture was still struggling for stability, but from the mid-1850s farming entered a period of increased profitability, reaping the benefits of improving methods, a growing population, and better means of transport for supplies and products. The extent of adoption of improved farming techniques was mixed. For example, some corn was being sown by seed drills, facilitating better weed control, but the old broadcast method was still also widely used. Drainage, a big factor in improving yields, was still badly needed on many farms, as noted in a report on the farms of the Londonderry Estate at Long Newton [34].

A general comment on the agriculture of the district at this time said, "The farm buildings are poor, and the tenants are too often in a similar predicament" [35]. These conditions were again reflected in the Long Newton report, where investment was being made to remedy the situation and to take advantage of the improving prospects for agriculture. At Middleton St. George, there was considerable farm house re-building during the nineteenth century.

The master of the day school in Middleton One Row lived in the School House, which together with the school room itself had been substantially rebuilt in 1828 at a cost approaching £100 [36]. There was also a schoolmistress listed as living in Middleton One Row, either assisting at the same school, which had about thirty pupils, or alternatively with a school of her own. Another schoolmistress was listed at Oak Tree, where there was a small nucleus of population.

By this date, the former Home Farm created by the Rev. Addison Fountaine around 1820 had become known as Middleton St. George Farm, and served also as a boarding school, with Michael Darling, the farmer, being noted himself as the schoolmaster. He had one male assistant. The twenty four scholars were aged from 8 to 15 years old. Three had birthplaces within five miles of the parish, twenty were born elsewhere in Durham, Yorkshire and Northumberland, and one was born in Scotland.

Despite being out of season, the Devonport Hotel had five visitors at the time of the census. Besides the innkeeper, his wife and 16 year old daughter, only one house servant was employed. There may of course have been additional domestic help in the season. The Queen's Head had only one visitor, but employed a groom and one house servant, in addition to the innkeeper's wife and 17 year old daughter. The Oak Tree Inn had a female innkeeper aged 77, and there was one lodger. The Hartburn Tavern at Goosepool was also a farm, run by the farmer, his wife, and one farm labourer

It is possible from the census to analyse the age structure of the population. A summary is given in the table below.

Age group	No. of males	No. of females	Total	No. born in parish	Percentage born in parish
0-10	38	41	79	39	49%
11-20	28	31	59	19	32%
21-30	12	15	27	3	11%
31-40	23	23	46	6	13%
41-50	9	17	26	5	19%
51-60	12	13	25	4	16%
61-70	5	5	10	2	20%
71-80	6	9	15	3	20%
81-90	-	1	1	-	-
91-	1	2	3	-	-
All ages	**134**	**157**	**291**	**81**	**28%**

A rather surprising feature is the low level of long-term residents, showing considerable mobility of the population. Out of the 291 inhabitants, excluding visitors and boarding scholars, only 84 had been born in the parish. An equal number were born outside the parish, but within a 5 mile radius. 109 had birthplaces elsewhere in Durham, Yorkshire and Northumberland, and 14 were born elsewhere in Britain. A frequent turn-over of farms is indicated by the stark fact that not one farmer had been born in the parish, and only one farmer's wife.

Excluding visitors and boarding scholars, there were 105 children in the parish. 26 of these were infants up to and including three years old, and the status of the other 79, aged from four to fourteen inclusive, was made up as follows.

Male scholars (listed ages 4-10)	11	
Female scholars (listed ages 5-11)	6	(and 1 aged 15)
Agricultural labourers (youngest aged 12)	3	
Blacksmith (presumably apprentice-aged 12)	1	
Male servant (at Hall-aged 12)	1	
Errand boy (aged 12)	1	
Female house servants (youngest aged 10)	3	
Dressmaker (aged 14)	1	
Unspecified sons or other male dependants	21	
Unspecified daughters or other female dependants	31	
Total no. of boys	**38**	
Total no. of girls	**41**	

Analysis of families indicates that early marriage was uncommon. There was only one married woman aged less than 30, and only two married men. Families where the wife was aged between 30 and 50 had an average of three children at home.

Under the influence of the spa and the railway, the social pattern of the parish was changing all the time, but there could be no forewarning of the transformation the second half of the century was to bring.

CHAPTER SEVEN - METAMORPHOSIS 1860 - 1880

THE COMING OF THE IRONWORKS AND THE CREATION OF A NEW VILLAGE

The census year 1851 was a significant one for the whole of the lower Tees area. In that year construction of the first blast furnaces to be built at Middlesbrough began, following the discovery of exploitable iron ore in the Eston Hills. This was the beginning of unprecedented expansion of the iron industry on Tees-side, and the creation of the planned towns that accompanied it.

The unbridled Victorian energy and enterprise were not confined to the immediate vicinity of Middlesbrough, but quickly spread to other locations beyond. In little more than a decade the industry had reached Middleton St. George. Land belonging to Palm Tree House Farm, lying between the Darlington to Yarm road and the railway was acquired for the building of blast furnaces and the establishment of the Middleton Iron Works. The choice of location was dictated by sound economic factors - the ready availability of raw materials, and the existence of the railway, critical for the movement of the heavy bulk materials. The coal and coke from the Durham coalfield were readily available and cheaply transportable. Similarly, limestone, for forming the slag in smelting, was easily brought in from Weardale. The Cleveland iron ore was also carried by railway, from the opposite direction. The railway provided the means of delivering the pig-iron product to processing works elsewhere, or for export. The eastern terminus of the Stockton and Darlington Railway had been extended to Middlesbrough in 1830, where extensive port facilities were situated and expanded for the rapidly growing trade.

No details have been uncovered as to the formation of the Middleton Iron Works, but it would appear that the promoters included Jonathan Westgarth Wooler, of the prominent family of business and professional men, and Squire Cocks who owned the land on which the ironworks were built. Construction took place around 1864, and there were originally two blast furnaces.

Unfortunately, not long after the ironworks were established, demand for iron products slumped. In mid-1866 the ironmasters reduced wages by 10%, and in July blastfurnacemen, puddlers, mill men and labourers all came out on strike. The two furnaces of the Middleton Ironworks were recorded as being idle. By the end of August the striking blastfurnacemen had been forced to accept the masters' terms, and returned to work [1].

Recovery was, however, slow, and the period between 1866 and 1870 was one of only moderate activity in the iron trade. The Franco-Prussian War of 1870 contributed to the dampening of demand. However, by 1872 there had been a substantial recovery, and it was reported that the smelters of pig iron had had in that year "the best end of the trade" [2]. The demand and price trend is illustrated by comparison of average bar iron prices per ton at Liverpool. It can be seen that the upsurge of demand towards the end of the period had resulted in a doubling of prices.

	£.	s.	d.
1864	7.	10.	0.
1865	7.	7.	6.
1866	6.	15.	0.
1867	6.	12.	6.
1868	6.	2.	6.
1869	6.	7.	6.
1870	6.	10.	0.
1871	6.	15.	0.
1872	13.	12.	6.
1873	15.	0.	0. approx

Some production costs also rose, and the Cleveland ironstone miners were seeking better returns. Over the period, the price of ironstone rose from 3s. 6d. per ton to 7s. 6d. per ton, and coal and coke in 1873 were about 40s. per ton. It was reckoned that pig iron could not be produced for less than 86s. per ton.

Middlesbrough and Cleveland were in the forefront of the booming iron business, producing two million tons of pig iron in 1873, and no doubt the Middleton Ironworks shared in the economic prosperity while it lasted. The works were owned by George Wythes & Co. By this time, there were three blast furnaces, all in blast [3]. By 1881 the number of furnaces had been increased to four [4]. Hodgkin's painting reproduced in Pl.22 gives a graphic view of the furnaces in operation.

While the location of the iron works was eminently suited to the availability of raw materials, there was no substantial source of labour in the immediate locality to meet the heavy demands of the enterprise. Consequently, resort had to be made to bringing labour in from outside, including many from a considerable distance. This in turn required the provision of housing, with the meeting of this demand attempting to keep pace with the construction and expansion of the works.

The first houses to be built were in a long terrace on the southern edge of the iron works site, with their front doors opening directly on to the road to Yarm. Squire Cocks, the last lord of the manor, saw to it that the name of his ancient forbears in office was perpetuated in the industrial developments by calling these houses Killinghall Row, although they are often referred to as "Old Row". Pemberton Terrace, named after his more recent predecessors, and with the added luxury of front gardens, followed later, and then the space between Killinghall Row and Pemberton Terrace was filled in by the building of more houses, with the less imaginative name of New Row. Other houses were built around "The Square", at the junction between the Darlington to Middleton One Row road and the road to Yarm. The railway had already been responsible for developments around the station at Fighting Cocks, and the additional impetus of the iron works and related activities resulted in more houses being constructed there and also along the road leading from there to the iron works. A little to the south, close to the junction of the Middleton One Row and Neasham roads, Chapel Row (now Chapel Street) was begun, later to be extended to its present length.

The emergence of this large new aggregation of housing changed within one decade the centre of gravity of the parish. The previous nucleus of population at Middleton One Row was still there, but was outweighed by that growing up around the iron works. The ironworks centred housing was originally known collectively as Killinghall, but with its continuing expansion that name was lost, the new village taking the name of the parish, Middleton St. George.

And what of the people at the heart of these momentous developments? The census of 1861 [5] shows much the same picture as in 1851, with the total population having actually suffered a small decline to 294. (The disappearance of the boarding school had contributed to this.) By 1871 the situation had changed dramatically, the population having exploded to 918, a more than threefold increase [6].

The most significant feature was the appearance of 470 people living in Killinghall and Fighting Cocks, whereas previously there had only been a few people at Fighting Cocks. The new ironworks community now made up over half of the total population.

The 1871 census shows a total of 133 men employed at the ironworks and the associated brickworks, set up at Fighting Cocks to utilise the local clay to meet the demands of the ironworks and its housing. Most of the ironworkers were described as labourers, but there were also the specialised tradesmen to provide the supporting services. A summary of the workforce occupations is given below.

Labourers	78
Furnace men	5
Engine drivers	4
Engine firemen / engine men	6

Fitter / engine fitters	4
Iron moulder	1
Pattern maker	1
Boiler smith	1
Blacksmith	1
White smith	1
Joiners / carpenter	3
Platelayer	1
Storemen	2
Overlooker	1
Draughtsman	1
Clerks	3
Brickmakers	3
Bricklayers & labourers	10
Plasterers	3
Masons	3
Excavator	1

Total 133

The question that needs to be asked is where did this labour force come from? The census returns, which give the place of birth of everyone entered, provide the answer. There were in total 288 adult males, and this included the 133 ironworkers, brickworkers and related trades. This group, directly attributable to the ironworks, were almost entirely incomers, only five of the men having been born in the parish. 14 had places of birth elsewhere in County Durham, and the largest number, 38, had Yorkshire birthplaces, spread widely over the county. Eight were Irish, three were Scots, and two Welsh. Surprisingly, two were Americans, with New York given as their place of birth. Discounting six whose birthplace was not known, this leaves 56 from other localities in England. These were widely dispersed over most of the country. A table of origins is given below, and the map in Fig. 26 shows graphically the areas from which the ironworkers and related trades were drawn.

Middleton St. George	5
Elsewhere in Durham	13
Yorkshire	38
Northumberland	1
Cumberland	3
Westmoreland	1
Lancashire	2
Cheshire	1
Nottinghamshire	3
Derbyshire	2
Leicestershire	1
Lincolnshire	6
Cambridgeshire	2
Norfolk	5
Staffordshire	9
Worcestershire	11
Shropshire	1
Huntingdonshire	2
London	1
Sussex	1
Bristol	1
Somerset	2

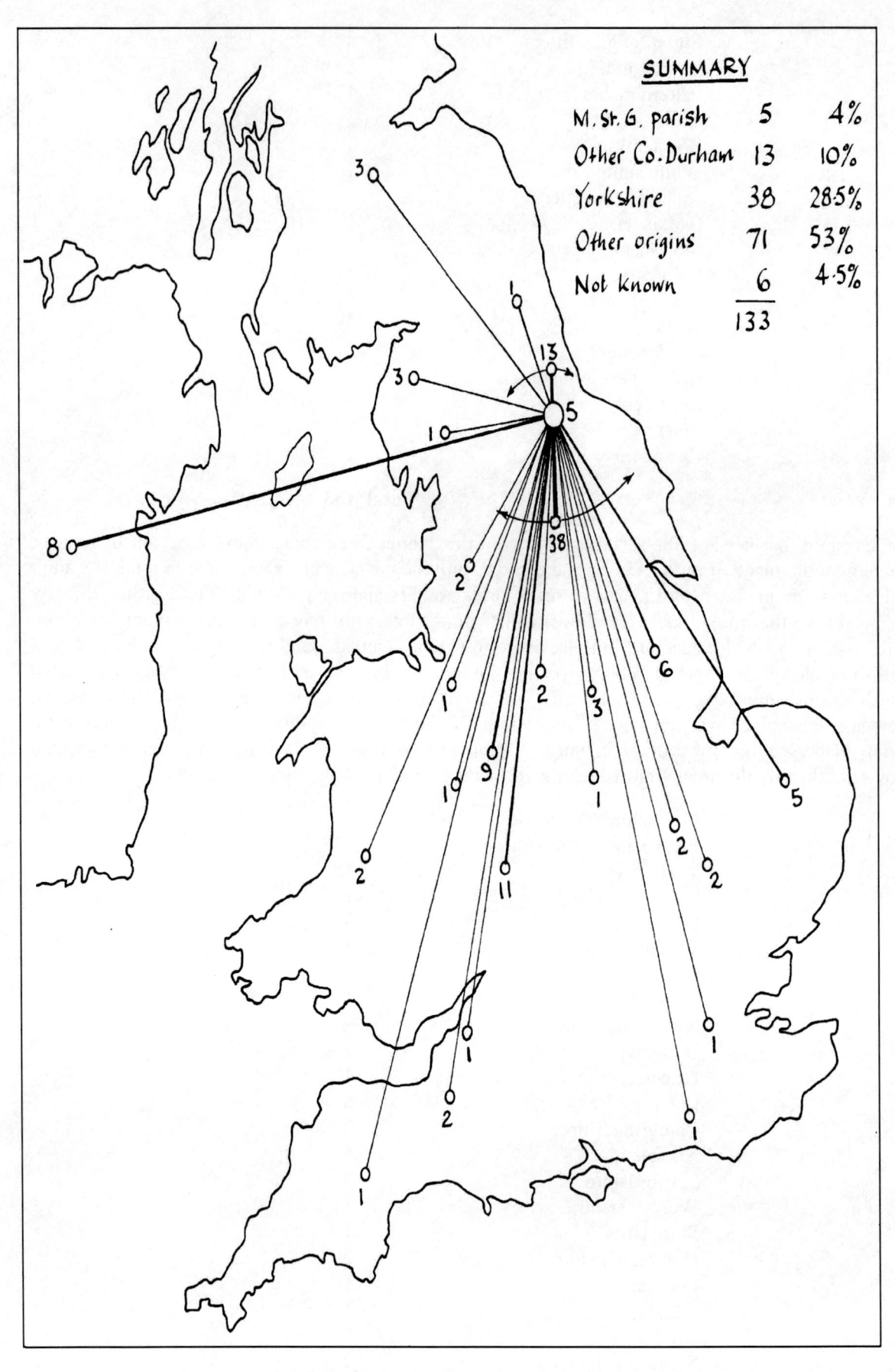

Fig.26 Origins of ironworkers, brick workers and related trades at Middleton St.George in 1871 census

Devon	1
Scotland	3
Ireland	8
Wales	2
U.S.A.	2
Not known	6

Total 133

Ireland, with its overpopulation and limited employment opportunities, was an obvious source of labour, but the significant numbers from Staffordshire and Worcestershire are at first sight surprising. However, the particular towns of origin, such as Dudley, Stourbridge and Wolverhampton, show more precisely that the incomers were largely from the heavily industrialised area west of Birmingham, where there would be a large pool of labour. Some of the Yorkshire workers were from the Leeds / Bradford area, but many came from the more rural areas, including some from nearby places just south of the Tees.

Some of the workers had obviously moved to Middleton St. George from previous employment in the ironworks on Tees-side, as several had children who had been born in Middlesbrough, or the other nearby iron towns.

There is no means of knowing how many were drawn from agriculture, but no doubt the attraction of better wages drew some from that source. To many, from whatever background they came, the attraction of employment in an industry seen to have an assured future, and with housing provided, would be an economic magnet.

There was probably difficulty in keeping the housing supply up with the demands of the increasing labour force. Consequently, the houses built for the ironworkers were used to the full. The 29 houses in Killinghall Row and Pemberton Terrace accommodated 187 people, an average of 6.4 persons per house. In some cases, two families shared a house. As an extreme example, John Isley lived with his wife and two children, together with seven others of a second family, comprising another ironworker, his wife and five children. Even when not sharing with another family, in nearly all cases the resident family had one or more boarders, exemplified by William Bradley, who, in addition to his wife and three children, had three boarders, all young single ironworkers.

Separated by a mile from the new Killinghall community, Middleton One Row remained a centre for visitors to the spa, and the location for several local services. Its population had grown from 130 in 30 houses in 1851, with three houses empty, to 229 in 40 houses in 1871. Pressure on accommodation was responsible for the fact that no houses were standing empty, and it would appear that five new houses had been built.

The Devonport Hotel was by this time run by Henry Tennick, with his son as ostler. The landlord of the other hostelry, the Queen's Head, was William Fishburn, who also had Middleton One Row Farm. Five of the heads of households were described as lodging house keepers, and twelve others also had boarders or visitors.

The meeting of ironworks accommodation demands extended to Middleton One Row. Two ironworks labourers and their families occupied houses of their own, and another ironworker lived with his wife's parents. The number of brick and stone workers resident in the village is indicative of the building activity in progress for the works and the associated housing. James Dodgson was one, a master mason employing eight men and two boys. Two of his masons can be identified, lodging in the village. Five bricklayers and a plasterer were also lodgers there.

Axel von Bergen, a Swedish civil engineer, was manager of the ironworks and lodged in the village. Charles Haigh was listed as an agent in the iron trade, and lodged with his wife in another household. The fine house of Middleton St. George Farm (Middleton Hall), which had in 1851 housed a boarding school, was in 1871 occupied by Charles E. Mueller, an iron merchant and ship owner.

He was born in Prussia, but had become a naturalised British citizen. His wife was Scottish, and they had three young children, with a governess, also from Prussia. Their household was completed by three servants, a cook, housemaid and laundress. He was not recorded in the census as farming the land, which was presumably let out.

The railway was another factor in the increased need for accommodation. William Barnard, born in London, was entered in the census schedule as railway agent and landowner. Two other properties were occupied by railway clerks and their families. Matthew Metcalfe was a railway gate keeper, and his stepson a railway labourer. A platelayer was another householder.

In the service sector, John Rodwell, the grocer, also kept the post office. There were two shoemakers, one with an assistant. Two females were listed as dressmakers. John Chambers, of a long established family, was a tailor. John Teasdale's unusual combination of occupations reflected the growing popularity of a new medium - "tailor and photographer".

Squire Cocks was not at the time resident at Low Middleton Hall, but was staying in Middleton One Row with Ann Graham, grocer, and three daughters. Their relationship was well known, one daughter being called Patience after the squire's mother. The squire's land agent, Michael Ogden, also lived in the village with his family, and a lodger, Thomas Parsons, a general medical practitioner.

George Bell was the resident cab proprietor, providing connections with the railway and transport for local journeys. Elizabeth Sutton was described as a horse dealer's wife, but her husband was obviously not present at the time of the census. They appeared to be of some substance, having a governess for their two children, and a groom and general servant.

The farming element was still strongly represented in the village, with ten houses occupied by agricultural labourers and their families. A police officer, John Robson, appears for the first time in the census. William Johnson was listed as a temperance agent - probably as a counter to the thirsty reputation of the ironworkers.

37 children were described as scholars, aged between 5 and 15. Margaret Moore was the schoolmistress. Other children from outside Middleton One Row no doubt also attended the school.

As mentioned earlier, the spa hotel venture had been short-lived. The demand for such accommodation had been greatly overestimated, and the project was just not viable. By 1861 the former hotel had become the Dinsdale Asylum, run by Dr. Donald Mackintosh, with 38 patients cared for by 21 attendants. Ten years later, in 1871, Dr. Joseph Eastwood had taken over as "physician and proprietor of licensed house for the insane", besides being farmer of 108 acres. The bath house was managed by Matthew Shipman, assisted by his wife and daughter.

In 1863 an attempt was made to bolster the spa. The Dinsdale Spa Improvement Company was established, with a capital of £2000, "to keep this favourite spa in that position of usefulness it has an undoubted right to hold". The Darlington and Stockton Times reported, "The spa and baths.....are undergoing a thorough repair, but so as not to inconvenience the visitors, it is intended, we learn, to throw the second class baths open to the public at about half the usual prices from one o' clock on Saturdays" [7]. In 1871 the bath house remained under the management of Matthew Shipman and his family.

The spa, together with the pleasant rural environment of Middleton One Row, did remain a considerable attraction, with the ironworks, out of sight about a mile away, not presenting too obvious a detraction. In April 1871, at the beginning of the season, about 55 visitors were accommodated in the Devonport, the Queen's Head, and in 18 private houses. A month later, the number of visitors had risen to about 100. By June the visitor total attained its zenith at about 150 persons. By the end of September the season was virtually over [8].

Mention has already been made of Fighting Cocks, at the northern end of the parish. This name given to the area was appropriated from the inn of the same name standing at the junction of the Darlington and Sadberge roads. The only buildings indicated at Fighting Cocks on the 1837 tithe map were the inn and Palm Tree House Farm. The following decades were to see considerable expansion and building activity.

The parish boundary between Middleton St. George and Dinsdale, apart from one minor deviation, follows the line of the old Roman road. The land of Palm Tree House Farm extended on both sides of the boundary, but the farmhouse itself, now demolished, was on the western side, as is the Fighting Cocks Inn. Both were therefore in Dinsdale parish, as was much of the subsequent expansion of Fighting Cocks.

Early information on the inn is lacking, but it is clear that the coming of the railway in 1825 was responsible for the prominent identification of Fighting Cocks as a stopping point and link to Middleton One Row and the spa. The early facilities were sparse, but later a proper station was built, and a coal and lime depot established. William Raine was the station master in 1871. There were two porters, both living with their families at Fighting Cocks, as did the signalman, who controlled the crossing over the Sadberge road. The innkeeper of the Fighting Cocks at this time was Thomas Dinsdale. His two teenage daughters worked as barmaids.

Even before the appearance of the ironworks, brickworks had been set up at Fighting Cocks. There was doubtless a strong local demand for bricks with the re-building of much of Middleton One Row in the expansion period of the spa. In addition, the railway provided a ready means for distribution of brick output to users elsewhere. From the 1860s, the ironworks and associated housing greatly expanded local demand. Only one brickmaker was listed at Fighting Cocks in 1871, but five bricklayers have already been noted as lodgers at Middleton One Row.

Demand for smithing services from the local agricultural community had doubtless been supplemented by requirements stemming from railway and ironworks activity. John Dobbing was the blacksmith at Fighting Cocks, and had an apprentice as a boarder in his household. He employed two other blacksmiths, both also resident at Fighting Cocks. One of them had come from Middlesbrough, probably through the ironworks connection. Closely allied to the blacksmith was the joiner / wheelwright / cartwright. In 1871 this position was filled by Robert Pallister, who had his workshop adjacent to the smithy. (Pl.32) He was assisted by his twelve year old son. He had the end house in a row extending along the Darlington road.

Squire Cocks had a corn grinding windmill at Fighting Cocks. John Burton was the miller in 1871. Apparently the sails were destroyed in a storm, after which the mill was converted to engine power [9].

Palm Tree House Farm at Fighting Cocks was farmed by the widow Elizabeth Horseman, helped by her two eldest sons. Two houses were occupied by agricultural labourers, one of whom had come from Ireland. Five ironworks labourers were lodgers in various households.

Water was an important requirement for the ironworks and the workforce, and a public supply was available. The Stockton, Middlesbrough and Yarm Water Company had been established in 1851 to serve the rapidly growing demands of Tees-side industry. They abstracted water from the Tees at Tees Cottage just outside Darlington and pumped it to a reservoir constructed at Middleton St. George near Fighting Cocks. From there it was fed by gravity through a single 15 inch pipe to Yarm, Stockton and Middlesbrough. It was not until a second pipe was installed in 1853 that the village was able to be connected and take advantage of a piped water supply [10]. The census of 1871 includes William Kitching, cab proprietor, living in the Water Works Cottage.

Gasworks at Fighting Cocks provided another public service. These did not appear in the 1871 census but were established in the same year.

Law and order at this end of the parish was maintained by a police sergeant, living at Fighting Cocks.

The ironworkers had a reputation for heavy drinking, and with this went incidents of disorderly conduct and petty crime. Around 1871 there was a suggestion that the village should have a police station and lock-up, but this came to nothing due to lack of funds. In 1877 another move was made, a seven foot long petition being presented to the Darlington County Branch of Magistrates, making a similar request, and also asking for the appointment of a local magistrate. The petitioners, including people from Sadberge, explained the background to their concerns, saying "This district has within the last six or eight years largely increased in population, and in consequence of the establishment of large ironworks in Middleton St. George a considerable portion of this additional population is of a very mixed and floating description, needing for the prevention of crime and preservation of the peace, the application of every provision the Law has wisely supplied" [11]. It appears that this time the appeal was successful, and a police station was established in The Square, conveniently close to the two public houses, The Killinghall Arms and The Havelock Arms, set up to quench the thirsts of the ironworkers [12]. (At a much later date this was superseded by a new police station in Middleton Lane, now a private house.)

Oak Tree, centred on the inn of that name, was another secondary nucleus of population. Its origin probably lies in the void in the agricultural community living space after the disappearance of the village of West Hartburn. By the nineteenth century it had developed into a distinct hamlet, and in 1871 its nine households contained a total of 44 people.

Elizabeth Chapman, a widow, kept the Oak Tree Inn. Her daughter and granddaughter lived with her, and at the time of the census they had one boarder. The brewery by this time appears to have been defunct. What was described as "The Old Brewery" was a farmhouse occupied by John Gell, who had the small 20 acre farm which encircled the hamlet. Beyond this, with its farmhouse to the south west, lay the much larger Oak Tree House Farm, extending to 138 acres. The farmer, Richard Robinson, employed two labourers, both of whom lived at Oak Tree. Another resident, George Mackay, was described as a gamekeeper, but with no definition as to his sphere of responsibility. The footwear business continued at Oak tree, with Isaac Teasdale as the boot and shoe maker. A brickmaker and railway platelayer were other residents.

Goosepool, east of Oak Tree, was recognised by the census as part of Middleton St.George, although at that time still within the parish of Long Newton. The Goosepool land was divided between two farms, High and Low Goosepool. High Goosepool stood remote, with William Dent farming its 129 acres. Low Goosepool had accumulated a small group of dwellings in addition to the farm.

John Thornton farmed the 185 acres of Low Goosepool, and was also innkeeper of the Goosepool Inn, otherwise known as the Hartburn Tavern. Jane Moore, widow of the previous blacksmith there, was described as a pauper, but the business was being continued by two sons and a grandson apprentice. Three other cottages were occupied by a labourer on the farm, a railway platelayer and a bricklayer.

Although displaced as the economic heart of the parish by the new industrial developments, the farms continued as the chief users of land and as a significant source of employment. Palm Tree House Farm at Fighting Cocks lost a substantial part of its land to the ironworks, but the other farms were largely unchanged. From about 1870 agriculture entered into another period of severe depression, due partly to a succession of bad harvests in the 1870s [13], but chiefly to the development of overseas food production and the shipping facilities to bring the products to the British market. Prices for grain and meat fell drastically and not until the turn of the century was their any upturn [14].

In the new make-up of the parish, the inadequacy and inconvenience of St. George's Church, standing in the fields near to Low Middleton, had become even more pronounced. At least as early as 1851 the Wesleyan Methodists had had a chapel at the east end of Middleton One Row [15], but adherents of the established church were still faced with a cross-country walk or ride to St. George's for worship. To the difficulties already faced by the inhabitants of Middleton One Row and visitors to the spa was added the need to cater for the new and even more distant industrial population. As a temporary expedient, some services were held in a room, converted for the purpose, at Fighting Cocks.

It was recognised that the only long-term solution was to build a new church, and the decision was taken to go ahead with this. The site chosen was at the western end of Middleton One Row, at the corner of Middleton Lane. Apart from being a pleasant location overlooking the river, the choice of site was no doubt motivated by being contiguous to the old-established nucleus of population, and at the same time within reasonable walking distance from the mushrooming new community to the north.

The Darlington-based J. B. Pritchett was appointed architect. He was of considerable local repute, and had been responsible for the highly regarded St. Nicholas' Church in Durham, and for the rebuilding of the chancel of St. Cuthbert's in Darlington. In common with other contemporary churches in the area, the design was neo-Gothic. The original concept was for a very basic nave and chancel arrangement, at an estimated cost of about £1300, but, before commencing, it was decided to add a bell tower at the south-east corner of the nave. This, together with external walling and perhaps other extras, brought the total cost to something over £2000. Construction was in granite, with a slated roof. The seating capacity was 300. The new church (Pl.18), dedicated to St. Laurence, was ready for use by the spring of 1871. The parish magazine records, "This church, long hoped for, but long delayed by a variety of untoward circumstances, was consecrated and dedicated to the worship of God, by the Lord Bishop of Durham, on Thursday, the 13th. day of April".

Corresponding with the need for a new church, thought was doubtless given to the provision of an associated rectory. It has already been remarked that the Reverend Addison Fountaine had built a fine house on his Forster Field Farm, where he lived during the later years of his period as rector. This was however his personal property, and was not available to his successors in the incumbency, for whom there was no accommodation provision. The need was becoming even more pressing with the new and expanded community to be served. However, the church itself was the priority, and the rectory had to wait a little longer. In the meantime, the rector was given the use of Low Middleton Hall, not required by the bachelor squire.

The rector at the time of the building of the new church was the Reverend Lyndurst B. Towne, aged 33. His wife, Elizabeth, had been married before, as she had a twelve year old son living with them, in addition to two infant children of their own. Another twelve year old boy in the household was described in the 1871 census as a pupil. They had three female servants, a cook, housemaid and nurse.

Half way along the road between Middleton One Row and Killinghall, Jonathan Westgarth Wooler had built a substantial residence called Almora Hall. (Pl.35) The name, taken from a town in northern India, reflects the Wooler family trading connections in the east. Jonathan's father, Joseph Wooler, was a member of the East India Company, and when he died Jonathan succeeded him in business in Mumbai (then Bombay). Returning to England in 1852, he lived for a number of years with his brother, William Alexander Wooler, at Sadberge Hall, before building his own house at Middleton St. George. He never married, and was in 1871 the sole resident of Almora Hall, apart from two servants. A gardener lived in the lodge at the entrance. In the 1871 census, Jonathan's occupation is given as "coal merchant" and in 1881 "coal owner". .

Jonathan Westgarth Wooler was a driving force in the building of the new church, and a substantial contributor to the building fund. He gave a separate donation towards the completion of the belfry and spire. Numerous fund raising events were also organised. One such was a fete held in the grounds of Almora Hall on the 2nd. and 3rd. of August 1871. Attractions included a flower show, archery and croquet, and the Darlington Philharmonic Band played. To encourage attendance, the railway offered single fares for the return journey to and from Fighting Cocks Station. A "fancy free" at the fete was the sale of goods left over from a previous fund raising event in Darlington, affording "the young ladies ample opportunity for making their usual successful attacks on the purses and susceptibilities of gentlemen." By the beginning of 1872 about £1950 had been secured, and big efforts were made to clear the outstanding debt [16].

Apart from the capital cost of the new church, the day-to-day financing was as ever a matter of concern. The rector outlined the position in 1871, saying that the old church rate used to produce £14 a year, against a current offertory total of about £44 over a four month period. There was a deficiency of £9.5s.11d. for the year, and he believed the offertory should not be less than £100 a year, with the hope for a future doubling of that figure.

In 1872 the rector displayed some grievance in reporting that "The income of the church derived from all sources in this parish is less than £200 a year; of this one half has by some means fallen into the hands of the patron of the living; thus I your parish priest have for my support less than £100 a year, and this not contributed by any of you, not even by those who pay tithes....."

The fact that the income of the living was "miserably small" was blamed for the frequent difficulty in finding a clergyman to occupy it, and for the lengthy vacancies. Jonathan Westgarth Wooler, in his capacity as churchwarden, took it upon himself to accommodate and entertain the visiting parson and his wife at Almora Hall for the interregnum week-ends.

It would be interesting to have more information on the attendance at the new church. A measure of the congregation increase may be indicated by the fact that there were 14 communicants at the last Christmas communion to be celebrated at St. George's Church in 1870, whereas there were 50 at the 1871 first Christmas communion at St. Laurence's. A note of the 1871 harvest festival recorded "Church crowded, many being unable to obtain seats." The rector commented on the service, "It is a very happy thing that the old-fashioned way of celebrating the Harvest Home has now nearly passed away; a few years ago, and in most of our villages it was the custom for the farmers to give their men a supper at the end of the harvest, and much rioting and drunkenness was usually the result: now, instead of this, the church's way of rejoicing has been revived, and throughout the land there are not many villages where a thanksgiving service is not held to God, the giver and ruler of the harvest."

The Church of England was not alone in looking to the spiritual welfare of the expanded population. They were in fact a little behind the Wesleyans, who had built a chapel on the road to Fighting Cocks in 1869. (Pl.19) This was closely followed by the United Methodist chapel built in 1872 at Middleton One Row.

Another shortcoming in the re-shaped parish was education. Around the time the ironworks were founded, the village school was recorded as having 21 boy pupils and 7 girls, all children of agricultural labourers, and each paying between 3d. and 6d. a week. This small school at Middleton One Row was clearly inadequate for the greatly increased population. The problem was a general one, and the Education Act of 1870 set out to remedy the situation, with the aim of education for all. The response at Middleton St. George was the establishment of a National School, for children above the age of six years.

The site for the new school building in Chapel Row, was chosen for its proximity to the ironworks, while minimising the distance from Middleton One Row. The land was given by Mr W. A. Wooler [17]. A temporary schoolroom was set up at Fighting Cocks, pending construction of the new building. By mid-1871 the new work was adequately advanced to allow school to start on 31 July. At this time, about £1250 had been collected for the new school, including £350 from Wythes and Cochrane, the owners of the ironworks.

By January 1872, 115 children were attending. There was a charge of 2d. per week for each pupil. At the beginning of 1873, the headmaster was Mr. T. Sangar. Mrs. Carter had just retired as schoolmistress, and was being replaced by Miss Rider. Miss Colvin was the infant schoolmistress.

One of the signs of the newly flourishing community was a revival of the parish magazine, from which much of the foregoing information has been taken. Quoting from the first issue of 1 May 1871:

"The parish is very different to what it was formerly, a new church has just been completed, new schools are in course of erection, a new Reading Room has been supplied at the Ironworks, many new residents have come amongst us, all showing that a new era has commenced with us."

The management of the ironworks was alert to the educational and social needs of their workforce, exemplified by the provision of the reading room referred to above. "The Middleton Iron Works Library and Reading Room is provided for the use of men employed on the Works. Subscription, 1d. per week, paid every three weeks. The Reading Room is open from 8 to 11 a.m., and from 6.30 to 10 p.m., and contains Chess Men, Draughts, Dominoes, etc., and the following papers are taken in-

DAILY
Northern Echo   Standard
Newcastle Chronicle   Manchester Guardian
Daily Telegraph

WEEKLY
York Herald   Darlington & Stockton Times
Reynolds   Irishman
Illustrated London News   Scotsman
Fun   Sporting Life (Twice a week)
Judy   Church Herald (Twice a week)
English Mechanic

MONTHLY
Chambers' Journal   Leisure Hour

The papers are sold by auction every 3 months. Books are given out every Monday and Thursday, between 7 and 8p.m.

Committee - M. Gill, G. Clarke, H. Cox, J. Egleston, S. Gladdis, T. Hope, W. Taylor, W. Bonsall, T. Milner.

Librarian - J. Campbell."

In the winter evenings the reading rooms hosted "Penny Readings", half of the proceeds going towards the new schools and half towards a piano for the room.

A concert for the benefit of the reading rooms was given at the conclusion of the 1871 readings, boosted by performers from Middlesbrough, "the local talent for the object being not quite adequate."

Night School classes were held in the National School on three evenings a week for "those whose education has hitherto been neglected, and who now feel their loss." The weekly fee was 3d.

An annual tea was laid on by the ironworks company for their employees. About 400 attended the function in the reading room in 1872 (either a very large room or quite a squash!), with a separate party for about 200 children the day after.

The church choir of boys and men, with the headmaster of the National school as Choirmaster, appears to have been a flourishing institution. In addition, singing classes held in the school were reported as making great progress. The new school was also the venue for Sunday School, held twice each Sunday, at 9.30a.m. and 2p.m. About 80 children were reported as attending in 1872.

The railway facilitated the introduction of another feature of social life - the trip to the seaside. The Stockton and Darlington Railway had extended its eastern terminus to Redcar in 1846, and an annual visit to the sea and sands was a highlight for many. The 1872 school treat to the seaside at Redcar, transported by what by then had become the North-Eastern Railway, was an early example of this.

The Middleton Ironworks Cricket Club was formed around this time. Difficulty was experienced in finding a ground, but eventually one was obtained temporarily for the 1871 season in the field opposite to Almora Hall. This "temporary" ground lasted as the home of the Middleton Cricket Club for some 80 years! Pl.34 shows an early team.

An inaugural match was played between the Ironworks and Middleton One Row on 27 May 1871, with the former winning by an innings. The scorecard showed a number of present day village names represented.

IRONWORKS

First Innings

B. Bosher,	c. Metcalfe,	b. T. Chambers	19
W. Dent,	b. Elliot		6
J. Fawell,	run out		8
H. Fawell,	b. Elliot		0
R. A. Dent,	c. Metcalfe	b. Elliot	33
M. Gill,	lbw,	b. Elliot	0
J. Slater,	c&b. Elliot		3
W. Raine,	c. Teasdale	b. Elliot	2
J. Campbell,	c. Parsons	b. Elliot	3
W. Dowson.	b. Chambers		4
R. Chambers,	not out		2
		Byes and wides	2
		Total	82

MIDDLETON-ONE-ROW

First Innings

T. Chambers,	run out		7	c. R.A. Dent,	b. W. Dent		5
J. Teasdale,	b. H. Fawell		0	b. W. Dent			4
C. Jackson,	c&b. H. Fawell		1	b. J. Fawell			13
Rev. L. B. Towne,			2	run out			0
R. Elliot,	c. Campbell	b. J. Fawell	3	b. H. Fawell			1
R. Moore,	b. H. Fawell		4	b. W. Dent			0
W. Lynas,	b. H. Fawell		0	b. J. Fawell			2
J. Metcalfe,	b. H. Fawell		1	not out			0
R. Pringle,	b. H. Fawell		0	run out			0
Dr. Parsons,	lbw,	b. H. Fawell	0	c. W. Raine	b. H Fawell		0
J. Chambers,	not out		0	b. W. Dent			0
				Byes and wides			5
		Total	18			Total	30

Forthcoming matches were to be played against Darlington North Road, Stockton Second Eleven, Ormesby Ironworks and Sadberge.

In 1873 the new school was still in debt, presumably on account of the balance of construction and fitting out costs still to pay. Prior to a sale of work, organised towards clearing the deficit, it was stated that the rector would match the £150 contributions of Squire Cocks, Mr. Wooler of Sadberge Hall, and Messrs. Cochrane of the ironworks.

At this time, the local administration of the parish was still in the hands of the church-based officers. Mr. W. A. Wooler of Sadberge Hall was guardian, and the churchwardens were Mr. M. F. Ogden and Robert Bamlett. The latter was also one of the overseers, the other being Anthony Dobbin. Mr. Ogden, churchwarden and Squire Cocks' land agent, was also assistant overseer and waywarden. Parish constable was Mr. J. W. Teasdale. The schoolmaster, Mr. T. Sangar, was organist and choirmaster.

CHAPTER EIGHT - FROM THE NINETEENTH CENTURY INTO THE TWENTIETH 1880 - 1914

CONTINUED DEVELOPMENT THROUGH TROUBLED TIMES

Boosted by the ironworks, the population continued to grow, and reached the thousand level by the last quarter of the century. The 1881 census listed for Middleton St. George parish 1081 people, with a further 81 living in the Fighting Cocks part of the village (parish of Dinsdale), and 22 at Goosepool (parish of Long Newton), giving a total of 1184 [1].

The short Pemberton Terrace had been extended to fill all the space available between it and Old Row. This "New Row" provided another 19 houses for ironworkers. More houses were also built in Chapel Row and elsewhere in the Killinghall area.

Middleton One Row did not expand significantly within itself, but was extended by the building of Tower Hill, by the ancient castle mound, and other large houses in that direction, including The Friary.

The greatest change occurred in the development of houses in Middleton Lane, the road between Middleton One Row and Killinghall. The lead taken by Jonathan Wooler, when he built Almora Hall, was followed by others, and some fifteen large, mostly detached houses had been constructed by 1881 [2].

One of these, Felix House, was occupied by Dr David Porteous, the general practitioner for the village and the area. The house had been designed for him by Axel von Bergen, the civil engineer who was manager of the ironworks. The house was named after the ship on which Dr. Porteous had sailed in the course of arctic exploration. The origin of the name, however, goes back further than this, stemming from Felix Booth, who made his money from gin, and was the sponsor of John Ross in his unsuccessful search for a north-west passage, and in his attempt to locate the lost expedition of Sir John Franklin.

Pemberton House, situated just before Middleton Lane reached Middleton One Row was in 1881 run as a school by the rector, the Reverend Christopher Jackson. In 1883 Pemberton House was taken over as the original premises of Barnard Castle School, whose new building was still under construction. The first term began in September, when 25 boarders took up residence. There were at the beginning also ten day boys. Numbers increased, and Violet Villa in Church Lane was taken over to provide additional accommodation. A wooden annexe to Pemberton House was damaged by fire at the beginning of 1885, but re-built and eventually transferred to Barnard Castle when the school moved to its new premises there in the autumn of 1885 [3]. Pemberton House was re-opened as a convalescent home in 1893, having been acquired by Sir Robert Ropner of the ship owning family.

The expansion of the village, alongside its iron smelting activities was not long sustained. By the 1880s imports of better quality ore from Spain and elsewhere were ousting the local high sulphur ore from Cleveland. This made it more economical to have blast furnaces closer to the port facilities. The rapid increase in steel production, as distinct from iron, contributed to the difficulties of ironworks using the less suitable local ore. In 1881 the four blast furnaces of George Wythes & Co. at Middleton were all out of blast [4], and in 1883 the works were shut down. They were to remain closed for the rest of the century.

The parish was obviously hard hit by the withdrawal of the main source of employment, which had been responsible for its re-shaping. The 1891 population had fallen to 871 from its census peak of 1103 in 1881. With the loss of the ironworks and the reduced population, the rateable value of the parish fell from about £14,000 in 1875 to only half of this by 1894.

Some alleviation of employment hardship was provided by the setting up of new industrial enterprises at Fighting Cocks. The Dinsdale Steel and Wire Works were established in 1882, using raw material from Sheffield and elsewhere. They were followed in 1887 by Richards and Tutt, with their adjacent Dinsdale Moor Ironworks. They took over the hearths of the blacksmith John Dobbin.

The second edition of the Ordnance Survey map, reproduced in Fig.27, shows the ironworks and the other industrial enterprises at Fighting Cocks, the associated housing and the spread of larger houses along Middleton Lane.

One of the side effects of the closure of the ironworks was the halting of plans for a Roman Catholic chapel, which intention had resulted in the name Chapel Row or Chapel Street, where the building would have stood. Some Irish labour element remained in the parish, but the lapse of ironworks support meant that the chapel was never built.

The established church was also affected. In 1883 the rector planned to have the east window of St. Laurence's Church embellished with stained glass, "but owing to the depression in trade and other causes, he could only raise enough money to fill in the centre light and the tracery" [5].

Despite the industrial downturn, extensive renovation work was carried out on St. George's, the parish church in the fields, commencing in June 1888 [6]. This included a new roof, new seating, new flooring, lime coating of walls internally, and a painted depiction of St. George in the east window. It was at this time that the black oak box pews were removed, and also a three decker pulpit. The cost was mostly met by the patron, Squire Cocks, and the rector, the Reverend Christopher Jackson, with a contribution also from Mr William Miller, the people's warden. Earlier, in 1881, Squire Cocks had financed the building of a tower at the west end, which survived until 1961, when it was declared unsafe and demolished. (Pl.11)

Away from the industrial village, Middleton One Row continued much as before, as did the farming community of the parish. The new larger houses in Middleton Lane were mainly the homes of prosperous families in commerce and industry, who, with improved communications, were no longer constrained to live where they worked.

In this respect the re-routing of the Darlington to Saltburn railway line was significant. The Darlington termination of the old line was North Road Station, which had been superseded for main line traffic by Bank Top Station. Moving the termination of the Saltburn line to Bank Top meant a new route eastwards out of Darlington, which by-passed Fighting Cocks before joining the old line by Oak Tree signal box. A new station was necessary for Middleton St. George, and its situation on the new route was much nearer to the centre of population than Fighting Cocks at the northern extremity of the parish. Fighting Cocks Station was closed to passenger traffic on 30 June 1887 (Pl.30), but remained open for coal and other freight. The new station, given the name Dinsdale, came into use the following day (Pl.31), offering greatly improved passenger facilities. These improvements, together with the fact that the station was considerably nearer to Middleton One Row, made it practicable and convenient for commuting to Darlington and Tees-Side, and thus opened up a much wider range of employment possibilities for the inhabitants of the parish.

With the ironworks themselves, the associated reading room was also defunct, and it was decided in 1885 that new facilities should be provided for the workers on the re-routing of the railway, and also for the local inhabitants. A house in Killinghall was taken and furnished as a Working Men's Institute. There were two reading rooms, a smoking room, and a room for games. This was said to have been greatly appreciated initially, but after only a year attendance had so greatly declined that the Institute was closed [7].

The new railway station was better situated than Fighting Cocks had been for visitors to the spa, but by this time its fortunes were severely failing. In an effort to arrest the decline, the bath-house premises were reorganised around 1880 to include visitor accommodation. A contemporary advertisement spells out the attractions. "The newly-built annexe is furnished with every comfort and contains a suite of rooms with first rate accommodation. It is situated in the beautiful Dinsdale Woods, overlooking the Tees. Angling can be had by visitors, and tickets for salmon fishing. From the beauty of the scenery it has a special recommendation for artists, and owing to the Sulphur Baths being under the same roof they can be used at all seasons." However, the great age of spas was over, and the improved facilities did not appear to have resulted in any sustained revival of patronage. This is borne out by Boyle in his 1892 "Guide to Durham", where he refers to the Dinsdale Spa simply as "a sulphur well, once extensively resorted to" [8]. Certainly by the end of the century it seems to have been no longer a significant commercial venture. The bath house in its later phase is shown in Pl.20, when from 1908 it served as the clubhouse for the Dinsdale Spa Golf Club.

A major event celebrated at Middleton One Row was Queen Victoria's Golden Jubilee in 1887. The weather was brilliant on 21 June, when there was a thanksgiving service, a public tea on the village green, and sports which included foot races and canoe races. Trees were illuminated by Chinese lanterns, and at about 10pm a large bonfire was lit [9].

With the population increasing through the 70s, so also was the demand for education. In 1885, the head teacher Mr. G. D. Atkinson reported that there were 210 children on the register, with an average attendance of 150 for the two months ending 3 April. The school warden, Mr. W.H. Wilkinson, listed 21 children who were not regularly attending, and warning notices were to be sent to the parents [10].

In this period, an acrimonious dispute arose as to the management of the school. This lasted several years and showed bitter personal rivalry. Funding for the school was the issue which initiated the dissension.

The National School was voluntarily supported, and this support was doubtless adversely affected by the shutting down of the ironworks in 1883. The school managers sought to put their finances on a more assured footing. The solution they saw was to transfer the school to a school board, as provided for in the 1870 Education Act, with the legal effect of making the school supportable from the rates. With the loss of the contribution from the ironworks, the major ratepayer in the parish was the North-Eastern Railway Company, whose line scythed through the parish. By adopting the planned strategy, almost half the cost of running the school would come from them [11].

The advice received by the managers was that they should close the school, to demonstrate that education facilities were not being provided, and that a school board was necessary to make good the deficiency. Accordingly, they wrote on 23 July 1884 to the Education Department, saying that the school was closed and that they would be unable to carry on in future. The closure of the school did in fact correspond with the beginning of the holidays, but there was no return until a school board was elected in the autumn. At the inaugural meeting on 6 November, the board and its appointed officers was confirmed as follows.

Christopher Blackett	Chairman	Farmer, West Hartburn Farm
John William Teasdale	Vice-chairman	Merchant Tailor, Middleton One Row
Jonathan Westgarth Wooler		Gentleman, Almora Hall
William Robinson		Innkeeper, General Havelock Hotel
William Horseman		Farmer & Contractor, Fighting Cocks

William Hodgson was appointed clerk and Edmund Backhouse treasurer.

The election was the point at which the managers of the National School became disenchanted with the scheme, although they themselves had proposed it. They had foreseen maintaining control by having a majority on the new school board, but this did not happen. Jonathan Westgarth Wooler was one of the National School trustees elected to the new board. His brother, Mr. W. A. Wooler, had given the land for the school, and Jonathan Westgarth Wooler himself had been a strong supporter and principal benefactor. When it became apparent that the National School group were not to be in control of the new school board, he showed his dissatisfaction by not attending the first meeting. John William Teasdale and William Robinson were of the opposite party, who appeared to have a three/two majority. The antagonism between the National School managers and the new school board immediately manifested itself.

Mr. O. B. Wooler, a solicitor and brother of Jonathan Westgarth Wooler, representing the National School managers, wrote to the new board, saying, as recorded in the minutes of that first meeting, "That the Schools were conveyed upon certain trusts inconsistent with the purpose for which the

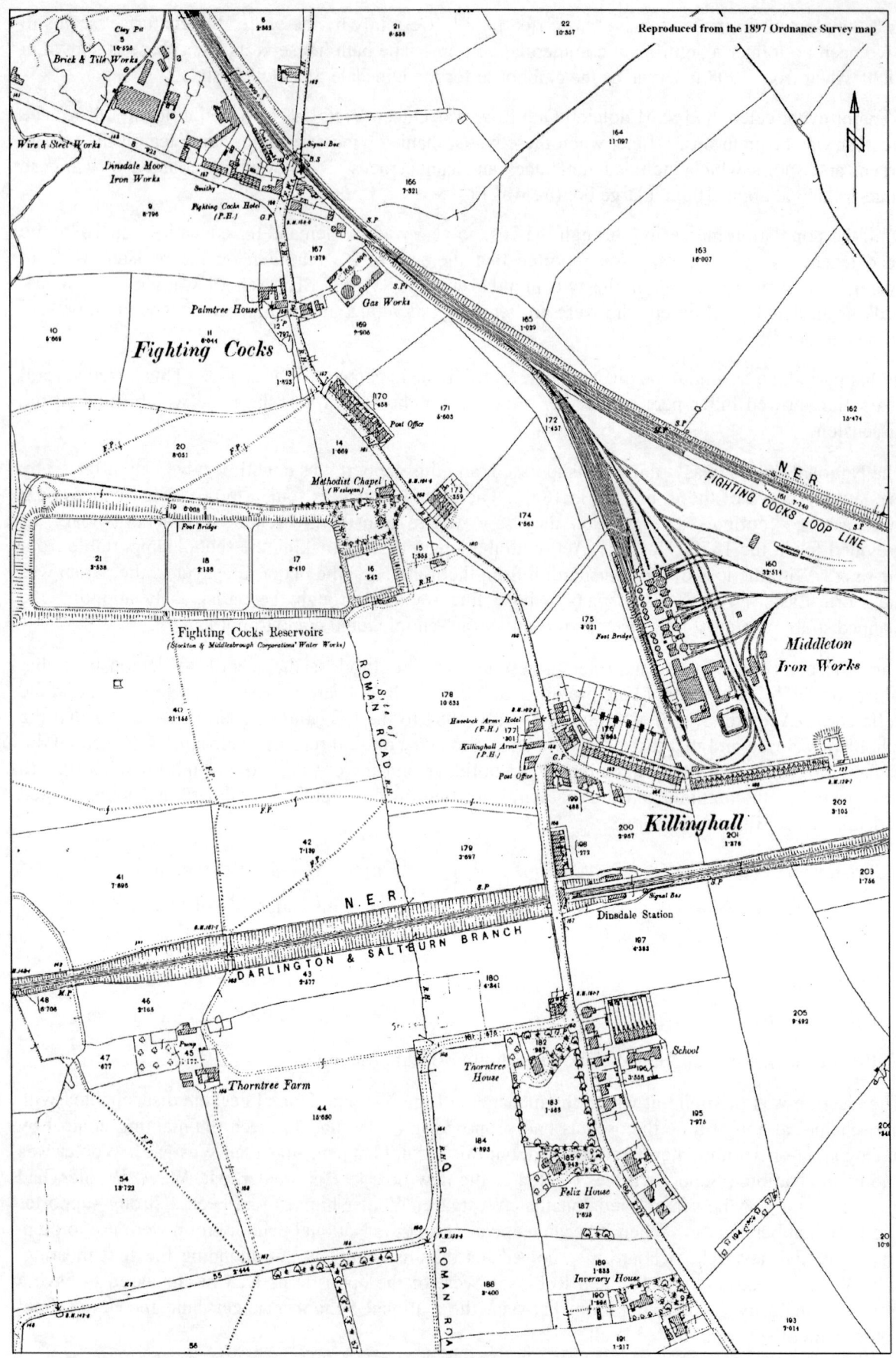

Fig. 27 The ironworks and other industrial enterprises at Killinghall and Fighting Cocks at the end of the nineteenth century. Showing the associated workers' housing and the development of large houses along Middleton Lane

Board had been called together and that the Schools could not be had for the purpose indicated. Also stating that private subscriptions had been received which would enable the schools to be continued on the voluntary principle." The board replied with a formal request that the schools be handed over to them. Squire Cocks expressed his concern, writing to the chairman of the board on 12 March 1885, "On my arrival at the Fighting Cocks Station I was greatly disappointed to find that the gentlemen who profess to be so anxious to save the pockets of the ratepayers had declined attending the meeting of the School Board. So far as I am concerned I should be too happy to do anything in my power to bring the matter to an amicable arrangement."

The Education Department was approached to try to resolve the impasse. They wrote on 20 March 1885 to Mr. J. W. Wooler, expressing their regret at the situation, wherein "the Trustees of the National School decline to confer with the Board upon the transfer of the School." They asked the trustees to consider again the terms of transfer, saying that, "An arrangement with the School Board under Section 23 of the Elementary Education Act of 1870 appears to be the best way of avoiding considerable delay and expense in making the necessary School provision."

The personal animosity was evident in a further letter dated 31 March 1885 from Mr. J. W. Wooler, in his capacity as a National School trustee, to the clerk of the new school board. "I must enter a protest to you as Clerk to the School Board against your having been made the tool of Messrs. Robinson & Teasdale to convey untruths to the Education Department regarding those Schools. It is well known that all the commotion, troubles and expense the parish has been put to is solely attributable to them and now that the people are beginning to see through them they get a petition and ask my friends to sign it with the object if possible of throwing the onus of building new Schools upon me. I protest against this. There is no necessity for new Schools in the parish. You have already confessed to the Education Department that there is ample School accommodation in this parish & if new Schools are to be built it will not be my fault but the fault of Messrs. Robinson and Teasdale. The memorial got up recently by Messrs. Robinson and Teasdale is utterly valueless as indicating the feeling of the parishioners on the question at issue as I know many of my friends signed it under a pure misapprehension of its real purport."

The Education Department had ruled that the school board should provide a school for not less than 245 children, with 12 June 1886 as the deadline for complying. In the event of default, the Education Department would appoint a fresh board, with power to acquire land for a new school, "including that on which the present School is erected." If taken to its conclusion, the ludicrous outcome could have been two schools competing for the same pupils.

When application was made by the National School for examination of the children, the Education Department refused to send an inspector, on the grounds that there was a school board and they were the appropriate authority for such a request. Mr. Wooler, for the National School, took the view that the school board was not effective and should have been declared in default.

In 1887 there was a further disruption due to William Robinson being disqualified as a member of the board, having been apparently declared bankrupt. The National School party saw this as an opportunity to take control of the school board, and supported the rector, the Rev. John Groves, as a candidate to fill the vacant place. Unfortunately for them, Squire Cocks entered the fray by accepting nomination, and was co-opted by a three against two majority, presumably with the benefit of the chairman's casting vote. This greatly incensed Mr. Wooler, who alleged unfair connivance.

Later in the year, when the three year term of the first school board had ended, a new board was elected, comprising:-

Jonathan Westsgarth Wooler	Chairman	Gentleman, Almora Hall
William Horseman	Vice chairman	Farmer & contractor, Palm Tree House, Fighting Cocks
Rev. Christopher Jackson		Pemberton House

William Kitching   Farmer, Waterworks, Fighting Cocks

John William Teasdale   Tailor, Middleton One Row

The position of Mr. Wooler as chairman indicates that the balance had finally shifted in favour of the National Schools faction. William Horseman had very likely always been on that side, and one or both of the new members were probably supporters.

However, the election of a new board did not in itself solve the problem, and the school was again closed between October 1887 and January 1888. The issue was eventually settled by an order made by the Education Department, authorising the school board to put into effect powers conferred within the 1870 Education Act to take over the existing school. A lease dated 29 June 1888 finally transferred the premises to the School Board.

Even after the settlement was reached, Jonathan Wooler remained aggrieved. Just six months before he died, he wrote on 4 February 1890 to the Education Department" to lay the cruel case of these schools before you....." He laid the blame on the previous school board, and spoke scathingly of some "notorious members". He maintained that the managers of the National School had been prepared to transfer it, but that the school board had been unreasonably difficult in agreeing the terms. He himself took the credit for minimising the time the school had been closed, remarking that if he had not done so "these poor children would have been running wild, and without any Education during all this time." He continued by drawing attention to the fact that during the three years of the dispute the grant previously made to the National School had been withdrawn. He sent an account for the running costs over that period, and asked for a retrospective grant to be made. A note attached to his letter in the Education Department file states that they had no power to make any such grant.

A different view to that of Mr. Wooler was expressed at the end of an Education Department memorandum explaining the reasons for the order they had made. "The School Board having been created, through the action of the Managers of the existing School, with the object of taking over that School, the Order carried out as nearly as practicable the arrangement which the Managers of the existing School originally proposed and which they appeared to consider, until their nominees were defeated at the election of the Board, to be the best for the parish" [12].

The "North Star" gave a more charitable summary of the situation in its obituary of Jonathan Westgarth Wooler, after his death on 20 August 1890. "The deceased gentleman also took the chief part in securing the election of the voluntary schools, to which for many years he contributed handsomely. On the closing of the local ironworks, and the consequent depression in trade in the neighbourhood, he was the means of securing the creation of a School Board, of which he ultimately became chairman" [13].

Bearing in mind that the Wooler family were concerted in their actions on this matter, their ambivalence in their attitude to the school board comes out in the obituary of William Alexander Wooler, Jonathan's brother, some nine months later, when it was recorded that "he fought hard against the establishment of a School Board for Middleton St. George" [14].

A further step on the education scene occurred in 1891 when elementary education became free for all. Parents no longer had to pay the previous school pence, and instead the government provided funding to the extent of ten shillings per year for each pupil.

The Rev. Christopher Jackson, chairman of the school board, issued a circular to parents and ratepayers, emphasising the need to maximise income by improving attendance figures, as the grant aid paid was calculated on average attendance and not the number on the roll. Apart from the financial aspect, the Rev. Jackson stressed that regular attendance was essential for progress, and also noted the importance of punctuality. "It is necessary that all should be in their places at the ringing of the School bell. By coming late, the Scripture Lessons are lost or only partially heard, while idle and dilatory habits are formed, which greatly interfere with the steady and punctual application so important in School work." [15].

The Local Government Act of 1894 introduced parish councils and brought the village level of government into the pattern we have today. Functions previously exercised by vestries and churchwardens were taken over by elected parish councils, which were given wide powers, albeit restricted by the amount of the rate they were allowed to levy [16].

Coincidentally marking the change from the old to the new, Squire Cocks, the last lord of the manor and the successor of the Killinghalls, died in November 1894, just a few days before the new form of parish administration came into effect. He was also the last to be interred beneath the chancel of St. George's Church.

The inaugural meeting of the Middleton St. George Parish Council was held in the Chapel Street Schools on 4 December 1894. The rector, the Reverend Christopher Jackson, was elected chairman for this initial meeting, which had the purpose of electing the parish councillors. On a show of hands, seven members were chosen, but there was clearly strong feeling amongst those present, and the result was challenged. A poll was requested, as provided for in the legislation, which resulted in a delay of a fortnight. On the results of the poll, the following were declared elected on 17 December 1894. Their occupations, noted in brackets, are as given in the 1891/1901 censuses.

William Kitching	Farmer at Fighting Cocks
Joseph Pybus	Farmer, West Hartburn
William Horseman	Wire Works Labourer
R. Seymour Benson	Managing Director of manufacturing engineers
R. A Luck, JP	Draper and Magistrate
John George Chapman	Coke and Iron Merchant
Charles John Wilson	Draper and Postman

Mr. Luck lived at The Villas. His drapery business was in Darlington, and continued into the 1950s. Mr. Benson lived at Castle Hill, which had previously been the West Farm of Middleton One Row.

At the first meeting of the newly constituted council on 5 January 1895, they elected from their number Robert Luck as provisional chairman, and William Kitching as vice-chairman and treasurer. The parish still had overseers, and John Campbell, the assistant overseer, was appointed clerk to the council. At a later meeting William Horseman was elected waywarden, with responsibility for roads and paths.

A recurring theme in the early years of the parish council deliberations was the village green at Middleton One Row. This does not conform to the conventional picture of a village green, but comprises mainly the steep river bank, together with the narrow grass-covered strip of land between the houses and the public roadway. Apart from being used for grazing sheep, it was then as now a public amenity area, frequented not only by the local people, but also by a considerable number of visitors. The virtual disappearance of visitors to the spa had been compensated by increasing numbers of day-trippers from the nearby towns, particularly at week-ends. Their outings were facilitated by the easy access provided by the railway, with Dinsdale Station being within easy walking distance from Middleton One Row.

In all these activities, the green was apparently used as a market place, with stalls erected for the sale of refreshments and other wares. It follows that there was a litter problem, and a proposal was made to impose a charge on stallholders to pay for the necessary clearing up. At a council meeting on 20 May 1895, it was agreed that a sum not exceeding 5s. be expended for the purpose of cleaning up the refuse on the village green after the Whitsuntide holiday. It was later reported that the actual cost had been 3s. Subsequent payments of varying amounts were made for the same purpose.

The problem, however, seemed more than that posed by random litter. On 18 October 1897 "Mr. W. Harrison reported that some person and persons were in the habit of tipping rubbish on the Village Bank at Middleton One Row". By this time, the council had come to the conclusion that better control would be exercised if they formally took charge of the village green. They had already assumed responsibility for maintenance other than waste clearance, such as making good of footpaths and repairing seats. After taking advice on the necessary procedures, a sub-committee was formed to draw up bye-laws for the regulation of the green and banks. This was followed by prolonged correspondence with the Local Government Board as to the details.

In the meantime, it was established that, under existing acts of parliament, "If any person wilfully lay any manure, soil, ashes, or rubbish, or other matter or thing on any town or village green, or do any other act whatsoever to the injury of such town or village green or to the interruption of the use or enjoyment thereof of a place for exercise and recreation, such person shall, for every such offence, be liable upon summary conviction to a fine not exceeding £2 over and above the damage occasioned thereby". A notice board to this effect was erected on the village green, and the clerk was instructed to write appropriately to one particular offender.

The owners of stints (the rights to graze sheep) on the green were consulted and asked for their agreement to the parish council taking over control of the green. They were not all co-operative, but it seems that the objections did not have the legal force to halt the process. Nevertheless, their grazing rights had to be maintained.

The sub-committee placed their proposed bye-laws before the full council on 17 October 1898, and these were approved. More correspondence with the Local Government Board followed, and modifications were requested. It took a further year for these to be implemented, and for the statutory publication of notices. The long procedure was finally completed by October 1899, allowing the parish council to enter into the next century with the power of control over their village green.

The Devonport Hotel was an early offender against the bye-laws at the beginning of 1900, when they cut a short length of access road between the hotel and the public road. In response to the council's complaint, "Mr. T. M. Hinde had an interview with the Clerk wherein he expressed regret that owing to an oversight a preliminary application had not been made to the council, but trusted that taking into account the great improvement that had been made, the council would not require the sods to be replaced. He also applied for permission to plant in front of the Devonport Hotel an ornamental tree to which he was quite willing to waive all rights and to allow to become public property". On the motion of Mr. R. Seymour Benson, the original complainant, it was decided to grant the requested permissions.

In 1901 subsidence of the village green bank caused considerable concern. On 14 March, "The chairman called attention to the very serious landslip which had occurred on the village bank and which was menacing the stability of the High Road through the village, and moved that the parish council be urged to use every means in their power and to petition the Darlington RDC to take immediate steps to deal with the serious landslip so as to prevent a further subsidence of the village bank".

The matter was further discussed on 15 April 1901, when it was decided that the remedy was to insert a slag-filled drain in the bank, to take away the overflow from a spring or well and also water drained from the Vicarage site. A cost of about £30 was foreseen. It was noted that a similar landslip a few years previously had been dealt with successfully with slag drains, paid for by the late Squire Cocks. On this occasion the adjacent property owners were approached for contributions towards the cost of the measures to ensure the stability of their properties. A generally favourable response seems to have allowed the work to go ahead, but until it was completed the dangerous state of the bank enforced closure of the lower footpath.

The pattern of roads in 1900 had developed over the centuries, to meet the needs of the local horse traffic. In the railway age, with increasing trade and movement, the limitations of the road system were painfully obvious. The parish council minutes make many references to the deficiencies.

The way to Long Newton was only a bridle road, and on 20 January 1896 the clerk was instructed to write to the Highways Board to draw their attention to its poor state of repair. A year later, the matter was still being discussed, but by this time Highways Boards had been superseded as the authorities for the maintenance of public roads by the newly formed Rural District Councils. A letter was read out from the Stockton Rural District Council, saying that they were liaising with the Darlington Rural District Council "with a view to try to come to some arrangement whereby the road can be made opened to all kinds of traffic and put in a proper state of repair". The owners of land adjoining the road were asked to give the land necessary for widening. Negotiations proceeded on this for some time, and it seems that by 1899 a measure of agreement was reached. When the minutes on the matter were discontinued in 1900, pressure was still being applied to get the up-grading works completed.

At this time the way to Long Newton took a different course to that which was eventually established, and which served for most of the twentieth century. As today, the road ran out of the village, past the ironworkers' houses, until taking an abrupt right turn under the railway, before turning sharply again to head towards Yarm. Just beyond this second turn, the way to Long Newton branched off, re-crossing the railway by a level crossing adjacent to the signal box. It then made its way by the still existing route to serve the farms of West Hartburn, Foster House and High Goosepool, before, until very recently, proceeding on to Long Newton.

For pedestrians there was a footpath taking the direct course, and cutting out the diversionary loop over the level crossing. This passed over the ironworks land, and was a cause of dispute. On 18 July 1910 it was recorded "that this Council having considered an application from the Darlington RDC for the consent of this Council to the stopping up of the public right of way leading from Fighting Cocks to Middleton One Row through the Linthorpe-Dinsdale Smelting Co's Works over the Fighting Cocks loop line to the Long Newton Road do hereby assent to the said proposal". Despite this agreement with the parish council, it would appear that relations between the Ironworks and the RDC were not so good, and five years later a dispute, bordering on legal action, was still continuing between them.

Further along the road to Yarm, the road took a severe double turn under the Goosepool railway bridge. As early as 1911, the emergence of motor transport was causing concern on this account. On 17 July "the Clerk was asked to communicate with the RDC Surveyor with respect to the dangerous character of the road at this point owing to the abrupt turn and ask him to have motor cautions erected and Mr J. Scott the representative of the parish on the RDC was instructed to bring the matter up before that council with a view to getting the corner eased by inducing the Rly. Co. to set back their fence a little". (The turn under the bridge still exists, and continued to be a danger until construction of the recent by-pass.)

The main road out of the village, connecting it to Darlington, also had serious shortcomings, even before the motor age. Amongst those affected were the emerging class of people with businesses in the town, who chose to live in the country. One such was Robert Luck, a member of the first Middleton St. George parish council, who took up the cause with the RDC, and followed up with a letter read to the parish council on 20 June 1898. "In consequence of a letter I wrote to the R.D.C., calling their attention to the very steep gradients on the banks at Morton Palms, a committee has been appointed to inspect & bring forward suggestions for their improvement. The steepness of the hills entail very great suffering & distress on draught horses particularly; and, passing over the roads, as I do, almost daily, I have witnessed many painful scenes, especially in winter weather. I am convinced if the road were improved we should not only enable our farmers & others to carry heavier loads to and from the town & thereby decrease the expense of carriage, but we should also get more residents in our neighbourhood, & thereby increase the rateable value, & so decrease our exceedingly high rates. I hope your council will take this matter up, & arrange to meet this committee. The date is not yet fixed, but it will probably be one day next week, & as soon as it is settled I shall be glad to advise you of it." Despite these representations, it would appear that nothing was done to alleviate the situation until the road was eventually re-routed in the inter-war years.

The road immediately fronted by the houses of Middleton One Row also came in for criticism at a meeting on 18 July 1897, but this was not a public highway, and hence the residents were responsible for its maintenance. Only four were prepared to pay and the repair project was abandoned.

Church Lane, leading from the west end of Middleton One Row and connecting with the old Roman road running down to the river, was also a private road, with a gate where it met the public highway beside St. Laurence's Church. In 1896 consideration was given to raising a rate to pay for repairs to the lane, but this does not seem to have happened, and the first moves were made towards take-over of the road by the Rural District Council, which did indeed happen not long afterwards.

A complaint to the Stockton Rural District Council was registered on 1 March 1897 about the poor state of the road from Low Middleton to Trafford Hill. This brought a rapid response, as a month later it was reported that the repairs were nearly completed.

The fact that most people travelled around on foot meant that footpaths and their maintenance were important and a frequent subject for parish council debate. Responsibility for their upkeep was often disputed.

Railway commuting was becoming more common, especially with the re-siting of the station, and access to it was therefore important. On 20 January 1896 the clerk was instructed to communicate with the Highways Board to ask them to repair the well-used footpath from Middleton One Row to Dinsdale Station.

The footpath through Middleton One Row itself was also in need of attention. The Highways Board agreed to do what was necessary within their area of responsibility, but some property owners were not so co-operative, and the executors of Squire Cocks disclaimed any liability. The parish council itself undertook to repair the badly deteriorated footpath at the east end of the village at a cost not exceeding 12s.

There was at this time no footpath alongside the road from Goosepool to Killinghall, and it was recorded that "in the winter months and during wet weather a footpath would be a great acquisition". Negotiations resulted in the Darlington RDC agreeing to supply and install the drainage, providing the local community did the rest of the work. On 18 April 1898 the parish council was able to report that the footpath from Goosepool to Killinghall was almost completed, and to pass a vote of thanks to the committee who supervised the work, to contributors towards the cost, and to farmers for their kind assistance in carting all the materials free of charge.

The ancient route between West Hartburn and Low Middleton via Oak Tree was another footpath requiring and receiving attention. This is the path that passed by the old church of St. George. Access to the church was also obtainable from the Low Middleton road, but it would appear that this was not without its difficulties. On 18 January 1897 it was reported that "foot passengers especially ladies were much inconvenienced in getting over some railings between the Low Middleton road and the field leading to Low Middleton church". Mr. C. H. Robinson, the owner of the land, was asked to provide a hand gate to facilitate access.

The River Tees was both parish and county boundary at the south of the parish. It was however no great barrier to communication, and there were fords at both extreme ends of the parish boundary. That on the west was at or near the site of the old Pounteys Bridge, and the eastern one was at Low Middleton. In the second half of the nineteenth century, children from the farms on the Yorkshire side came over the river to school at Middleton One Row, and presumably continued to do so after the school was established in Chapel Row. Ford usage was inherently inconvenient and uncertain, being subject to river conditions. To overcome this, a ferry plied between Low Middleton and Low Moor on the Yorkshire side. (Pl.29)

Some time before 1912 the ferry had ceased to operate, and this was a source of complaint at the parish council meeting on15 January 1912. " Mr. J. Scott mentioned the fact that the Public Ferry Boat which used to ply across the Tees at this point and has done so from time immemorial was no longer provided and he proposed that the clerk be instructed to write to the Rural District Council and ask them to ascertain whose duty it was to provide a boat and especially to find out whether the onus was on any adjoining landowner to maintain a boat at this point as otherwise the road and footpaths leading to it on both sides of the river are useless and to draw attention to the fact that the ancient cottage on the Over Dinsdale estate known as the "Boathouse" has recently been rebuilt and converted into an ordinary cottage also to point out the importance of this question having regard to the fact that there is no public bridge over the River Tees between Yarm and Croft and this ancient ferry is situate about midway between these places".

At a subsequent meeting on 15 April it was recorded that enquiries from old inhabitants on both sides of the river had confirmed the antiquity of the ferry service, and it was decided to continue to press for its re-establishment. Sights were, however, set higher than this, and the parish council agreed to send a resolution to Durham County Council, supporting the Darlington RDC in a proposal for a bridge over the Tees on the line of the old Roman road, where a bridge had previously existed. Neither the ferry nor the bridge obtained the necessary support for action to be taken. Any need for schoolchildren to cross the river was obviated when a school was built near Girsby.

Gas lighting had been installed in the parish in the latter part of the nineteenth century, with gas supplied from the gas works at Fighting Cocks, owned by a company set up in 1871. In 1893 there were said to be 32 public lamps in the parish. Supply arrangements were regulated under contract between inspectors appointed under the Lighting and Watching Act and the Middleton and Dinsdale Gas Company. In 1896 the parish council took over the powers, duties and liabilities previously vested in the inspectors.

In answer to complaints about the state of some of the lamps, the gas company responded that repairs and servicing were normally done after the close of the lighting season, but they undertook to attend immediately to broken lamps.

A new contract for a year was entered into between the parish council and the gas company. The terms are interesting:

1. The company to supply gas to all lamps - not less than 14 candlepower each burner, consuming not less than 5 cu. ft. of gas per hour.

2. Lamps to be lit at dusk and extinguished at 10pm (Saturday 10.30pm). Lamps not to be lighted two days before and two days after the full moon.

3. The company to clean and repair as necessary

4. Lighting Period 1st September 1897 to 31st March 1898

5. Charge for season £44

It can be seen that the duration when lamps were illuminated was severely curtailed to when it was considered to be really necessary. For five months in the spring and summer (April to August) there was no lighting. The parish council asked that the lighting period be extended for a fortnight at each end, and agreed to pay an extra £4.10s. for this.

The contract was renewed on an annual basis, and the charge went up to £50 when it was agreed to provide a light in Chapel Street, which had previously been entirely unlit.

A letter from the Middleton and Dinsdale Gas Company dated 20 October 1900 dealt with complaints about lighting between Chapel Street and Fighting Cocks, and made a counter complaint of vandalism. Their representative wrote, "I have made enquiries and find that no irregularity has occurred on the part of our workmen. The lamps have been lighted regularly but we have to complain that frequently the village lads have mischievously put them out on various occasions. Our Works Manager has complained to the Police both about this and about damage which has been done to the lamps and I hope will not leave any further cause of complaint".

Sewage drainage was provided in the parish, with filter beds before discharge into the river, but most houses then, and for a long time afterwards, had only earth closets and ash pits, which required manual emptying by the householders.

Even these primitive facilities were not universally available. On 20 April 1896 the clerk drew the attention of the North Eastern Railway Company "to the fact that the signalmen employed at the cabin at the railway crossing between the highway to Yarm and West Hartburn were not provided with privy, earth closet, or any convenience, a great nuisance being created thereby and to ask the railway company if they will kindly supply the necessary accommodation".

On 1 March 1895 attention was drawn to the bad state of the drains at Middleton One Row, and later in the year plans for improved sewage disposal were discussed. In October a letter was sent to the RDC about the offensive smells from the sewers in the parish.

On 15 February 1896 the parish council met a committee of the RDC at the sewage garden. "The committee considered the effluent most satisfactory, but with a view of removing all possible grounds of objection by the County Council, they decided to cut several new trenches to spread the sewage over a larger surface of land than it is at present." It was agreed that this should be done. The sewage farm was also a market garden, and the tenant, Mr. Parlour, claimed that he would lose up to £100 on account of the extended sewage beds. He eventually accepted £10 in compensation.

A complaint about drain smells near the Friary was registered on 19 July 1897 by the occupant, Mr. W. P. Barnard. "Also the disagreeable smell arising from ash pits in connection with various houses in the parish on account of the ash pits not being regularly cleaned out causing them to be very unsanitary and injurious to health especially those connected with Belle Vue Terrace near Dinsdale Station and also others at Middleton One Row." Arising from this, the RDC served notices on persons in default. However, further complaints continued, and at the beginning of 1898 the clerk was instructed to write to the RDC to point out that it was " a difficult thing for persons in this parish to comply with the Sanitary Inspector's notices to clean out their ash pits owing to the lack of any public deposit and to request that the RDC will organize some system of scavenging in the parish".

The appointment of a scavenger was discussed at a subsequent meeting. The Local Government Board advised that the RDC could accept responsibility for cleansing of privies and ash pits, or could delegate to the parish council. The latter course was adopted, and the parish council initiated enquiries as to how other parishes coped with the scavenging problem.

The RDC sanitary inspector, Mr. Croad, advised the system adopted at Cockerton, quoting him as follows. "The appointment of a man as scavenger, who will clean out all the ash pits and make arrangements with some farmer to lead and take the refuse, for every load received the farmer will give a receipt, and the scavenger will be remunerated by the District Council at the rate of 6d. per load, as vouched by the farmer's receipts. Mr. Croad states that the scavenger would have no difficulty in arranging with some farmer or farmers to take the refuse and that in Cockerton the farmers give 4d. per load for it, so that the scavenger is really getting 10d. per load for his labour."

The scavenging post was advertised in local newspapers, and several tenders were received. Thomas Blair was selected as the first contractor for the work, and his tender of £14 per annum was accepted. He undertook the responsibility of checking when clearing needed to be done "so that no nuisance occurs due to accumulation of refuse or rubbish". If the council required, he had to clean as requested within 48 hours of their notice to do so. All refuse had to be disposed of "so as not to be a danger to health". A poster was then displayed to advertise the scavenging service, with the request that those wishing to make use of it should send a postcard to Mr. Blair. Authority was granted by the Local Government Board for the cost of the service to be considered a special charge on the parish.

When Thomas Blair's contract was renewed the following year, his charge went up to £20, on the grounds that "the manure is nearly all pots, tins etc. and it has cost me more than this last year getting out than what it is worth". John Applegarth was his successor in 1900 at the same charge.

The rateable value of the parish in 1895 was £6769. The poor rate was a substantial call on the parish, being charged for 1894 at 2s.1d. in the pound. A sanitary rate of, 10d. in the pound was levied on domestic and other properties, with a reduced rate of $2^{1/2}$ d. for land. The lighting rate amounted to 3d. in the pound, reduced to 1d. on land. Valuation for rates was initially made by the overseers, but was subject to approval by a county rating committee. The ironworks continued to be a major contributor to the rates. In 1895 they complained about their £250 rateable value assessment.

The Darlington Poor Law Union received the money from the poor rate, being the body responsible for care of the poor and for providing the workhouse in Darlington. The local overseers received their salaries from it. In 1895 at Middleton St. George the overseers were John Pybus and William Miller. It was they who had the responsibility of calling the meeting to elect the first parish council. John Campbell, the assistant overseer, had been appointed clerk to the parish council, and on account of this it was requested that his salary be increased to £10 per annum.

The parish council itself was elected annually, until triennial elections were introduced by an act of 1899. The first parish council to take office for a three year term, commencing in 1901, consisted of the following seven members:

> R.Seymour Benson
> William Henry Wilkinson
> Eugene Carter Tompkins
> John William Teasdale
> Joseph Pybus
> William Horseman
> William Miller

Around the turn of the century the ironworks re-opened after a certain amount of reconstruction carried out by the new owners, the Linthorpe Dinsdale Smelting Company. The furnaces were progressively brought back into production over a number of years [17]. The intention was to allow the use of foreign ores, and to yield a product more suitable for the making of steel. This was good news for the parish, and the parish council were well aware of the contribution the company's operations made to the economy of the parish. At the same time, they were exposed to complaints about the danger to health and the environment arising from these operations. This was probably why complaints in 1901 were channelled through the Rural District Council. On 25 March "it was decided to call the attention of the Darlington RDC to the nuisance which is being caused by the discharge of smoke and dirt from the Lancashire Stoves and the Blastfurnaces of the Dinsdale Smelting Company who are now smelting manganiferous iron ore". On 3 June 1901 it was reported that the DRDC had been in touch with the Dinsdale Smelting Company, who "had taken legal opinion and were informed that their operations did not contravene the law, but as the company had expressed their willingness to consider any suggestion the Council might make, a committee had been appointed that day to await upon the Directors of the Company in order to try and bring about some amicable settlement, as although they were anxious to safeguard the interests of the community at the same time the Council did not wish to cripple the Company in the legitimate conduct of their business".

In 1904 it was proposed to embellish the centre of the ironworks village by the installation of a fountain combined with a gas lamp in the middle of the road junction at the Square. The Linthorpe Dinsdale Smelting Company suggested replacing the fountain by a drinking trough, and offered to defray the cost, up to a maximum of £15. This was accepted, and the trough and lamp were erected the next year. (Pl.36)

The question of a recreation ground was first raised in 1895, but no further action was taken at that time, as it was considered that the cost would be too great. However, a little later enquiries were made about the possibility of purchasing some land to the north of Dinsdale Station for a recreation ground for children belonging to the parish. Solicitors, representing the owner, Sir Henry Havelock-Allan, advised that the land, amounting to about a quarter of an acre, could be made available on a 15 year lease at an annual rent of £12.10s. Negotiations again stalled, and it was not until 1907 that an agreement was signed to take the field adjacent to Dinsdale Station as a recreation ground.

On 19 October 1896 it was agreed to ask the executors if some of the money left by the late Squire Cocks could be applied to charitable purposes for the good of the parish. The chairman subsequently saw Mr. Barron. one of the executors, who explained their intentions in that respect. "It was the intention of the Executors to purchase the house and field occupied by and belonging to the Rev. C. Jackson for the purpose of a convalescent home and to endow the same with £300pa. The field would be laid out and used as pleasure grounds also to build six almshouses and to erect a building containing two large rooms which could probably be used for parish purposes."

There was clearly some difficulty in erecting the almshouses where proposed. It was decided to draw up a petition to the executors, making a number of other suggestions, including the endowment of beds at convalescent homes at Redcar and Grange over Sands, and scholarships for boys at Barnard Castle School and Darlington Grammar School. None of these alternatives seem to have been taken up, but the almshouse scheme was pursued. The almshouses were eventually built as the Cocks Memorial Homes in 1903 on the site where they still stand, between the Square and Fighting Cocks.

After the early mushroom growth of Killinghall to meet the needs of the ironworks, expansion still continued, but in a more piecemeal fashion. Houses in Station Road had been built in the 1880s at a cost of about £100 each, and building extension of the Water View end of the row continued up to the end of the century. The rating assessments for 1904 included Mrs. Rhodes' new house at Middleton One Row, Mr. Brown's two new houses in Castle Hill Road, and Mrs. Craig's new house in Middleton Lane. Since the turn of the century the new rectory had also been completed. Middleton One Row continued as a separate village centre, with its shops and post office. One shop also served as a small temperance hotel. The Queen's Head Inn was defunct, being last licensed in 1880.

The Ropner Convalescent Home at the south end of Middleton Lane figured in parish affairs. On 18 July 1898, the parish council complained "that as patients are being brought to the Home in the last stages of consumption it is very detrimental to the health and comfort of the residents in the parish, and to ask if the said committee will kindly see that such cases are not sent in future". The secretary of the Convalescent Home replied that they had instructed their medical officers not to send sufferers from phthisis who were a danger to the health of others and not likely to obtain any permanent benefit themselves. Another complaint was that the residents of the Home were taking up the seats on the village green, which would appear to be a natural thing for them to do as they took the air along the Front. The response of the Convalescent Home was to install three additional seats for the use of their patients.

Around 1900 the former spa hotel, which had subsequently served as a mental hospital, became a school for retarded children.

The concept of a new rectory became an imminent reality when the foundation stone was laid by Thomas Metcalf Barron on 21 June 1902. During the building period, the Rev. Christopher Jackson died and was succeeded by the Rev. Walter Andrews. The new rectory was completed on 19 October 1903, allowing him to move in with his family [18]

Dr. Stanley Steavenson succeeded Dr. Porteous in the medical practice, and also took over residence in Felix House. He kept a herd of pure white goats to provide milk for consumptives, and in 1908 established a sanatorium for sufferers. Wooden chalets were erected in the grounds to provide the fresh air environment recognised as being an essential part of treatment. Dr. Steavenson was always a motoring enthusiast. A seemingly unlikely association with the sanatorium was a motor haulage business, which he set up with a workshop in the grounds. This apparently provided employment for patients [19].

People with long term mental disorders were cared for in a private asylum established in the premises originally built by the Rev. Addison Fountaine, and afterwards successively known as Home Farm, Middleton St. George Farm, and then Middleton Hall. Considerable additions and modifications had been made in 1897 to set up the institution, and the asylum continued to serve in the same capacity throughout the first half of the twentieth century [20].

The railway was the main artery in and out of the village, and between 1896 and 1898 requests were made to the North-Eastern Railway Company to arrange for more trains to stop at Dinsdale Station. In 1905 a suggestion was made to change the name of the station from Dinsdale to Middleton St. George as the existing title was "a confusing misnomer". However, there was no support for the motion, and, despite the confusion, the name has continued to the present day.

In 1895 moves were afoot to improve the postal service, a second daily collection over the whole year being requested, instead of the current arrangement wherein this was operative over the summer season only. A Sunday delivery was also requested. A year later it was agreed that mail would be delivered to West Hartburn and Goosepool on six days a week, instead of the existing arrangement for delivery on only three days a week. This would seem to imply that the Sunday delivery had not been agreed.

Telegraphic connection was also an issue at this time. On 21 October 1895 "the clerk was instructed to ask the Highways Board to kindly effect an early settlement with the Post Office authorities with respect to telegraph poles on the highways as the residents of Middleton One Row are much inconvenienced by the delay in securing telegraph connections, the necessary guarantee for bringing telegraph wires to the village being forthcoming". The connections to the system were eventually made, and a telephone exchange was set up in a house in Salisbury Terrace, which lasted until the system was automated.

Queen Victoria had her Diamond Jubilee in 1897, and on 15 April it was agreed to call a public meeting to decide how it could be best celebrated in the parish. Details of the outcome are lacking, but on the day two ex-Crimean War cannon were fired on the green. These had been brought from where they had stood at Tower Hill, and were at some later date disposed of for scrap. The school recognised the occasion by declaring a holiday on 22 June [21].

The big event at the end of the Edwardian era was the new school, following assumption of responsibility for education by the county council. Although only some forty years old, the Board Schools were already antiquated and unsuitable for the growing population and aspiring educational standards. The new building, opened in 1911, provided modern premises, with much increased accommodation and better facilities, including a domestic science room for the girls. Apart from those who were in a position to have private or higher education, all the education needs of the parish were met by the school from starting at the age of five to leaving at fourteen. More recently, the same building continued in use as a primary school, surviving a destructive fire in 2003, before being replaced by a completely new building in modern style, which was officially opened in 2006.

CHAPTER NINE - THE TWENTIETH CENTURY AFTER 1914

A SKETCH OF THE UNFOLDING SCENE TO THE PRESENT DAY

As in all conflicts, the logistic problem during the Great War was to take away the young men for the front line while at the same time keeping the home front going efficiently to supply the needs of war and everyday living. The generally adopted solution was to bring women into what were traditionally men's jobs. However, at Middleton the ironworks was the major employer, and blast furnace work was hardly suitable for women, although doubtless some peripheral jobs were taken over by them. Perhaps the older men had to take a greater share of the heavy and arduous work. The war effort would require full production from the ironworks, although at the beginning of 1915 it was reported that 60 of their men had enlisted in the forces. About half of these had families or other dependants who were in receipt of half pay from the company.

Concentration on the war effort did not, however, stifle all other considerations. There was an acrimonious dispute at the time on the issue of pollution, and the RDC were threatening legal action against the company. The parish council had previously made their own representations on smoke from the works, but they were clearly at this time extremely anxious not to upset the company, with possible adverse effect on their operations. It was resolved on 25 January 1915 "that the Clerk be instructed to write to the Darlington RDC protesting against the proposed action to be taken against the Linthorpe-Dinsdale Smelting Co. by that Council and to point out that if the action succeeds the result will be disastrous to this parish as it will involve the closing down of the works which pay £300 per week wages, (and) over £600 per annum in rates". Reference was also made to the half-pay benefits to servicemen's families, which would cease. It does not appear that the complaint in this instance originated with the parish council, as it was recorded that "this Council considers it a very high handed proceeding on the part of the Rural D.C. to ignore them in the matter as they consider they had a right to be consulted this being a purely parochial matter". If there had been any local complaint, then the matter had certainly got out of hand [1].

The war effort inevitably halted normal development in the parish, but there were changes associated with the conflict. The original Pemberton House, which had become the Ropner Convalescent Home, was put into service as a Red Cross hospital for the war years and for some time afterwards. The fledgling transport business set up by Dr. Steavenson played its part, and was employed in the carriage of oxygen cylinders. Forty men did not return after the war, having given their lives, as recorded on the war memorial by St Laurence's Church.

The coming of peace allowed the suspended development of the parish to recommence, but problems of ironworks viability were a brake on progress. The position worsened when there was a two month shut-down in 1921 due to the coal strike. The industry was in poor shape, and many pre-war customers were now able to produce their own iron. The increasing use of scrap in steel production was another factor in the reduction in demand for pig iron [2]. An early casualty was Charles Ingram's wagon works, which had been established to maintain ironworks rolling stock, and was closed down around this time.

Yet again the pollution problem raised its head. In 1923 the Ministry of Health received a petition of 15 signatories alleging nuisance caused by the smoke from the works. A special meeting of the parish council was convened to consider the situation. It was observed at the meeting that most of the signatories had come from elsewhere and had only been in the neighbourhood for a few months. One was said to be unknown and three were not householders. Despite the petition being presented to nearly all households, less than 1% had signed. Reference was made to the comparatively good health of the parish, and to the fact that none of the medical establishments had made any complaint.

At the conclusion of the meeting it was resolved "that this Council is of the opinion that no nuisance is caused by the smelting operations of the L-D Co., and would deprecate any action being taken by the Min. of Health, which can only result in the closing of the Works, and the consequent throwing out of employment of 300 workmen, to say nothing of the serious loss to the Par. of the accruing rates; and we are of the opinion that the petrs. wish to close the Works, although they ostensibly make use of the plea of smoke, because they object to working men living so near, as was evidenced a short time ago, when a petition was successful in prevailing upon the RDC of D. to build council houses in a position different from that originally chosen for them".

At the time of this case, the ironworks' wage bill was said to be some £300 per week, with £1600 per annum paid in rates. The men were paid per shift, with average earnings around £1 a week [3].

Production continued in a stuttering fashion for more than a decade after the cessation of hostilities, but the works finally closed down in 1931. This was part of the wider depression afflicting the country, and unemployment was rife in the parish. The ironworks offices were still in use, but only for paying out the "dole" to those out of work. A view and description of the ironworks in their final form can be seen in a recent study by Frank Richardson [4].

Agriculture continued to provide some employment, but for only a small proportion of the population. Farms remained mixed, but with a predominance of grassland. Until the Second World War horses remained the main source of motive power.

There was a post-war demand for new houses, and council houses were planned for Middleton St. George in the early 1920s. From the foregoing comments relating to the alleged smoke nuisance, it is clear that the originally planned site was rejected. The new houses were eventually built around this time and called Thorntree Gardens, as the estate was bought from Thorntree Farm, on the Low Dinsdale side of the parish boundary.

Public works schemes were promoted to help provide employment. One such was the re-routing of the road to Darlington, which had provoked concern before the turn of the century. The horses which had laboured up the severe gradients near to Morton Palms had by this time been partly replaced by motor transport, but the hills still presented a difficulty. John Forbutt ran a motor bus service to the town, and there are memories of his vehicle sometimes having to struggle to surmount the rises. The filling of the depression for the smooth sweep of the new road removed the troublesome gradients.

Another change in the road system was the solution of the long-standing Long Newton road problem. A new length of road was made, branching off the Yarm road just before it passed under the railway bridge, and linking directly with the existing road to Long Newton, cutting out the level crossing by the Oak Tree signal box. The new link road was taken under a bridge carrying the goods line on the course of the old Stockton & Darlington Railway, which had previously been an obstacle.

In respect of public services, gradual improvement of sanitary arrangements was made throughout the period. Nevertheless, a considerable number of earth closets were still in use at the outbreak of the Second World War. By this time the farmed-out scavenging system, which was still operational in the 20s, had been replaced, for those still not on mains sewage, by a motorised clearing service operated by the RDC.

An aftermath of the ironworks was a huge mountain of slag left over from the smelting process. There was a use for this in road-making, and two crushing plants were set up for this purpose. One was operated by the county council, and the other by a company under the name Clokes Extension Ltd.

In 1924 Clokes Extension offered to supply electric light and power to the village. The response to this is not clear, but conversion of houses to electricity proceeded in a piecemeal fashion once a public supply became available some time later.

1925 marked the centenary of the Stockton and Darlington Railway. A great cavalcade of locomotives and rolling stock passed through the parish on the original line, and grandstands were set up in adjacent fields.

Also in 1925 there was a change in the status of the old school building. This was taken over by the Parochial Church Council and became known as the Parochial Hall [5]. Apart from providing for the Sunday School, it was used for dances and other community activities.

The facilities of St. Laurence's Church were improved by the addition in 1926 of a western extension, providing vestry accommodation [6].

A sign of the times was the opening of the Lyric Cinema, situated between Station Road and Water View, in 1936. The owner was Mr. Carter Crowe of Newcastle-upon-Tyne. He converted the premises which had been built in the nineteenth century as Raikes Hall, and which had subsequently been used for a number of community purposes.

One of the personalities spanning the inter-war years was Dr. Steavenson. His sanatorium continued for a number of years, and the haulage business remained a going concern. In his general practice, he was to be seen in his later years doing his calls in his SS Jaguar, which at the time was very impressive [7]. By then, the still growing parish and surrounding area had two general practitioners, Dr. William Meikle having his home and surgery at Brackendale on the opposite side of Middleton Lane.

The coronation of George VI in 1937 was celebrated in the parish, with one recalled source of entertainment at the festivities being a very challenging "greasy pole", which was then a popular feature as such events, despite leaving contestants in a very sticky state after their efforts!

Ownership of an extensive swathe of land within the parish changed hands in 1938. Of the five farms accumulated by the Rev. Addison Fountaine in the first half of the nineteenth century, four of them - Foster House, White House, High Goosepool and Low Goosepool - had remained as one estate. The Middleton St. George Estate, as it was called, comprising most of the ancient West Hartburn and extending to 623 acres, was sold and broken up at this time into its constituent farms [8]. West Hartburn Farm itself, which was a separate entity, was also sold in this period by the Cowan owners, except for a smaller part retained by themselves as the new Highfield Farm.

The one single element of the war having the greatest impact on the parish was undoubtedly the Royal Air Force aerodrome. This transformed a large area of the landscape, and brought about an interface and social intermingling with the local population.

The prospect of war resulted in the start of construction of the airfield in late 1938. The site was in the south-east of the parish, extending right up to St. George's Church, with a continuation into Long Newton parish. Middleton St. George Farm was obliterated by the airfield and the farmhouse and other buildings were demolished. Low Goosepool Farm lost half of its land, and Oak Tree House Farm also gave up a substantial area.

Construction appears to have been beset with problems, including shortage of materials, and continued through 1939 and 1940. The slag heaps left over from the ironworks contributed towards the base material for runways. With mechanisation still comparatively rudimentary, a large labour force was required, which was a boost to local employment. The building works had reached a stage which allowed R.A.F. staffing to commence in the autumn of 1940, with the station officially opening on 15 January 1941. Officially R.A.F. Middleton St. George, the station was more commonly known as Goosepool, after its immediate location.

Apart from the airfield itself, a wireless station was established in a field opposite the council slag works, with a number of high, lattice construction radio masts. Another detached establishment was the "Waffery", built further along the road from the wireless station towards Low Middleton, on land belonging to Oakland Farm. As the name indicates, this accommodated the WAAF contingent of ground staff.

The original aircraft to be based on the aerodrome was the Armstrong Whitworth Whitley, a twin-engined bomber, known as the "flying coffin", not from any vulnerability to disaster but from its fuselage shape. The first plane to land on the new airfield was the inaugural Whitley, which flew in from Dishforth on 9 April 1941.

The Whitleys of 78 Squadron were joined by the four-engined Handley Page Halifaxes of 76 Squadron in June 1941. Together they operated from Goosepool on night bombing raids over Germany and occupied Europe until the Whitleys moved to nearby Croft in October 1941. There they changed over to Halifaxes before returning to Goosepool in June 1942. Shortly before this, at the end of May, both 76 and 78 Squadrons had joined in the first of the "thousand bomber" raids. Both squadrons moved on to Linton-on-Ouse in September 1942.

From this time the Royal Canadian Air Force assumed duties at Goosepool, providing most of the aircrew and ground staff. Their squadrons were responsible for operations from Goosepool for the remainder of the war.

In October 1942, RCAF 420 Squadron arrived at Goosepool, flying twin-engined Wellingtons. These were followed in January 1943 by RCAF 419 Squadron, who came across from Croft with their Halifaxes and commenced operations from Goosepool. They subsequently adopted the name "Moose Squadron" after their first commanding officer, the late John (Moose) Fulton.

By May 1943 Goosepool had lost its Wellingtons, 420 Squadron having been posted abroad. However, within a month they were replaced by more Wellingtons of RCAF 428 Squadron, who were transferred to Goosepool from Dalton, near Thirsk. Soon after their arrival, they were superseded by Halifaxes, as already being flown by 419 Squadron.

At the end of 1943 the first Avro Lancasters arrived at Goosepool for training purposes. They were four-engined bombers, with improved speed and striking capacity. By April 1944 the Lancasters had joined the Halifaxes in operational flights. As the number of Lancasters increased, the remaining Halifaxes were withdrawn. The Lancasters played their part in the intense bombing missions over Germany for the remainder of the war. (Pl.38) Shortly after the cessation of hostilities, the remaining aircraft left for Canada, with great ceremony and sentiment.

The history of Goosepool throughout the war, and indeed beyond, has been recorded by Stanley Howes, with comprehensive operational information. His book is readily available, and repetition of details here would be superfluous. I am grateful to him for the chronology of events, on which I have drawn [9]. In a separate publication, David Brown also provides valuable information on Goosepool [10]. Mr Howes' book reproduces the most evocative photograph of the times, showing ground crew servicing a Lancaster bomber with St. George's Church in the background; a dramatic link over the centuries between the Middle Ages and the war years.

These simple facts do not of course tell of the human drama behind the operations from Goosepool. Many aircraft were lost on sorties, and many of their crews perished. Even on home ground, crashes occurred, particularly when taking off with heavy bomb loads or when limping home after a raid.

The best remembered of many feats of heroism was that of Pilot Officer William McMullen, the Canadian pilot of a stricken Lancaster of 428 Squadron, which had caught fire on a training flight on 13 January 1945 and was endeavouring to return to base. When it became clear that they could not reach the airfield, he ordered the crew to bale out, but stayed at the controls himself to steer the doomed aircraft clear of the town of Darlington. He was killed when the plane crashed near to Lingfield Farm, only a short distance outside the built-up area. When the area was subsequently developed for more housing, Lingfield Road was re-named McMullen Road, and a monument stands there in his memory.

Another notable hero was Pilot Officer Andrew Mynarski, also of the RCAF. He was the mid-upper gunner in a Lancaster of Moose Squadron, when it was attacked and disabled in flames over France on 13 June 1944. His valiant attempts to free the trapped rear gunner resulted in his being badly burned before managing to bale out. He reached the ground alive, but died soon afterwards. For his outstanding bravery he was posthumously awarded the highest honour of the Victoria Cross. At a ceremony in 2005, a monument to him was unveiled at the airport from which he flew some sixty years earlier.

Middleton received a royal visit on 11 August 1944, when King George VI, Queen Elizabeth and Princess Elizabeth, the present queen, came to Goosepool to present decorations to men of both squadrons. The visit was of course secret and hence not publicised. Despite this, most of the population were out to see the royal car cavalcade passing through the village as it made its way from Darlington to Goosepool.

Bombs, armaments and other equipment were delivered by rail to Fighting Cocks goods station, and then by road to the aerodrome. The bombs were transported on low trailers pulled by tractors. In the early days the bombs were relatively small in size, but later, when the blockbusters of 4000lb. and more appeared, there was only one to each trailer.

Bombs were not the only things dropped over enemy territory from Goosepool. Amongst the debris from locally crashed aircraft, could be found bundles of propaganda leaflets, designed to sow the seeds of discontent on the German fatherland by discrediting Hitler and the leadership.

The presence of the aerodrome inevitably had considerable effect on the parish, providing civilian jobs and contributing to the local economy. In addition, the large number of young men, and some women, based there and wanting to get away from their service stresses in an often uncertain existence, led to a significant social impact. The aerodrome did provide for leisure activities, but there was always a desire to seek contacts and entertainment outside.

The Oak Tree Inn, very near to the airfield, was a popular meeting place for conviviality, and the Devonport and the other public houses in the village, the Killinghall Arms, the Havelock Arms and the Fighting Cocks, were also well patronised.

Dancing provided an opportunity for meeting local girls, and the relationships which developed ranged from the usual fleeting friendships to more regular associations, and even to marriage. Local dances in the Parochial Hall were consequently always well attended, and so were the dance halls of Darlington and Stockton.

After an evening "on the town", the revellers often returned on the train from Darlington or Tees-side. The last trains were sometimes illicitly stopped when the communication cord was pulled as the train passed the aerodrome. By the time the guard was able to get along to investigate, all had disappeared into the darkness, leaving only a row of open doors. By this means, the long walk from Dinsdale Station to Goosepool was avoided.

Over Dinsdale Hall was used as accommodation for aircrew. One of their outings from there was to Middleton One Row, only two fields away, but on the opposite side of the river. Stepping stones provided a rather hazardous way across, and much amusement was caused by those attempting to get across dry-shod.

The high casualty rate in bombing operations inherently led to an attitude of living for the day, and not surprisingly there were plenty of incidents and petty infringements of the law. The local police sergeant and constable were frequently in action to deal with the drunk and disorderly, and offences such as riding a bike in the dark without lights.

The Lyric Cinema was in great demand, particularly in the period before the aerodrome got its own cinema. There were three different programmes each week, and every evening there was a "little picture" and the main feature or "big picture", with the "News" in between. Queues were normal, and sometimes the doors had to be closed with disappointed filmgoers still waiting [11].

Not all was hedonistic, however. The undenominational mission hall next to the Lyric received a new lease of life, when evangelical services were organised by Canadian airmen. These were very well attended by people from the village and from Darlington. The children's services and related activities were especially popular.

The army also appeared in the village, but in a very transitory fashion, with squads of soldiers billeted in various premises for short periods. Castle Hill housed an Irish unit at one time, and the skirl of their pipes resounded through the village on their weekly practice parade from Middleton One Row to Fighting Cocks.

The Home Guard was much in evidence on their exercises and parades, with Great War veteran Sergeant Walley in charge. The Air Raid Precautions (ARP) men underwent training to deal with emergencies, and were responsible for ensuring the black-out was observed. Air raid shelters, above and below ground, were constructed everywhere, and the school had to give up most of its garden to that end. The carrying of gas masks, in brown cardboard boxes, by schoolchildren was enforced for a while, but the requirement was then relaxed.

In the early part of the war, the school roll was greatly increased by the arrival of evacuees from Tyneside. The children were given temporary homes with local families. However, this situation did not last long, as the pull of home, or the parents' reluctance to be without their children, proved stronger than the threat of bombing, and most of the evacuees returned home after only a short stay.

The aerodrome might have been expected to have been a target for enemy action, but did not suffer a single attack. Apart from a stray incident of bomb unloading, the biggest risk to the parish was during raids on Tees-side industry, when the sirens sounded, and people went into their shelters until the all-clear.

The war effort was all pervading, as was the home food production campaign. The allotments, which had served to help feed families during the depression, were used to the maximum, as exhorted by the "Dig for Victory" campaign, during the period of rationing in the war years and afterwards. When the season came for tomatoes to be available from Mr. Vardy's greenhouses, behind the corner of Chapel Street, buyers hurried to collect their strictly rationed allowance.

In the war years local services met a large proportion of daily household needs, with anything else bought on shopping trips on the crowded bus to Darlington. The village supported a CWS store and six other general dealers, including one at Middleton One Row. There was also a butcher, a greengrocer, an outfitter and haberdasher, a newsagent and a post office, and there were two shoemaker/cobblers. These were supplemented by mobile grocery, butchery, greengrocery and fish deliveries, and at least two milkmen. Two fish and chip shops were hard pressed to meet the nightly demand. Petrol rationing was a restriction on the relatively few people with cars, but Arthur Mudd managed to provide a taxi service on special occasions with his stately Rolls Royce.

Avoiding waste was a watchword, and re-cycling schemes were set up. To encourage salvage and re-cycling of paper, there was a military style scheme, whereby children were awarded ranks, depending upon the amount of paper brought in to the depot. A small collection would make the donor a corporal, with the award of the appropriate stripes, and a big haul might make him or her a captain, more splendidly embellished to the envy of friends. Needless to say, this was the reason for the disappearance of many once treasured books and magazines, which might otherwise have survived today.

Monetary collections were made for servicemen's causes and for the war effort. Middleton contributed to a motor torpedo boat, but it is not clear now whether the amount raised was sufficient to pay for it completely or just to sponsor it.

With the end of the war, life began to return to a more normal peace-time style. There had, however, been a significant change since the period of recession, which had only ended in the run-up to the conflict. The returning servicemen had higher expectations, and the post-war Labour government had set out their social revolution. Women, drafted into men's jobs in the wartime, were not all prepared to relapse into menial employment, such as domestic service, or to be simply house-bound mothers.

Always of first importance was employment. The ironworks had gone for good, although the blast furnaces still stood as a reminder of what had been. However, the smaller Dinsdale Moor Iron Works of the Richards family at Fighting Cocks, which had flourished in the war years, continued as a major employer. At starting and finishing times, there was a steady stream of bicycles making their way to and from the works. When they closed in 1954, the adjacent scrap works of Arnott and Young were able to expand and fill the void.

Many found their work in Darlington and on Tees-side, helped, in the virtual absence of private cars, by the good transport system of trains and buses. ICI at Billingham, and later at Wilton, provided jobs for many Middleton men. Another source of employment was the aircraft scrap establishment set up at Urlay Nook in the wartime. This was subsequently turned into a Royal Navy supply depot, which required a large influx of workers. Allens West station on the Darlington to Saltburn railway line was built to bring in the workforce. The nearby British Chrome and Chemicals works were another local employer.

The aerodrome also continued to provide civilian jobs after the departure of the Canadian bomber squadrons. Between 1945 and 1947 it served as a Fighter Command base, flying twin-engined Mosquitoes. After that it served another ten years under Flying Training Command, with aircraft including the jet-powered Meteors.

Since the war years, the aerodrome had become more self-contained, and social contacts with the personnel based there were very much less, although a few did live in the village. Many trainees and staff now had at week-ends the opportunity to go home to their families, wherever that might be. This situation changed from 1950, when married quarters began to be built, and a considerable number of service families joined the local population. More married quarters were added in 1955.

In the late forties and the fifties the Parochial Hall flourished as the home of the Middleton St. George Operatic and Dramatic Society. Their productions, including "Our Miss Gibbs", "The Quaker Girl", "The Mikado" and "The Young Mrs. Barrington", always played to full houses. The Lyric Cinema continued to provide entertainment until television and changing life styles resulted in falling attendances and final closure at the end of the fifties. (Pl.37)

The blast furnaces of the ironworks had stood idle since their closure. In 1947 they were demolished, together with the brick lift towers and other ancillary buildings. (Pls.26 & 28) The engine house was allowed to remain, as being a building which could be adapted for other usage.(Pl.23)

Another feature to disappear around this time was the blacksmith's shop at Fighting Cocks, (Pl.33) where Bert Knott had been the last smith. The sharp upsurge of mechanisation on farms had largely eliminated the need for horses. The houses and cottages along the Darlington road beyond the smithy were also demolished.

The need for new housing was met by the building of more council houses as an extension of Thorntree Gardens. The site of the new houses had been used as the first post-war football field for the Middleton St. George football Club, who were district championship winners in successive seasons. When they had to give up their pitch they moved to a new one in a field near Fighting Cocks.

A few years later, the village cricket team was also to lose its pitch off Middleton Lane, which had been used "temporarily" for about 80 years. It had to make way for the building of St. Anne's Gardens, but its loss proved in the long run beneficial both to the cricket club and to the village as a whole. The opportunity was taken to make a completely new pitch on waste ground behind the Cocks Memorial Homes, and at the same time to form the Cricket and Social Club, with its own premises adjoining the pitch. This proved an immediate success, and a bowling green was added later. It continues both as sporting and social facility for the community. The success extended to notable achievements on the field, attested by the team's league championship and cup-winning performances.

Still on the sporting front, the Dinsdale Spa Golf Club left the club house by the river, which they had inherited from the spa, and built modern premises, with improved facilities and better access, on the road to Neasham.

Other developments took place in the area west of The Square. A small field adjacent to the Cocks Memorial Homes was taken for the building of old people's bungalows. Next to these was the "Works Field", which had belonged to the ironworks. This was made into the community playing field, realising a very long standing objective [12]. Across the road, further housing was built where Lamb's Garage had previously stood.

Changes in water supply arrangements resulted first in the construction of a pumping station adjacent to the reservoirs, and finally when this and the reservoirs became no longer necessary, the complete closure of the establishment. This opened the way for its conversion into the Water Park for leisure activities, including fishing and canoeing. The pump house became a new village hall, filling a void which had existed since the Parochial Hall (the old Board School) had been demolished for the building of houses on its site in Chapel Street.

The immediate post-war years saw the last fires to blaze in the waiting rooms of Dinsdale Station. Thereafter economies took their toll, the number of porters was reduced, and the once-splendid gardens deteriorated from lack of resources to attend to them. Finally, in the Beeching era, the whole station arrangement was changed. The ticket office and associated premises, which stood beside the road and spanned the rail tracks, were demolished, as were the waiting rooms on the platforms. The station became unmanned with a minimum of facilities. The old station at Fighting Cocks, which had continued as a goods depot, finally closed on 9 March 1964 [13].

The rail sidings which had served the ironworks were taken over as part of a British Rail facility for the production of long lengths of welded rails for track renewal. Another usage was as the last parking place for steam locomotives, due to be scrapped and replaced by diesel power. (Pl.39) There was pathos in the fact that this stretch of line, which had seen the momentous passage of the pioneering "Locomotion" in 1825, also took part in the final demise of the steam locomotive about a century and a half later.

The school also changed, with the legislation which transformed the pattern of education. Secondary education for all led eventually to the village school being devoted entirely to young children, with secondary education being provided at a purpose-made school at Hurworth-on-Tees.

There was no halt to the expansion of the village. After a public inquiry in 1962 [14], the building of St. Anne's Gardens had bridged most of the remaining gap between Middleton St. George and Middleton One Row. Substantial developments off Church Lane contributed towards meeting the ever-increasing housing demand. When they were no longer required, the gas works were demolished, and the site was used for many years by Stiller, a large and successful haulage company. When they left, this was also taken over for more housing. The population increase was not accompanied by any expansion of village shopping services, which suffered a slow decline as mobility increased and the attractions of urban supermarkets increasingly prevailed.

Goosepool aerodrome changed from Flying Training Command to Fighter Command in 1956, progressing through Meteors and Vampires to Hunters and finally the much more advanced Javelins and Lightnings. It also assumed a separate function as a base for the V-bombers, principally Vulcans, strategically important in the Cold War period. They had their own dispersal area and facilities, including ground crew quarters, constructed at one side of the airfield. By 1964, however, defence requirements had changed, and the aerodrome closed in that year, bringing to an end its service as an RAF airfield.

The departure of the RAF allowed the acquisition of the airfield by a consortium of local authorities, who established a management structure and had the necessary work carried out for conversion to a civil airport. Flights to Heathrow commenced by the end of 1964, but the venture was not a commercial success. Autair operated scheduled flights to Luton from the beginning of 1967, but the travelling time into London was a big disadvantage of the arrangement, and a return was eventually made to Heathrow. From 1969 British Midland Airways became responsible for developing the service, and for the opening of other routes. Dan Air also played a part by providing flights to Amsterdam, which linked with many continental and worldwide destinations.

Within the new airport, many of the RAF buildings were surplus to requirements and put to other uses. The headquarters and administration block became from 1968 to 1977 a College of Education, and an airfield fire training school was established in adjacent buildings. The previous officers' mess has become the well-established St. George's Hotel.. A number of accommodation blocks were developed into Trees Park, a residential home for the elderly. This has more recently become St. George's Hospital, providing psychiatric care.

Middleton Hall, in the shadow of the airport, changed its function in the opposite direction. Having in the 50s lost its long-established role as a mental hospital, it became a care and nursing home. The subsequent introduction of retirement apartments began its extensive development as Middleton Hall Retirement Village.

The end of the millennium saw the closing down of Durham Tube, the successor of Arnott & Young and the earlier iron and steel firms at Fighting Cocks, ending the long tradition of metal manufacturing in the area, with the loss of another provider of employment in the village. It did however allow re-development of the area for further housing.

For a long time the idea of a by-pass for the village had been considered. This eventually became a reality when the road between Darlington and Yarm was taken on a completely new line around the northern end of the village, removing the disturbance of the ever-increasing through traffic. The new road afforded much improved access to the airport, and also eliminated the dangerous turn under the Goosepool railway bridge, which had long been a cause for concern. At the same time the opportunity was taken to provide a new direct link from the main road to Long Newton, cutting out the previous way via West Hartburn, which became a dead-end farm access only.

The re-shaping of the road system came at the end of an eventful twentieth century, with the local scene constantly changing to adapt to national and global pressures and the unprecedented technological advances of the century. There is no sign of any lessening of the rate of change or any diminution of developments affecting the face of the village and parish.

POSTSCRIPT - INTO A NEW MILLENNIUM

With the entry into a new millennium, the last structure belonging to the ironworks finally disappeared. The engine house had stood for over seventy years after the closure of the works, as a reminder of the enterprise which had created the village in the nineteenth century. Now, this too could not survive the march of progress. When Hadley's engineering business came to an end, the old building became redundant, and was eventually demolished in 2004 to make way for more new housing.[1] (Pls.23,24,26)

The fact that employment in the immediate locality of the village is perhaps lower than it has ever been does not mean that there has been any reduction in the size of the community. On the contrary, the village continues to grow and flourish. Globalisation of business, unrestrained use of private cars, good public transport including a fast rail link to London, the airport on the doorstep, and not least the IT revolution, have all combined towards a situation where working practices are increasingly flexible and the need to live close to one's workplace has become less important.

In these conditions, what prospect is there for the community today? It is often said that an established population finds it hard to integrate with newcomers, and that incomers have little sense of identity. This is not necessarily so, and historically it has not been the case at Middleton. Looking at the facts, the agricultural population in the eighteenth century showed considerable mobility, and in 1851 almost 70% of the population had been born outside the parish. When the ironworks arrived there was a large influx of workers and their families from all directions. The wide diversity of origins has not prevented the existence of a strong sense of community in the past, and there is no reason why it should do so in the challenging conditions of today.

Interest in the history of the parish and the area is one sign of identification and community spirit. Some residents have comparatively recently produced privately work based on their own studies, and a local history group has been formed to stimulate interest and to provide a vehicle for research by members.[2] There is ample scope for this.

It will probably be obvious that much of the information in the last chapter comes from my own personal memories. The scope for deeper study of this period in particular is great, and one very worthwhile task for the local history group is the recording of people, places and events while they can still be recalled. The author hopes that this book will be an incentive towards that end.

REFERENCES

(See Bibliography for fuller details of sources)

ABBREVIATIONS

DCRO	Durham County Record Office.
DUL	Durham University Library Special Collections.
PRO	National Archives (Public Record Office).
Surtees	The History and Antiquities of the County Palatine of Durham, Vol.3, unless noted otherwise.
Sur. Soc	Surtees Society
VCH	Victoria County History, Durham, Vol.3, unless noted otherwise.

Where references are repetitive, after the first full reference a shortened form is used, e.g. "Sharp" to signify "Sharp, Sir Cuthbert. Memorials of the Rebellion of the Earls of Northumberland and Westmoreland".

CHAPTER ONE - EARLY HISTORY

1. Proceedings of the Society of Antiquaries of Newcastle-upon-Tyne, 1924, 198-9.
2. Whellan, History, Topography and Directory of Durham, 702.
3. Cramp & Lang, A Century of Anglo-Saxon Sculpture, 3.
4. Selkirk, The Piercebridge Formula.
5. The Anglo-Saxon Chronicle (Everyman Edition), 53.
6. Domesday Book (Penguin Edition), 787, 792, 802, 811-813, 855, 874, 875.
7. Proceedings of the Society of Antiquaries of Newcastle-upon-Tyne, 1889/90, 131.
8. Green, Anglo-Saxon Sundials, 489.
9. VCH, Vol.1, 240.
10. Haigh, Yorkshire Dials, pl.11, facing p.141.

CHAPTER TWO - THE MIDDLE AGES

1. Red Book of the Exchequer, Rolls Ser. vol.1, 440.
2. VCH, 294.
3. Red Book of the Exchequer, Rolls Ser. vol.1, 442.
4. Surtees, Vol.1, cxxvii.
5. VCH, 295.

6 Roberts, Dunsford and Harris, Framing Medieval Landscapes: Region and Place in County Durham, 232.

7 Roberts, Rural Settlement in Britain, 104.

8 Larson, Local Law Courts in Late Medieval Durham, 97 et seq.

9 VCH, 295.

10 VCH, 295.

11 VCH, 295.

12 Longstaffe, The Tenures of Middleton St. George and some Account of the House of Killinghall, 74.

13 Longstaffe, The History and Antiquities of the Parish of Darlington, Pedigree of Allan.

14 Longstaffe, The Tenures of Middleton St. George, 75, 77.

15 Surtees, 221.

16 Hutchinson, The History & Antiquities of the County Palatine of Durham, vol.1, 386.

17 Surtees, 221.

18 Sur.Soc., Bishop Langley's Register, vol. IV, 142,143.

19 VCH, 296.

20 VCH, 296-7.

21 VCH 297.

22 Still & Pallister, The Excavation of One House Site in the Deserted Village of West Hartburn, 187-206.

23 Still & Pallister, West Hartburn 1965 Site C, 139-148.

24 Pallister & Wrathmell, The Deserted Village of West Hartburn, Third Report : Excavation of Site D and Discussion.

25. Natrass, Witch Posts and Early Dwellings in Cleveland.

26 Glenn, Romanesque and Gothic Decorative Metalwork and Ivory Carvings in the Museum of Scotland, 44-46.

27 Surtees, 226.

28 VCH, 296.

29 VCH, 297.

30 VCH, 298.

31 VCH, 298.

32 VCH, 298.

33 VCH, 297 (note).

34 Sur.Soc. North Country Wills, 168.

35 VCH III, 297.

36 VCH, 298.

37 VCH, Vol.1, 355.

38 Surtees, 225 (note).

39 Surtees, 239.

40 VCH, Vol.1, 357-8.

41 VCH, 217-219.

42 Surtees, 225.

43 VCH, 297.

44 Surtees, 226.

45 VCH III, 295.

46 VCH, 299.

47 VCH, 298.

48 VCH, 298 (note).

49 I am indebted to Mrs Janet Gettings, who pointed out this feature to me, as shown in her unpublished 1994 dissertation on the Medieval History of Middleton St. George.

50 Longstaffe, The Tenures of Middleton St. George, 86.

51 Ryder, The Medieval Cross Grave Slab Cover, 106 and pl.46.

52 Proceedings of the Society of Antiquaries of Newcastle-upon-Tyne, 3rd ser. IV, 1910.

53 VCH, 299.

54 Sur.Soc., Fasti Dunelmensis, A Record of the Beniliced Clergy of the Diocese of Durham down to the Dissolution of the Monasteries and Collegiate Churches, 177

55 Longstaffe, The Tenures of Middleton St. George, 77, 78.

56 Sur.Soc., Registers of Tunstall and Pilkington, nos.11 & 12.

57 DCRO EP/Mi.SG, London Gazette abstract noting order of the Charity Commissioners made 27th February 1900.

58 Valor Ecclesiasticus (Record Commissioners), v, 317.

59 Sur.Soc., Historiae Dunelmenensis Scriptores Tres, cccv.

60   Surtees, 228, 229. All the following references to the bridge are also from Surtees in the same place.

61   Longstaffe, The History and Antiquities of the Parish of Darlington, 351 (note).

62   McNamee, The Wars of the Bruces, 86 & 88.

63   VCH, 299.

64   Sur.Soc. Historiae Dunelmensis Scriptores Tres, clxxxvi.

65   VCH, Vol.2, 211.

CHAPTER THREE - THE SIXTEENTH CENTURY

1   VCH, 296, 297.

2   Surtees, 222.

3   Sur.Soc., North Country Wills II, 114.

4   VCH, 296., Surtees, 222.

5   Longstaffe, The Tenures of Middleton St. George, 82.

6   DCRO, Turton Papers, Pt. A, No.1.

7   Sur.Soc., Wills and Inventories, 133.

8   Longstaffe, The Tenures of Middleton St. George, 86.

9   VCH, 296.

10   VCH, 298.

11   VCH, 297, 298.

12   VCH, 219.

13   Surtees, 225 (note).

14   Longstaffe, The History and Antiquities of the Parish of Darlington, 113.

15   PRO, S.P. 12/51.

16   Sharp, Sir Cuthbert. Memorials of the Rebellion of the Earls of Northumberland and Westmoreland, 258-60.

17   PRO, S.P. 15/17.

18   Sharp, Memorials of the Rebellion, 159, 160.

19   Sharp, 140-142.

20   Sharp, 144-145.

21	Sharp, 130.
22	Sharp, 135
23	Black, The Reign of Elizabeth (The Oxford History of England), 112.
24	Longstaffe, The History and Antiquities of the Parish of Darlington, 110.
25	Reid, The Durham Crown Lordships in the Sixteenth and Seventeenth Centuries and the Aftermath.
26	Surtees, 230 (note).
27	PRO, Durham Orders in Chancery, 1632, no.122.
28	DUL, Inventory of William Mitchell.

CHAPTER FOUR - THE SEVENTEENTH CENTURY

1	DUL, Inventory of Marmaduke Andrew, 1611.
2	VCH, 296.
3	DUL, Inventory of William Allonson, 1619.
4	DUL, Will and inventory of Lawrence Langley, 1610.
5	DUL, Inventory of Agnes Hutchinson, 1606.
6	DUL, Inventory of Dorothy Pinkney, 1610.
7, 8	A True Certificate of all the Recusants within the Archdiocese of York.
9	Northern book of Compositions 1629-32.
10	Longstaffe, The History and Antiquities of the Parish of Darlington, 132-3.
11	Longstaffe, The Tenures of Middleton St. George, 94, 95.
12	Sur.Soc., Durham Protestations, 174.
13	Sur.Soc., Durham Protestations, 91.
14	Sur.Soc., Records of the Committees for Compounding, 260. (Following entries from this source abbreviated to "Compounding".)
15	Compounding, 61, 260.
16	Compounding, 260.
17, 18	Longstaffe, The Tenures of Middleton St George, 95.
19, 20	Compounding, 227.

21, 22	Compounding, 226.
23	Compounding, 7
24	Compounding, 14, 15.
25	Compounding, 19, 20.
26	Compounding, 35.
27	Compounding, 39.
28	Compounding, 65-68.
29	Compounding, xxxii, xxxiii.
30	Compounding, 106, 107.
31	Compounding, 311.
32	Compounding, 72, 73.
33	DUL, Mickleton & Spearman Papers, MS2, pt.2, fol.258 (dorso)
34	DCRO, Parish Register of Middleton St. George.
35	<u>VCH</u>, 295.
36	PRO, Hearth Tax Returns 1666.
37	Pallister, <u>Burial in Wool</u>.
38	Longstaffe, <u>The Tenures of Middleton St. George</u>, 97.
39	Longstaffe, <u>The Tenures of Middleton St. George</u>, 93.
40	DCRO, Middleton St. George parish register.
41	DCRO, Middleton St. George parish register.
42	Longstaffe, <u>The History and Antiquities of the Parish of Darlington</u>, 113.
43	DUL, Inventory of William Killinghall 1644 (filed under 1649).
44	DUL, Inventory of John Killinghall 1651.

CHAPTER FIVE - THE EIGHTEENTH CENTURY

1, 2   VCH, 296.

3   Plan of Red Hall Farm 1726 - Havelock Allan papers.

4   1759 Land tax assessment.

5   Sur.Soc., Newcastle Hostmen's Company, 291.

6   North Yorkshire County Record Office, Barton Estates Survey Book 1757.

7   DCRO, 1789 Land tax assessment.

8   DCRO, 1798 Land tax assessment.

9   Longstaffe, The History and Antiquities of the Parish of Darlington, 368. (Contribution on Agriculture by Henry Chaytor, Esq.)

10   Watson, The Reign of George III (Oxford History of England), 519, 520.

11   Gall, The Durham Ox 1796-1807, "Agricultural Super Star", (Durham Biographies, Vol.3.)

12   Walker, Dinsdale and Croft (5th ed.), 2.

13   Parish register of St. Swithin, Bath.

13   Darlington parish register.

14   Middleton St. George parish register.

15   Robinson, Middleton St. George and the Mid-Tees Valley. Mr Robinson, who had some opportunity to study the building, is firmly of the opinion that some of the earlier structure still survives.

16   Robinson, Middleton St. George and the Mid-Tees Valley. Insurance details were traced by Mr Robinson through the Guardian Royal Insurance fire mark.

17   For a full view of the community, the parish registers of both Middleton St. George and Dinsdale are relevant.

18   Grigg, Population Growth and Agrarian Change, 99.

19   1830 Charity Commission Report on the Charities of Middleton St. George.

20   Northern Despatch, 21 April c.1960, From Today's Local Anniversaries. The original provenance has not been traced.

21   Pallister, The Dinsdale Spa.

22   Peacock, Observations upon the Composition and Uses of the Water, at the New Sulphur Baths, at Dinsdale.

23   Walker, Dinsdale and Croft (5th ed.), 104 et seq.

CHAPTER SIX - THE FIRST HALF OF THE NINETEENTH CENTURY

1   VCH, 296.

2   DCRO, 1806 Land Tax Assessment.

3   DCRO, 1814, 1821 and 1826 Land Tax Assessments.

4   Longstaffe, The History and Antiquities of the Parish of Darlington, 257.

5   Parish Register of St. Peter, Leeds.

6   Monumental inscription in St. George's Church.

7   Surtees, 225.

8   The baptisms of all the children except William are recorded in the Middleton St. George parish register.

9   Diary of the Reverend William Addison Fountaine.

10   Longstaffe, The History and Antiquities of the Parish of Darlington, lvii.

11   Longstaffe, The History and Antiquities of the Parish of Darlington, 342-7.

12   Jeans, History of the Stockton and Darlington Railway, 42. The rector's name was included in the act which received the royal assent on 19th April 1821.

13   Parish register of St Swithin, Bath

14   Parish register of St. Saviour, Bath.

15   VCH, 298.

16   Notes by the Reverend John Groves.

17   Tithe map for Middleton St. George.

18   Pallister, The Dinsdale Spa.

19   Peacock, 7, 8.

20   Walker, An Analysis of the Waters of Dinsdale and Croft (numerous editions).

21   Sur.Soc., A Memoir of Robert Surtees.

22   Walker, An Analysis of the Waters of Dinsdale and Croft (3rd ed.).

23   Walker, An Analysis of the Waters of Dinsdale and Croft (2nd ed.), 20.

24   Mackenzie & Ross, Vol.2, 79.

25   Head, A Home Tour through the Manufacturing Districts of England in the Summer of 1835, 309.

26   Granville, Spas of England and Principal Sea-Bathing Places, Vol.1, The North, 216.

27   The Stockton and Darlington Railway has been well researched, and railway historians will be familiar with the primary sources. The main threads are usefully collated in the Northern Echo Railway Centenary Supplement of 1925, and this has provided much of the information used in the writing of this chapter.

28   Head, A Home Tour through the Manufacturing Districts of England in the Summer of 1835, 309.

29   Granville, Spas of England and Principal Sea-Bathing Places, vol.1, The North, 216.

30   Parson & White, History, Directory, and Gazeteer, 1827.

31   Pigot & Co's New Commercial Directory 1828-9.

32   Slater's Royal National Commercial Directory 1848.

33   1851 Census for Middleton St. George.

34   A Report on the Southern Estate Farms (Long Newton) 1854.

35   Longstaffe, The History and Antiquities of the Parish of Darlington, 368. (Contribution on Agriculture by Henry Chaytor, Esq.)

36   1830 Charity Commission Report on the Charities of Middleton St. George.

CHAPTER SEVEN - METAMORPHOSIS 1860 - 1870

1   Hempstead, Cleveland Iron and Steel, Background and 19th Century History, 131,132.

2   Griffiths' Guide to the Iron Trades of Great Britain (1873), 6.

3   Griffiths' Guide to the Iron Trades of Great Britain (1873), 260.

4   Edwards, Chronology of the Development of the Iron and Steel Industries of Tees Side, 92. (Other commentators say that the number of furnaces had risen to four as early as 1874.)

5   1861 Census for Middleton St. George..

6   1871 Census for Middleton St. George.

7   Darlington and Stockton Times, 2 May 1863.

8   Middleton St. George Parish Magazine, 1 May 1871.

9   Richardson, Industrial Village to a Dormitory in 150 Years, 23.

10   Information kindly provided verbally and in notes by Mr J.F. Prentice.

11 Darlington and Stockton Times, "Seven -Foot Plea comes to Light at Darlington", 21 May 1960.

12 Northern Echo, Article by Chris Lloyd "Quarrelsome Irish and the fight for souls", 3 Dec.2003.

13 Ashworth, <u>An Economic History of England 1870-1939</u>, 53.

14 Court, <u>A Concise Economic History of Britain</u>, 200 et seq.

15 Hagar and Co's Directory of the County of Durham (1851), 262.

16 Middleton St. George Parish Magazine, May 1871-Jan.1874, from which the following details relating to completion of the church and other matters are also taken.

17 Deed Poll conveying land, 28 December 1871.

CHAPTER EIGHT - FROM THE NINETEENTH CENTURY INTO THE TWENTIETH 1880 - 1914

1 1881 Census for Middleton St. George and Dinsdale.

2 Backing up the particulars from the 1881 census, an undated map from around this period shows thirteen houses built, with further plots marked for others.

3 Hitchcock, <u>The History of Barnard Castle School - 1883-1933</u>, 9-16.

4 Edwards, <u>Chronology of the Development of the Iron and Steel Industries of Tees-Side.</u>

5 Notes by the Reverend John Groves.

6 Diocesan Faculty 13 August 1888 (Ep Mi.SG 48).

7 Notes by the Reverend John Groves.

8 Boyle, <u>Guide to Durham</u>, 662.

9 Notes by the Reverend John Groves.

10 Middleton St. George School Minute Book, 6 Nov.1884-3 Jan.1891.

11 Minutes of Middleton St. George School Board, 1884-91 provide most of the information for this account of the school dispute.

12 PRO E.D. 2/145, 1890. Education Department Memorandum.

13 North Star, 21 August 1890.

14 North Star, 5 May 1891.

15 Note to Parents and Ratepayers of the Middleton St. George School Board District. (1891)

16 DCRO, Middleton St. George Parish Council Minutes, which are the source of most of the following information.

17 Hay, The Middleton Ironworks, 1864-1947.

18 Notes by the Reverend John Groves.

19 Northern Echo, article by Chris Lloyd, "TB sanatorium with a real Alpine pedigree", 31 December 2003.

20 Walford, Middleton Hall - A Rough History.

21 Minutes of Middleton St. George School Board 1891-1904.

CHAPTER NINE - THE TWENTIETH CENTURY AFTER 1914

1 DCRO, Middleton St. George Parish Council Minutes. The PC minutes are also the source of much of the quoted information for the first two decades of the period.

2 Stuart, The Cleveland Iron Industry, 46.

3 Ovens, The Parish of Middleton St. George in the 19th and Early 20th Centuries. His account of the ironworks includes details of working practices and rates of pay as recalled by a retired ironworker.

4 Richardson, Industrial Village to a Dormitory in 150 Years, 29-32.

5 Transfer of old school buildings (Ep/Mi.SG 49).

6 Diocesan Faculty 3 April 1926 (Ep/Mi.SG 48).

7 Memories of Dr. Steavenson in "More escapades of an eccentric doctor" by Chris Lloyd in the Northern Echo, 7 January 2004.

8 Sale (20 June 1938) papers in possession of Mr. G.W. Pattison of Foster House.

9 Howes, Goosepool, The History of RAF and RCAF Middleton St. George and Teesside Airport.

10 Brown, Aerodromes in North Yorkshire and Wartime Memories.

11 For reminiscences of the cinema, see "Spotlight falls on faded film glory of the Lyric", by Chris Lloyd in the Northern Echo 16 April 2003.

12 Richardson, Industrial Village to a Dormitory in 150 Years, 49-58.

13 Holmes, The Stockton and Darlington Railway 1825-1975, 93.

14 Reported in the Northern Echo, 14 April 1962.

Many of the events noted in this chapter do not have documentary references, as they are directly from the author's own memories and the recollections of others.

POSTSCRIPT - INTO A NEW MILLENNIUM

1. Wheeler, The Middleton Ironworks: Survey of the Blowing Engine House. (carried out at the time of demolition.)

2. A very recent contribution by the Middleton St. George Local History Group is their DVD "Middleton St. George, Documents from the Past", produced in 2006.

BIBLIOGRAPHY

MANUSCRIPT PRIMARY SOURCES

Durham Probate Records held by Durham University Library, Special Collections

1576 Inventory of William Mitchell (DPR I /1 /1576 /M-)
1583 Will of Rowland Johnson (DPR I /1 /1585 / J-)
1606 Will and inventory of Agnes Hutchinson (DPR I /1 / 1606 / H10)
1610 Will and inventory of Lawrence Langley (DPR I / 1611 / L2)
1610 Inventory of Dorothy Pinkney (DPR I / 1 / 1610 / P1)
1611 Inventory of Marmaduke Andrew (DPR I / 1 / 1611 / A6)
1619 Inventory of William Allanson (DPR I / 1 / 1619 / A3)
1644 Inventory of William Killinghall (DPR I /1 / 1649 / K1) Filed under 1649
1651 Inventory of John Killinghall (DPR I / 1 / 1651 / K1)

Other documents held by Durham University Library, Special Collections

1837 Tithe commutation map and schedule for the township of Middleton St. George
       Tithe commutation map and schedule for the township of Long Newton

1523 Deed of sale of sale of one third of the manor of Middleton St. George by Thomas Cambe to Elizabeth Killinghall (Turton Papers, Pt. A, No.1)

1618 Mickleton & Spearman Papers, MS2, pt.2. A view taken of the comon and private armies of this ward (Stockton) before Sr. Georg Conyers & Sr. Rauffe Conyers knights deputye lieutenants for the said ward the seconde of October 1618.

Parish registers held by the Durham County Record Office

Darlington
Dinsdale
Middleton St. George

Other parish registers

Parish register of St. Peter's, Leeds
Parish register of St. Swithin's, Bath
Parish register of St. Saviour's, Bath

Durham Quarter Sessions records held by Durham County Record Office

Land tax assessment 1759 (Q/D/L 94)
Land tax assessment 1789 (Q/D/L 97)
Land tax assessment 1798 (Q/D/L 100)
Land tax assessment 1806 (Q/D/L 102)
Land tax assessment 1814 (Q/D/L 106)

Land tax assessment 1821 (Q/D/L 108)

Land tax assessment 1826 (Q/D/L 112)

Other documents held by Durham County Record Office

1854	Report on the Southern Estate Farms (Long Newton) by Mr. A. Graham, up to 1st. October 1854. Londonderry Papers (D / LO E 513(1) 1854)
1871	Deed Poll 28 Dec.1871, by W. A. Wooler, conveying land in Chapel Street for school
1884-1891	Middleton St. George School Board Minute Book (E/SB 222)
1891-1904	Middleton St. George School Board Minute Book (E/SB 223)
1887	Records of Interest. Rev. John Groves, Rector, containing notes of appointment of incumbents, alterations to the church, etc 1883-1904. Volume inscribed "Presented by W. A. Wooler, Middleton St. George" (EP/ Mi. SG 14)
1888	Diocesan Faculty (13 Aug.) for repairs to church (EP/Mi. SG 55)
1891	Note to Parents and Ratepayers of the Middleton St. George School Board District
1894 onwards	Middleton St. George parish council minutes
1925	Agreement for transfer of old school building to parish council (EP/Mi. SG 49)
1926	Diocesan Faculty for building of vestry at St Laurence's Church (EP/Mi. SG 56)

Estate records in North Yorkshire County Record Office

1726	Plan of Red Hall Farm - Havelock Allan Papers
1757	Barton Estates Survey Book (including Middleton St. George farms) - Havelock Allan Papers

Census returns and enumerators' sheets for Middleton St. George and (Low) Dinsdale

1841, 1851, 1861, 1871, 1881, 1891, 1901

Documents held in National Archives (Public Record Office)

1569	Muster Roll for the Stockton Ward of County Durham (SP 12/51)
1570	Letter (11 Jan.) from Queen Elizabeth to the Earl of Sussex, complaining about tardy retribution (SP/15/17)
1632	Complaint of enclosure at Middleton-One-Row. Durham Orders in Chancery, No.122
1666	Hearth Tax returns for County Durham (E179/106/28)
1890	Education Department Memorandum (ED 2/145)

No longer extant

1821-3	Diary of the Rev. William Addison Fountaine. The quoted extracts from the diary are taken from an article entitled "A Durham Parson Woodforde" printed in the Church Times of 29 December 1961. The article was written by H. T. Kirby, who had the great fortune to find the diary in a second-hand bookshop. He submitted it to a foremost publishing house, who lost and presumably inadvertently destroyed it! We must be grateful to Mr Kirby and the Church Times for what has survived.

PRINTED DOCUMENTARY SOURCES

A True Certificate of all the Recusants within the Archdiocese of York. Cecil Papers 228/1. Printed in Catholic Record Society, Vol.53

Bishop Langley's Register - The Register of Thomas Langley Bishop of Durham 1406-1437, Vol. 4 (Surtees Soc., Vol.170, 1955)

Charity Commission Report on the Charities of Middleton St. George, 1830.

Charity Commission Report on the Charities of Middleton St. George, HMSO, 1900 (DCRO EP Mi. SG 48), reciting the 1830 Report.

Domesday Book, Penguin Classics Edition 2003

Durham Protestations - Durham Protestations or the Returns made to the House of Commons 1641/2 for the Maintenance of the Protestant Religion for the County Palatine of Durham, for the Borough of Berwick-upon-Tweed, and the Parish of Morpeth (Surtees Soc, Vol.135, 1922)

Education Department Memorandum 1890 (PRO E.D.2/145)

Fasti Dunelmensis - A Record of the Beneficed Clergy of the Diocese of Durham down to the Dissolution of the Monasteries and Collegiate Churches (Surtees Soc., Vol.139, 1926)

Historiae Dunelmensis Scriptores Tres - Gaufridus de Coldingham, Robertus de Graystanes, et Willielmus de Chambre (Surtees Soc., Vol.IX, 1839)

London Gazette. Abstract noting Order of the Charity Commissioners made 27 February 1900 (DCRO EP/Mi. SG)

Newcastle Hostmen's Company - Extracts from the Records of the Company of Hostmen of Newcastle-upon-Tyne (Surtees Soc., Vol.105, 1901)

North Country Wills - North Country Wills being abstracts of wills relating to the counties of York, Nottingham, Northumberland, Cumberland, and Westmoreland, at Somerset House and Lambeth Palace 1383-1558 (Surtees Soc., Vol.116, 1908)

North Country Wills II - North Country Wills 1558-1604 vol. II (Surtees Soc.,Vol.121, 1912 I)

Northern Book of Compositions 1629-32 Printed in Catholic Record Society, Vol.53

Records of the Committees for Compounding, etc, with Delinquent Royalists in Durham and Northumberland during the Civil War, etc 1643-1660 (Surtees Soc., Vol.111, 1905)

Red Book of the Exchequer. Printed in Rolls Ser.

Registers of Tunstall and Pilkington - The Registers of Cuthbert Tunstall Bishop of Durham 1530-9 and James Pilkington Bishop of Durham 1561-76 (Surtees Soc., Vol. 161, 1946)

School Inquiry Commission, Vol. xix, Northern Division, 1869

The Anglo-Saxon Chronicle, trans. G. N. Garmonsway. Dent Everyman Library, 1953

Valor Ecclesiasticus (Record Commissioners, V)

Wills and Inventories illustrative of the History, Manners, Language, Statistics, &c of the Northern Counties of England from the Eleventh Century downwards, Part 1 (Surtees Soc., Vol.2, 1835)

PRINTED BOOKS

Ashworth, William	An Economic History of England 1870-1939 (London 1960)
Black, J.B.	The Reign of Elizabeth (Oxford History of England) (1936)
Boyle, J.R.	Guide to Durham (London 1892)
Brown, David	Aerodromes in North Yorkshire and Wartime Memories (Stockton on Tees 1996)
Court, W.H.B.	A Concise Economic History of Britain from 1750 to Recent Times (Cambridge 1954)
Cramp, R. J. and Lang, J. T.	A Century of Anglo-Saxon Sculpture (Newcastle upon Tyne 1997)
Edwards, K. H. R.	Chronology of the Iron and Steel Industries of Tees-Side (1958)
Glenn, Virginia	Romanesque & Gothic Decorative Metalwork and Ivory Carvings in the Museum of Scotland (2003)
Granville, A. B.	Spas of England and Principal Sea-Bathing Places, Vol.1, The North (1841, re-published Bath 1971)
Griffiths	Griffiths' Guide to the Iron Trade of Great Britain (1873)
Grigg, D.B.	Population Growth and Agrarian Change (Cambridge 1980)
Hagar	Hagar and Co's Directory of the County of Durham (Nottingham 1851)
Head, Sir George	A Home Tour through the Manufacturing Districts of England in the Summer of 1835 (1836, re-published London 1968)
Hempstead, C.A. (ed)	Cleveland Iron and Steel - Background and 19th. Century History
Hitchcock, R.C.	The History of Barnard Castle School, 1883-1933 (West Hartlepool, 1935)
Holmes, P.J.	The Stockton and Darlington Railway 1825-1975 (Ayr 1975)
Howes, Stanley D.	Goosepool - The History of RAF and RCAF Middleton St. George and Teesside Airport (Darlington 2003)
Hutchinson William	The History & Antiquities of the County Palatine of Durham (1823)
Jeans, J. S.	History of the Stockton and Darlington Railway (1875, republished Newcastle upon Tyne 1975)
Liddy, C. D. and Britnell, R. H. (eds.)	North-East England in the Later Middle Ages. (Regions and Regionalism in History Series) (Woodbridge 2005)
Longstaffe, W. H. D.	The History and Antiquities of the Parish of Darlington (Darlington, London and Newcastle 1854)

Mackenzie, E. and Ross, M.	An Historical, Topographical, and Descriptive View of the County Palatine of Durham (1834)
McNamee, Colm	The Wars of the Bruces (East Linton 1997)
Parson & White	History, Directory, and Gazeteer, of the Counties of Durham and Northumberland, and the Towns and Counties of Newcastle-upon-Tyne and Berwick upon Tweed,etc.,by Wm. Parson & Wm. White 1827
Peacock, John	Observations upon the Composition and Uses of the Water, at the New Sulphur Baths, at Dinsdale near Darlington, in the County of Durham (1805, second edition with additions 1829)
Pigot	Pigot Co's New Commercial Directory, for the Counties of Cumberland, Durham, Northumberland, West Moreland, and Yorkshire for 1828-9
Reid, D. S.	The Durham Crown Lordships in the Sixteenth and Seventeenth Centuries and the Aftermath (Durham County Local History Society) (1990)
Richardson, Frank	Industrial Village to a Dormitory in 150 Years. Middleton St. George.and Surrounding Area. (Privately published, Bedale (2003)
Roberts, B. K.	Rural Settlement in Britain (1977, 1979 London)
Ryder, P. F.	The Medieval Cross Grave Slab Cover (Architectural and Archaeological Society of Durham and Northumberland) (1985)
Selkirk, Raymond	The Piercebridge Formula (Cambridge 1983)
Sharp, Sir Cuthbert	Memorials of the Rebellion of the Earls of Northumberland and Westmoreland (London 1840. Re-published Durham 1975)
Slater	Slater's (Late Pigot & Co) National Commercial Directory and Topography of the Counties of Chester, Cumberland, Durham, Lancaster, Northumberland, Westmoreland, and York, etc.,1848)
Surtees, Robert 1823	The History and Antiquities of the County Palatine of Durham (1823)
Surtees Society	A Memoir of Robert Surtees, Esq. M.A., F.S.A., Author of the History of the County Palatine of Durham, Vol.xxv (1852)
Victoria County History	The Victoria History of the County of Durham (1905, 1908)
Walker, Thomas Dixon	An Analysis of the Waters of Dinsdale and Croft, with Practical Observations on their Powers, illustrated by Cases, to which is added remarks on Bathing; intended for the Use of Invalids (Second Edition 1928)
Walker, Thomas Dixon	As above (Third Edition, improved, 1835)
Walker, Thomas Dixon	Dinsdale and Croft, Parts I and II (Fifth Edition 1864)
Watson Stephen	The Reign of King George III 1760-1815. (The Oxford History of England) (1936)
Whellan	History, Topography and Directory of the County Palatine of Durham (1856)

REPORTS AND ARTICLES IN JOURNALS AND OTHER PUBLICATIONS

Gall, John — The Durham Ox 1796-1807 "An agricultural Super Star", <u>Durham Biographies,</u> vol.3, ed. G.R.Batho (Durham County Local History Society) (2003)

Green, A.R. — Anglo-Saxon sundials. <u>Society of Antiquaries Journal</u>, vol.VIII (1928)

Haigh, the Rev. Daniel Henry — Yorkshire Dials. <u>Yorkshire Archaeological Journal</u>, vol.V (1879)

Hay, T.T. — The Middleton Ironworks, 1864-1947. <u>Cleveland Industrial Archaeology Society Newsletter</u> no.72 (1999)

Larson, Peter, L — Local Law Courts in Late Medieval Durham (In Liddy & Britnell - <u>North-East England in the Later Middle Ages</u>, qv)

Longstaffe, W.H.D. — The Tenures of Middleton St. George and some Account of the House of Killinghall. <u>Archaeologia Aeliana</u>, new ser.(ii) (1858)

<u>Middleton St. George Parish Magazine,</u> May 1871-January 1874

Nattrass, Mary — Witch Posts and Early Dwellings in Cleveland. <u>Yorkshire Archaeological Journal</u>, vol.39

Northern Echo — <u>Centenary of the Stockton and Darlington Railway Supplement</u> (1925)

Ovens, David — The Parish of Middleton St. George in the 19th and Early 20th Centuries. <u>Durham County Local History Society</u> Bulletin 21 (1978)

Pallister, A. — Burial in Wool. <u>Durham County Local History Society</u>, Bulletin 9 (1968)

Pallister, A. — The Dinsdale Spa. <u>Durham County Local History Society</u>, Bulletin 14 (1972)

Pallister, A. and Wrathmell, S. — The Deserted Village of West Hartburn, Third Report: Excavation of Site C and Discussion. <u>Architectural and Archaeological Society of Durham and Northumberland</u>, Research Report No.2, Medieval Rural Settlement in North-East England (1990)

PSAN — Note of Visit. <u>Proceedings of the Society of Antiquaries of Newcastle-upon-Tyne</u>, vol.4 (1889/90)

PSAN — Note of Visit. <u>Proceedings of the Society of Antiquaries of Newcastle-upon-Tyne</u>, 3rd ser.IV (1910)

PSAN — Note of Roman lamps from Middleton St. George. <u>Proceedings of the Society of Antiquaries of Newcastle-upon-Tyne</u>, 4th ser., vol.1 (1924)

Roberts, B. Dunsford, H. & Harris, S. — Framing Medieval Landscapes: Region and Place in County Durham (In Liddy and Britnell - <u>North-East England in the Later Middle Ages</u>, qv)

Still, L. and Pallister, A.1964   The Excavation of One House Site in the Deserted Village of West Hartburn, County Durham. <u>Archaelogia Aeliana</u>, 4th ser., Vol.XLII (1964)

Still, L. and Pallister, A.1967   West Hartburn 1965 Site C. <u>Archaelogia Aeliana</u>, 4th ser., Vol.XLV (1967)

Wheeler, J.S.   The Middleton Ironworks: Survey of the Blowing Engine House. <u>The Cleveland Industrial Archaeologist</u>, no.29 (2004) (Memoirs of the Cleveland Industrial Archaeology Society)

NEWSPAPERS

Contemporary reports and local history articles and items, as noted in references

North Star

Northern Echo

Northern Despatch

Darlington and Stockton Times

UNPUBLISHED SECONDARY SOURCES

Gettings, Janet   The Medieval History of Middleton St. George (Dissertation for BA Archaeology/History, University of Durham, 1994)

Robinson, Leslie   Middleton St.George & the Mid-Tees Valley (Privately desktop printed) (Copy in Darlington Public Library)

Stuart, Alberta D.   The Cleveland Iron Industry (1936) (Copy in Middlesbrough Public Library)

Walford, Jeremy   Middleton Hall - A Rough History (Photocopy notes - at Hall)

Women's Institute   Village History (late 1950s) (Copy in possession of author)

INDEX OF NAMES AND PLACES

Where personal names appear in a variety of spellings, they have been gathered together and listed under the most recognisable common form.

	Page		Page
Adamson, Thomas	115, 127	Ascough (Askew), Alan	68
Addison, Joseph	111	James	66-68, 70, 71
William	110	Family	70, 77
Addison Fountaine, David	110	Ashby, Thomas	38
Dorothy	110	Atkinson, G.D.	147, 149
Joseph	110	Auclet, William de	46
Lucy	110		
Mary	110	Baard, Godfrey	25, 32
Rosamund	110	Ralph	32, 38, 42, 44
William	110	Roland	32
Rev. William	109-113, 115, 117, 121, 123, 125, 130, 139, 161, 165	William	46
		Backhouse, Edward	149
Aerodrome, Airport	165-171	Bales, James	66
Addy, John	61	Balliol, John de	38
Aislaby	22, 79	Family	25, 40
Alande, Robert	54	Balmer, Watson	82, 83, 109
Allan, George	84	Bamlett, Robert	143, 145
Jane	84	Family	79
Allen, James	87	Band, John	70
Margaret	87	Bank, Thomas	51, 63
William	87	Bankes, Robert	54
Allonson, Christopher	66, 69	Barnard, William	21, 138, 158
Isobel	69	Barnard Castle School	147, 160
John	70	Barron, Thomas Metcalf	160
William	63	Batmeson, Ralph	66
Almora Hall	141, 142, 147, 149, 151	Bath,	110, 112
Andell, George	66	Baxter, Thomas	126
Anderson	111	Bell, George	138
Andrew, Henry	66	John	82, 83
John	55	Bellanby, Cuthbert	66
Marmaduke	54, 61-63	Belle Vue Terrace	168
Andrews, Rev. Walter	160	Benson, R. Seymour	153, 154, 159
Anniser	21	Bergen, Axel von	137
Appleby, John	54	Berwick	51
Applegarth, John	159	Bewick, William	111
Arnott & Young	167, 169, 171	Black Path	21
Arthur, Ralph	55	Blackett, Christopher	149

Blacklock, Robert	55	George	82, 109
Blackwell Grange	84	Jane	86
Blair, Thomas	158, 159	John	138, 144
Blakiston, Edmund	52	R.	144
Blast furnaces	133 et seq.	Thomas	86, 109
Blenkinsopp, Miles	54	T.	144
Blenkiron, William	126	Chapel Row, Street	134, 142, 147, 148, 156, 157, 168, 170
Bolton, Robert	46		
Bonsall, W.	143	Chapman, Elizabeth	140
Booth, Felix	147	John George	153
Bosher, B.	144	Charles I	65
Bowes, Sir George	55	Chaytor, Nicholas	65
Brackendale	165	Chipchase, John	66
Bradfute, Rev. James	88	Christelow, John	87
John	88	Mary	82
Marion	88	Thomas	87
Bradley, William	137	Family	86
Braskewe, Thomas	54	Church House Farm	68, 79, 82, 85, 88, 113, 115
Brasse, Richard	66		
Brewster, Matthew	126	Church Lane	147, 156, 170
Brito, Nicholas	46	Cirisy, Peter de	46
Brown, Betteres	63	Clarke, George	115, 129, 130
David	166	Clavering, Sir Thomas	82, 109, 113, 115
Leonard	70	Clementson, Rev. William	111, 112
Mr.	160	Clifton (Bristol)	111
Bruce, John	82, 83	Clokes Extension	164
Family	25	Coates, Mr.	125
Bryndelawes, William	47	Cochrane, Messrs.	145
Burn, Matthew	113	Cockerton Hall	109
Burton, John	82, 83, 139	Cocks, Elisha	110
		Elizabeth	109
Cacheside, Ralph	55	Henry A.W.	113, 115, 117, 133, 134, 138, 139, 145, 148, 151 153, 154, 156, 160
Cambe, John de	34, 44		
Robert de	32, 38		
Walter de	34, 47	Sally	109
William	53	Cocks Memorial Homes	160, 169, 170
Thomas	51	Coke, Thomas	113, 115
Family	39, 51, 52	College of Education	171
Campbell, J.	144, 153, 159	Colling, Charles	83
Carter, Ann	129	Richard	63
William	113	Robert	63, 83
Mrs.	142	Colpitts, Joseph	113
Casse, Rev. William	57, 63, 66	Colvin, Miss	142
Castle Hill	153, 168	Consclyffe, John	47
Cecil, William	56	Conyers, Christopher	46
Chambers, Ann	115	Sir John	38

Sir Ralph	68	Devonport Inn, Hotel	109, 130, 137, 138, 154, 167
Conyers Darcy, Sir	70		
Copeman, Christopher	66	Dinsdale, church	47, 71, 87, 88, 110
Ronald	66	manor,	25, 27, 29, 52
Cottage Farm	115, 129	manor house	40
Cottam, John	54	parish	17, 39, 40, 56, 57, 87, 88, 115, 117, 127, 129, 139, 147
Council School	161, 168, 170		
Cowan family	165		
Cowper, Rev. Charles	111	Dinsdale, Low	22, 48, 49, 118, 164
Cox, H.	143	Dinsdale, Over	22, 157
Craig, Mrs.	160	Dinsdale Asylum	138
Cricket Club	144, 169, 170	Dinsdale Moor House	113, 115, 129
Croad, Mr.	158	Dinsdale Moor Ironworks	147, 169
Croft-on-Tees	21, 22, 48, 89, 121, 166	Dinsdale Spa	88, 89, 109, 120-2, 126, 127, 148, 149, 160
Crouch, Gilbert	68		
Crowe, Carter	163	Dinsdale Spa Golf Club,	149, 170
Cully, Ann	69	Dinsdale Spa Hotel	120, 121, 127, 138, 160
Mary	69	Dinsdale Spa Improvement Co.	138
Thomas	66, 69	Dinsdale Station	148, 153, 156, 160, 161, 167, 170
Cummings, George	86		
Thomas	86	Dinsdale Steel & Wire Works	147
Cunningham, James	58	Dinsdale, Thomas,	139
John	54	Dishforth	166
Thomas	71	Ditchburn, Elizabeth	126
Curry	110	Dixon, John	121
		Dobbin(g), Anthony	127, 145
Dale, Anthony	66, 70	John	125, 139, 147
Elizabeth	69	Dodgson, James	137
James	66, 69	Donking, John	129
John	70	Downs, Thomas	82
William	66, 69	Family	109
Dalton-on-Tees	21	Dowson, W.	144
Dalton (near Thirsk)	166	Dryden, Catherine	129
Darling, Michael	129, 130	John	109
Darlington	17, 32, 51, 55, 65, 86, 111, 121, 123, 125, 126, 127, 166-9	Jonathan	82, 115
		Duncan, Davies	70
Davison, Thomas	87	Dunn, John	55
Dawson, Richard	129	Dowson, W.	144
Thomas	66	Durham	29, 36, 47, 48, 49
Dent, R.A.	144	Durham, Lord	120, 121
William	140	Durham, Earl of	121
W.	144	Durham Tube Ltd	171

East Middleton Farm	87	Foster, Francis	71
Eastwood, Dr. Joseph	136	Fountaine, Mary	110
Eden, Capt	67	Fowler, Jonathan	111
Edward I	48, 49	Freare, Christopher	66
Edward III	42	Margaret	70
Eeles, John	113	William	71
Thomas	115	Friary, The	21, 147, 158
Egglescliffe	27, 88		
Eglestone, j	143	Gaines, John,	51, 61
Elgy, Robert	115	Gargrave, Thomas	56
Elizabeth I	54, 55, 69	Garrett, Thomas	127
Elizabeth, late Queen Mother	167	Garth, John	109
Elizabeth, Princess	167	Mrs.	109
Elliott, R	144	Gascoyne, Ninian	82, 87
Ellis, Capt. Robert	67	Edward	82
Thomas	126, 127	Family	109
Elstob, James	66	Gasworks	139, 157, 170
Emmonson, George	70	Gates, Robert	71
Errington, Colonel	67	Gell, John	140
Eryholme	22	George VI	165
Ewbank, Christopher	64	Gibson, Christopher	66
Isobel	64	Gilesgate Moor, Durham	49
		Gill, M.	144
Fawcett, Jane	64	Gingerbread House	88
Fawell, H.	144	Girlington, Ninian	51
J.	144	Girsby	22, 157
Felix House	147, 160	Gladdis S.	143
Felton, Anthony	39, 52	Glanville, F.	109
Field House	113, 115, 117	Goosepool	17, 33, 38, 39, 52, 67, 112, 121, 125-8, 140, 147, 155, 156, 161
Fighting Cocks	87, 121, 123, 125-7, 134, 139, 140, 142 147, 148, 157, 169, 171	Goosepool, Low	115, 123, 125, 129, 140
Fighting Cocks Inn	21, 123, 125, 139, 167	High	115, 129, 130, 140, 155,
Fighting Cocks Station	141, 143, 148, 149, 167, 170	Gosforth	25
Fishburn, William	137	Gowland, John	66
Fordham, Bishop	32	Graham, Ann	138
Forster Field Farm,	82, 87, 88, 109, 110,	Patience	138
Foster House Farm	113, 115, 117, 121	Grange, The	51, 61
	125, 129, 141, 155, 165	Granville, Dr. A.B.	121, 126
Forsyth, Thomas	127	Great Stainton	67
Fortune, Anthony	126	Greaveson, John	66
John	129	Groves, Rev. John	151

Hadley, C.N.	171	Hothwaite, John de	46
Haigh, Charles	137	Howes, Stanley	166
Hall, Christopher	66, 67	Huddart, Thomas	90
Thomas	67	Hugh, rector	46
Hanson, Ann	115	Hull, Isobel	86
Nicholas	126, 127	Thomas	87
Harrison, Francis	54	Hunter, William	115, 127
James	127	Hurworth-on-Tees	170
Robert	82, 83, 109	Husband, John	169
William	66	Hutchinson, Agnes	64
W.	153	Richard	64
Hartburn, East	34	Robert	64
Hartburn Tavern	123, 129, 130, 140	Thomas	64, 66
Hartburn, West	see West Hartburn	Hygebald, Bishop	22
Haughton-le-Skerne	60, 66, 88		
Harland, Ann	113	**I**anson, Thomas	87
Havelock-Allan, Sir Henry	160	Ibbotson, Carr	109
Havelock Arms	140, 149, 167	Ingleby Barwick	21
Head, Sir George	120, 126	Ingledew, James	126, 127
Heighington, Richard	51, 52	Ingram, Charles	163
Henry II	25	Isley, John	137
Henry VIII	46, 54	Iton, Richard	66
Henderson, Robert	113		
Herdewyk, Thomas de	46	**J**ackson, Christopher	87, 115, 124
Hick, Stephen	66	Rev. Christopher	147, 148, 151-3, 160
High House	127	C.	144
High Scroggs Farm	113, 115, 129	Harriet	127
Highfield Farm	165	Family	86
Hilton, Colonel	67	James, Matthew	126
Robert	71	James II	77
Hinde, T.M.	154	Jameson, Matthew	115
Hoar, George, Sen.	82	Ralph	54
Jun.	82	John, rector	42
William	82	Johnson, Cuthbert	51, 57
Family	85, 109	John	66, 69
Hodgkin, J.	134	Rowland	51, 61
Hodgson, William	149	William	127, 138
Hodson, George	67		
Home Farm	113, 115, 130, 161	**K**ay, Francis	79
Hope, T.	143	William	79
Horseman, Elizabeth	139	Ketton	83
William	149, 151-3, 159	Killinghall, Anne	65, 72
Horsely, Marmaduke,	70	Elizabeth	46, 52, 72, 79
Owen	66	Francis	38, 51, 52, 64, 66, 71, 72

Killinghall, Henry	52, 54-6, 63, 65, 72	Long Newton	17, 25, 34, 38, 55, 57, 62, 63, 67, 70, 130, 140, 145, 154, 155, 163, 164
Hugh	32, 51		
Isobel	65		
Jane	84, 113		
John	32, 38, 42, 44, 46, 52, 57, 58, 65, 66, 67, 69 70, 72, 73-77, 79, 84 87, 88	Low Middleton, manor	25 et seq., 51, 56, 57, 64, 68
		manor house	30, 84
		Low Middleton Farm	30, 82, 87, 113, 115, 117
		Low Middleton Ferry	154
Margaret	67, 72, 79	Low Middleton Hall	30, 84, 138, 141
Robert	46, 51, 79, 84	Low Moor Bottom	88, 156
Thomas	32	Luck, Robert A., JP	153, 155
William	38, 51, 52, 65-8, 70, 72, 73, 77, 79	Lynas, W	144
Family	32, 39, 46, 51, 52, 56, 65, 73, 77, 79, 120	Lyric Cinema	165, 167, 169
Ironworks village	134, 147, 148, 156, 160	Mackay, George	140
		Mackintosh, Dr. Ronald	138
Killinghall Arms	140, 167	Maddock, Richard	51, 52
Killinghall Row	134, 137	Mainchforth, Katherin	67
Kirkburn	24	Maltby	22
Kitchin, William	139, 152, 153	Margeris, John	127
Knott, Bert	169	Marley, Robert	66, 70
		Thomas	66
Lambton, William Henry	88, 120	Martin, Robert	66, 71
Lamb's Garage	170	Mary Queen of Scots	54
Lamson, Rowlly	55	Mary Tudor	54
Langley, Cardinal, Bishop	32	Masterman, Mr.	82, 83
Langley, Lawrence	63, 65	Maud, Mr.	113
Margaret	63	Mawer, Richard	62
Lawson, Henry	65	Robert	66
Layfield, William	54	McMullen, Pilot Officer William	166
Lesley, General	65	Meikle, Dr. William	165
Lickley, Thomas	66, 69, 70	Merrington, William de	46
Lingfield Farm	166	Metcalfe, J.	144
Linthorpe Dinsdale Smelting Co.	155, 159, 161, 163	Matthew	138
Linton-on-Ouse	166	Methodist/Wesleyan chapels	140, 142
Lodge, William	66	Mewburn, Francis	112
London, William de	44, 46	Meynill, John de	38
Londonderry Estate	130		

Middlesbrough	133, 135, 137	William	129
Middleton, Ann	82	Moorie, Francis	66
Cuthbert	70	Morton	59, 60
Ely	82, 83, 109	Morton Field	57
George	79, 87	Morton Palms	155, 164
John de	46	Motte	21, 39, 47
Michael	82, 83, 88	Mueller, Charles E.	138
Thomas	66	Mudd, Arthur	168
Family	86, 87, 88	Myres, George	55
Middleton & Dinsdale Gas Company	157	Mynarski, Pilot Officer Andrew	166
Middleton Hall	44, 110, 137, 161, 171	Naismith, Cuthbert	55
Middleton Hall Retirement Village	171	Naseby, Margaret	86
		National School	142, 145, 149-152
Middleton Ironworks	133-137 et seq., 159, 163, 164, 169, 173	Nether Middleton	See Low Middleton
		New Row	134, 147
Middleton Lane	140, 141, 147, 148, 160 165	Newcastle	65
		New Hall	51, 61, 63
Middleton Moor	57	Newton Francis	66, 70
Middleton One Row	References throughout	Noble, Rev. William	88
early manor	See Over Middleton	North Eastern Railway Co.	143, 149, 158, 161
Middleton One Row East Farm	79, 113, 115	Norton	21, 64
Middleton One Row Farm	115, 129, 117, 137		
Middleton One Row West Farm	115, 129, 153	Oakland Farm	165
Middleton St. George	References throughout	Oak Tree	87, 123, 125, 126-8, 130, 156, 164
manor	See Lower Middleton		
Middleton St. George Estate	165	brewery	140
Middleton St. George Farm	68, 82, 113, 115, 129, 130, 137, 161, 163	Oak Tree Farm	82, 115, 140
		Oak Tree House Farm	61, 79, 113, 115, 117, 129, 140, 165
Mill House	87		
Miller, William	148, 159	Oak Tree Inn	123, 126, 127, 130, 137, 167
Milner, T.	143		
Mission Hall	168	Ogden, Michael	138, 145
Mitchell, William	58, 60-2	Old Byland	24
Moore, Jane	140	Old Row	134, 147
Margaret	138	Oliver, Ralph	111
Robert	126, 127	William	82, 83, 109
R.	144	Family	109
Thomas	127	miller	110

Orpyn, James	46, 52	Potts and Robson	115
Over Dinsdale Hall	167	Pounteys Bridge (Pons Teys)	21, 39, 47, 48
Over Middleton, manor	25 et seq., 51, 52, 54-6	chapel	47
Overton, George	121, 123	Pounteys Lane	21
		Preacher, William	83
Pallister, Robert	139	Pringle, R.	144
Thomas	128	Pritchett, J.B.	141
Palmer, William	126, 127	Pudsey, Michael	67, 68
Palm Tree House Farm	21, 79, 87, 113, 115, 129, 133, 139, 140, 151	Puiset, Hugh, Bishop	17, 25, 32
		Pyburn (Pybron), Elizabeth	129
Parlour, Mr.	158	John	113
Parochial Hall	165, 167, 169, 170	Pybus, Joseph	159
Parrott, John	54		
Parkinson, Anne	52	**Q**ueen's Head Inn	127, 130, 137, 138, 160
Parsons, Dr. Thomas	138, 144		
Pattison, Robert	84, 85	**R**aikes Hall	165
farrier	110	Raine, Christopher	66
Paul Hartburn	52, 67	William	139, 144
Paul, Ralph	52	Rattray, Lucy	110
Peacock, Dr. John	89, 111, 118, 120	Raynarte, Richard	54
Pease, Edward	112, 121, 123	Reading Room	143, 148
Pemberton House	147, 151, 163	Recreation Ground	159, 170
Pemberton Terrace	134, 137, 147	Red House, The, (Red Hall)	51, 61, 63, 70, 79
Pemberton, William	79, 82, 88-90, 109	Redcar,	143
Winifred	90	Readman, Francis	66
Family	79, 86, 88, 120	Redmayne, Robert	46
Peverall, Mary	112	Renny, Edward	66
Pickersgill & Longstaffe	126	Rhodes, Mrs.	160
Piercebridge	21, 22	Richard I	25
Pinchard, John	88	Richard II	32
Mary	87	Richards, family	169
Family	86	Richardson, Bartholomew	66
Pincher, Jane	126	Christopher	82, 113, 115
Pinkney, Dorothy	64	Frank	164
Margaret	70	Margaret	82
Margery	67	Robert	70
Place, Family	120	Thomas	69, 82
Porteous, Dr. David	147	Family	79, 83, 86, 109

Richards & Tutt	147	Scroggs Farm	82, 113, 115, 129
Riddell, Sir Thomas	67	Thomas	58, 66, 69
Rider, Miss	142	Seamer, Robert	66
Ripon	65	Sedgefield	54, 62
Robert the Bruce	38	Settrington, Ralph	46
Robert III of Scotland	49	(or Richard) de	
Robson, John	138	Shield, William	115
Robinson, Anthony	113, 131	Shildon	125
Betty	111	Shilveden, Geoffrey de	46
C.H.	156	Shipman, Betsy	127
John	88	Matthew	138
Richard	140	Shuttlington, Alan de	46, 47
Thomas	71	Siward	25, 39, 40
William	88, 149, 151	Slater, J.	144
Family	86	Smart, John	71
Rodwell, John	138	Smith, John	87
Roman Catholic chapel	148	William	82, 87, 88, 128
Roman road	21, 39, 47	Family	109
Ropner Convalescent Home	147, 160, 163	Smithy	169
Ropner, Sir Robert	147	Sockburn	22, 42, 87, 88
Ruthall, Thomas, Bishop	36	Spooner, Cuthbert	66, 70
		Spring House	88
Sadberge	21, 29, 34, 38, 48, 51, 60, 67, 88	Square, The	121, 134, 140, 159
		Stanhope	79
Hall	141	St. Anne's Gardens	169, 170
Wapentake	25, 48	Station Road	21, 160, 165
Sadbyere, William	47	Steavenson, Dr. Stanley	160, 163, 165
Sadbury Field	57	Stelling, Anne	64
Sadler, John	66, 67, 68, 69	Constance	64
Sir Ralph	55	William	64
William	46	Stephenson, George	112, 121, 123
Salisbury terrace	161	Robert	121, 123
Sangar, Mr. T.	142, 145	St. George's Church	22, 27, 42, 44, 52, 63, 64, 72, 84, 87, 88, 112, 140, 142, 148, 153, 156, 165 166
Savill, William	66		
Scarlet, Christopher	71		
School	87, 142, 145, 149-152, 161, 169		
		St. George's Hospital	168
Scott, J.	155, 156	St. George's Hotel	171
Scott & Co.	126	Stiller (hauliers),	170

Stockdale, Thomas	115, 129	Tennick, Henry	137
Stockton	86, 121, 123, 125, 125-7, 167	Teysdell, John	47
		Theakston, Marmaduke	111
Stockton & Darlington Railway	112, 117, 121-7, 133, 143, 164	Thompson, James	54
		John	71
Stockton, John	66	Thomas	70
Stockton, Middlesbrough & Yarm Water Co	139	Family	86
		Thornaby	22
St. Laurence's Church	44, 141, 142, 148, 163, 165	Thornborough, Robert	54
		Thornton, John	129, 140
Stodhoe	29, 39, 40, 56, 57, 62	Thomas	113, 115, 129
Story, Richard	66	Thorntree Gardens	21, 164, 169
Strafford, Earl of	65	Thorntree House Farm	115, 129, 164
St. Saviour's Church, Bath	112	Todd, John	46
Surtees, Alexander	47	Tompkins, Eugene Carter	159
Elizabeth	51	Tower Hill	39, 147, 161,
Gocelin	40	Towne, Rev. Lyndhurst B.	141, 144
H.G.	121	Elizabeth	141
Marmaduke	52	Townshend, Lord	83
Ralph	52	Trafford, Manor	27
Robert	47, 118	Hill	156
Thomas	52	Trees Park	171
Thomas, Sir	40, 42	Tull, Jethro	83
Family	39, 40, 51, 52	Tunstall, Ralph	70
Sussex, Earl of	55	Turner, William	47
Sutton, Elizabeth	138	Tyler, Watt	32
Tailbois, Ralph	51	Urlay Nook	121, 125, 169
Taylor, W.	143	Usher, Margaret	127
Teasdale, Isaac	127, 140		
Teasdale, John	127, 138	Vardy, Mr.	168
J.	144	Victoria, Queen	149, 161
John William	145, 149, 151, 152, 159	Villas, The	153
James	112	Violet Villa	147
Robert	127		
Tees	17, 22, 39, 44, 49, 52, 56, 65, 120, 156	Walker, Thomas Dixon	118, 120
		Walley, sergeant	168
Teesside	169	Walton, Henry	113

Walworth, William	32
Family	32
Ward, George	66
Water Park	170
Water View	160, 165
Water Works Cottage	139
Watkins, Mrs.	111
Wedderburn, Mrs.	111
Welton, John de	46
West Hartburn	25, 27, 34 et seq. 51, 52, 56, 57, 60, 63, 64, 67, 68, 71, 153, 155, 156, 161, 165
West Hartburn Farm	82, 87, 90, 109, 115, 117, 128, 140, 149, 155, 165
Weston, George	113
Wetherill (Wetherelt), Ann	69
Christopher	71
John	66, 67, 70
Marmaduke	54, 55, 59, 66, 69, 70, 71
Matthew	69
William	71
Thomas	66, 69
Family	85
Whaley, Rev.	79, 82, 109
Wharton, Lady	82
Family	109
Wheat Sheaf Inn	123
White House Farm	63, 82, 88, 113, 115, 128, 130, 165
White, Mr.	111
William, rector	42, 45
William, son of Siward	25, 39, 40
William the Conqueror	17
Wilkinson, Henry	71
John	111
Richard	67
Thomas	66, 79
William	71
William Henry	149, 153
Mr.	111
Family	86, 87
Wilson, Charles John	153
George	54
Marmaduke	58, 66, 69
Ralph	70
Roger	70
Family	86
Woar, Matthew	71
Woodhouse, George	86
Thomas	86
William	109
Wooler, Jonathan Westgarth	133, 141, 142, 147, 149, 151, 152
Joseph	141
Octavius B.	149
William Alexander	141, 142, 145, 149, 152
Working Men's Institute	148
Worsall	22
Wray, Capt. Christopher	67
Wrenn, Sir Charles	52, 63, 64
Katherine	38
Margery	39
William	38, 39, 51
Wright, Edward	87
Francis	113
Ralph	82
Family	86
Wrightson, Thomas	115
Mr, jun.	82
Mr, sen.	82
Family	85
Wynghous	39
Wythes & Cochrane	142
Wythes, George & Co.	134, 147, 39
Yarm	47, 48, 49, 86, 87, 110, 125, 127, 171